LONDON

THE ESSENTIAL INSIDER'S GUIDE

ROBERT KAHN
SERIES EDITOR

FANG DUFF KAHN PUBLISHERS
NEW YORK

16 Hampstead, Hampstead Heath & Highgate

15 Islington

14 Regent's Park

6 Bloomsbury

7 Clerkenw

4 Soho & Fiztrovia

5 Trafalgar Squar Covent Garde & Holborn

13 Holland Park & Notting Hill

3 Mayfair

12 Kensington Gardens & Hyde Park

2 St. James's, Westminster & Whitehall

1 The Sou Bank, Bankside Bermond

11 From Hyde Park to the River

19 Southwest & West of London

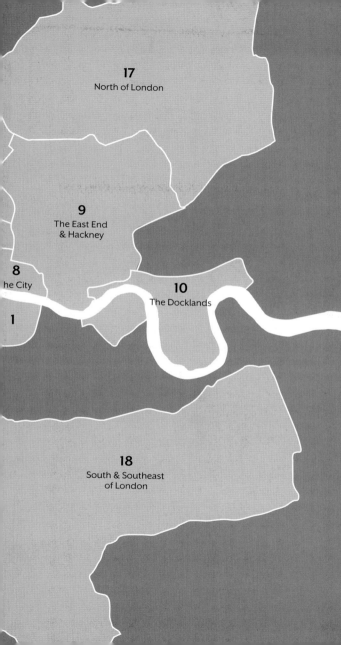

17
North of London

9
The East End
& Hackney

8
he City

1

10
The Docklands

18
South & Southeast
of London

First published in the United States of America
Fang Duff Kahn Publishers
611 Broadway, 4th floor
New York, NY 10012
www.fangduffkahn.com

Editors: Tim Adams and Helen Gordon
Design: Ingrid Bromberg Kennedy, In-Grid Design
Printed in China through Asia Pacific Offset

ISBN: 978-0-9830795-3-8
Library of Congress Number: 2011929609

Distributed by Publishers Group West

City Secrets books may be purchased at special quantity discounts for
business or promotional use. For information, please contact us at
info@fangduffkahn.com.

Every care has been taken to ensure the accuracy of the information in
this book. However, the publisher is not able to accept responsibility for
any consequences arising from the use of this guide or the information
it contains. If you do encounter a factual error, please let us know.

TABLE OF CONTENTS

1 The South Bank, Bankside & Bermondsey 12

2 St. James's, Westminster & Whitehall 32

3 Mayfair 52

4 Soho & Fiztrovia 66

5 Trafalgar Square, Covent Garden & Holborn 82

6 Bloomsbury 106

7 Clerkenwell 128

8 The City 140

9 The East End & Hackney 158

10 The Docklands 190

11 From Hyde Park to the River 202

12 Kensington Gardens & Hyde Park 222

13 Holland Park & Notting Hill 232

14 Regent's Park 246

15 Islington 260

16 Hampstead, Hampstead Heath & Highgate 270

17 North of London 288

18 South & Southeast of London 298

19 Southwest & West of London 312

   Index of Contributors 324

   Index 343

PREFACE

When I was working on this book, I occasionally had in mind a particular short story by Robert Louis Stevenson. The story tells of a young man who, visiting a large city (not unlike London) for the first time, stumbles through a door in an unpromising side street and finds himself in a secret walled garden. The garden is full of the most extraordinary plants and flowers, and there is a party going on, to which the young man is welcomed. He is offered wonderful food and wine, makes new friends, falls in love. The next day he plans to visit the walled garden again, but, try as he might—it is a sad story—he can never find the door in the side street, and the city becomes foreign to him once more. The story seemed a little parable of what we all hope when we visit new cities: we hope to become insiders, to have access to a version of what London cab-drivers call "the knowledge": an intimate geography of the kinds of places that make the city come fully alive. In a city as vast and accidental as London, this kind of knowledge is only ever partial and often eccentric. The idea of this book was a simple one, then: to gather together a selection of highly personal impressions from a number of people who know the city best and love it most—notably its writers and its artists, its architects and its historians—and to build an anecdotal guide to London's best-kept secrets. The response was, in many ways, exhilarating. Everyone we invited to contribute, it seemed, had a favourite corner table, or a street or building or park or shop, which held for them special significance. Moreover—perhaps surprisingly—most were more than willing to share these haunts with discriminating strangers. The result, we hope, is an insight into the London that Londoners might carry in their heads. Though most familiar landmarks are represented, if somewhat obliquely, this book does not pretend to be comprehensive; rather, it aims to open the door to a city no one has told you about before.

TIM ADAMS
London

HOW TO USE THIS BOOK

This is a highly subjective guidebook which reflects the personal tastes and insights of its contributors. We asked architects, painters, writers, and other cultural figures to recommend an overlooked or underappreciated site or artwork, or, alternatively, a well-known one about which they could offer fresh insights, personal observations, or specialized information. Respondents were also invited to describe strolls, neighborhoods, events, shops, and all manner of idiosyncratic and traditional ways of spending time in London. These recommendations have been organized into nineteen areas, each with an accompanying map keyed to the text by numbers.

Two icons appear throughout the book, to reference restaurants and shops. In addition there are four transporation symbols: ⊖ for the Tube, **LO** for the London Overground, **DLR** for the Docklands Light Railway, and **RAIL** for the london Rail. For directions we recommend the Journey Planner available through the Transport for London website: www.tfl. gov.uk.

The editors are delighted with the high number of unusual and delightful recommendations included here. We acknowledge that London provides an endless number of rich experiences and it is our hope that you will be inspired by the enthusiasm of our contributors to discover secrets of your own.

USEFUL WEBSITE

London A–Z map (www.a-zmaps.co.uk): The maps are available as an app, as well as in book format.

The Transport for London Journey Planner (www.tfl.gov.uk): Provides travel information to and from any destination in London.

Visit London (www.visitlondon.com): A comprehensive online guide to London, it includes general information and an up-to-date schedule of events, exhibitions, etc.

The London Guide (www.londontourist.org): A comprehensive online guide.

Context London (www.contexttravel.com): For the erudite traveler, we recommend Context London, a network of architects, art historians, archaeologists, and historians living in London who lead urban walking seminars.

English Heritage (www.english-heritage.org.uk): Several essays in this book refer to "Blue Plaques." These plaques are put up by English Heritage and designate places where important people in history lived and worked, and/or buildings with historical significance.

There are also several references to "Grade I" and "Grade II" buildings. Buildings are graded by English Heritage to show their relative architectural or historic interest. Grade I buildings are of exceptional interest; Grade II are particularly important buildings of more than special interest.

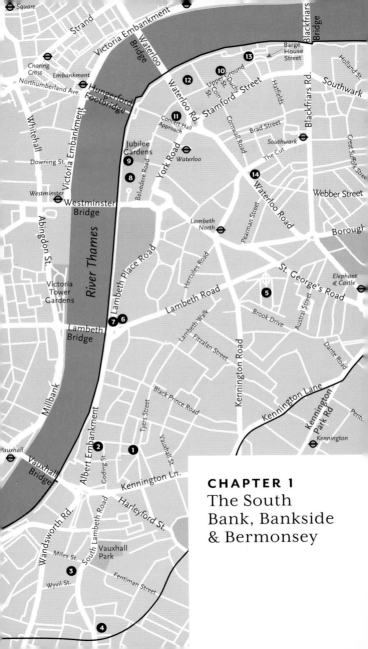

CHAPTER 1
The South
Bank, Bankside
& Bermonsey

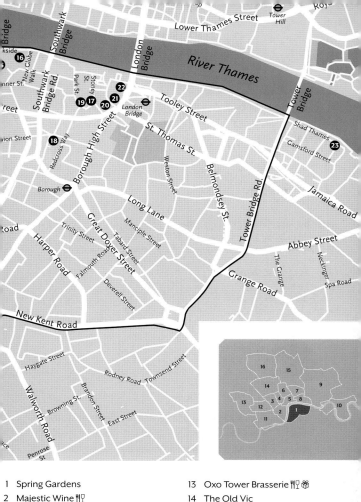

1   Spring Gardens
2   Majestic Wine 🍴♔
3   Keybridge House
4   Estrela 🍴♔
5   Imperial War Museum
6   The Knot Garden
7   South Bank Stroll
8   County Hall Restaurant 🍴♔
9   The Millennium Wheel
10 Gourmet Pizza Company 🍴♔
11 The Topolski Century
12 Royal National Theatre

13 Oxo Tower Brasserie 🍴♔🎁
14 The Old Vic
15 Tate Modern
16 Shakespeare's Globe Theatre
17 Monmouth Coffee Company 🍴♔
18 Red Cross Garden
19 Borough Market 🍴♔🎁
20 Southwark Cathedral
21 Bermonsey Market 🎁
22 Rosie's 🍴♔
23 Design Museum

The South Bank, Bankside & Bermondsey

THE SOUTH BANK

Vauxhall Walk
⊖   Vauxhall

1.1   **Spring Gardens**
Tyers Street, opposite Vauxhall City Farm SE11
www.vauxhallandkennington.org.uk/springgardens.shtml

1.2   **Majestic Wine**
Arch 83
Goding Street SE11
020 7587 1830; www.majestic.co.uk

1.3   **Keybridge House**
80 South Lambeth Road SW8

1.4   **Estrela**
111 South Lambeth Road SW8
020 7793 1051

Just a ten-minute stroll across the bridge from Tate Britain is Vauxhall. Despite its extraordinary layers of history, this is an area entirely untouched by tourists. Indeed, not much touched by any North Londoners, who have always exercised a disdainful prejudice about the South. During his career as an official at the Post Office, the novelist Anthony Trollope abolished the South London postal district. Officially, South does not exist. London has only SW and SE. Yet Vauxhall is the essence of this nonexistent area: tough, gritty, not at all pretty—but fascinating, and an extraordinary central-London secret.

Start by visiting Spring Gardens. First mentioned by diarist Samuel Pepys in 1662, this was perhaps the very first urban theme park. Famous for drinking, whoring, and music, it was home to a rehearsal for Handel's "Music for the Royal Fireworks" in 1749 that drew an audience of twelve thousand. In 1785, it became Vauxhall Pleasure Gardens. Entertainments included a reenactment of the Battle of Waterloo, although its "dark walks" were perhaps better suited to private activities. Hilariously, contemporary chroniclers described the whole site as a "gay exhibition"; hilarious because the current Vauxhall Tavern sports similar expertise. Tamer amusements can be found at Majestic Wine on Goding Street, where the obliging staff will let you taste without obligation. The Russian word for railway station is "vokzal" because Russia's first railway ran from St. Petersburg to the pleasure gardens created at Pavlovsk in imitation of Vauxhall.

From Spring Gardens, head for the apparently unappetising South Lambeth Road, passing along the way the bogglingly conspicuous headquarters of MI6 (the Secret Intelligence Service) on the south of Vauxhall Bridge, designed in ripe PoMo by Terry Farrell. Soon you will find Keybridge House, an astonishing Brutalist building from the seventies, and the source of many local rumours about spies and spying. It was built as the government's phone-tapping centre, and has an appro-priately sinister aspect. Very few come and go from this vast structure, but large black automobiles slide silently in and out of the underground car park. There are regular stories in the tabloids of spooks from MI6 and Keybridge House losing their laptops, filled with vital security data, in the neighbouring tapas bars of what's now known as Little Portugal. The best of these is Estrela, where the food is as good as anywhere in Portugal itself, but the atmosphere invigoratingly Lusitanian. Portuguese football plays all day; people munch rice cakes and quaff cold Sagres beer.

Nearby is Tradescant Road, a reminder that the influential plant collector John Tradescant (1608–1662) lived here. Tradescant brought back magnolia from Virginia and became head gardener to King Charles I. To be honest, Tradescant Road is a sordid little cut. But see it soon: the Mayor's ambitious development plans are going to wipe out this secret and strangely unspoilt part of London.

STEPHEN BAYLEY
Stephen Bayley created the Boilerhouse Project at the V & A and was responsible for the Design Museum in London. He is a columnist for the Times.

1.5 Imperial War Museum

Lambeth Road SE1
020 7416 5000; www.iwm.org.uk
Lambeth North or Waterloo

This is only a London city secret to those whose kneejerk reactions are prompted by at least two of the three words in the name; their loss, for the museum is both shocking and inspiring, and even at times, as it should be, almost fun. Since the British have grown so selectively vague about their own history—never mind everyone else's—and long since passed up the chance for a Museum of the British Empire on Hyde Park Corner, this is the only world-class historical museum in England. (There is a second IWM in Manchester and there are outposts elsewhere.) In recording the trail of human conflict and suffering—military and civilian—across the entire twentieth century, its brief is to be scholarly and popular as well as educational and entertaining. It is hard to imagine it being better or more movingly done. The range of presentation methods is one of its most striking features, from the pop Trench and Blitz "Experiences" to the meticulous curating of personal memorabilia and major war paintings by John Singer Sargent, Stanley Spencer, Edward Ardizzone, John Piper, and Paul Nash. A tall atrium displays the dinosaurs of war—Spitfire, Mustang, Focke-Wulf, doodlebug, V2, Monty's tank—as if they were creatures in a museum of natural history. Temporary shows are scrupulously well focussed and extend, with wit and imagination, the idea of war's aftermath—Dior's "New Look," for example, in 1947. During the "Ministry of Food" exhibition, they baked the state-approved National Loaf to the original recipe every day. There's an excellent shop (lots of books), and a terrific café, where you will probably need to reflect quietly on what you have seen.

The permanent Holocaust Exhibition is outstanding, and should be allowed two hours, ideally three. (Entry is ticketed, and attendance by children is discouraged.) Again, diversity of communication keeps the brain receptive and keen: maps, charts, and the old home movies of the condemned; an SS ledger of executions completed in a neat copper-plate hand; a sewer grid from Lodz, a glaring, bone-white model of Auschwitz under snow. The remorseless industrialisation of genocide—backed by hard evidence acquired, or loaned, from Germany, Poland, and Ukraine—is both tempered and made even more terrible by the filmed witness of surviving British Jews.

MICHAEL RATCLIFFE

Michael Ratcliffe has been Literary Editor and Chief Book Reviewer of The Times, and Theatre Critic of The Observer.

1.6 The Knot Garden

1983
Museum of Garden History
Lambeth Palace Road SE1
020 7401 8865; www.museumgardenhistory.org
⊖ Lambeth North or Waterloo

The Knot Garden is an oasis of calm in one of the busiest parts of London. It was created out of the churchyard of St. Mary's Lambeth (1370, restored 1851), now the Museum of Garden History. It contains the fine Tradescant Sarcophagus. John Tradescant was gardener to Charles I, and the knot garden is planted with flowers of that period. St. Mary's is next to Lambeth Palace, which is off Lambeth Palace Road. To find the Knot Garden you walk through the museum, which in itself is interesting, and where you can have tea.

CLAYRE PERCY
Clayre Percy is editor, together with her daughter, Jane Ridley, of The Letters of Edwin Lutyens to His Wife, Lady Emily, and The Letters of Arthur Balfour and Lady Elcho.

1.7 South Bank Stroll

From Lambeth Bridge to the Tate Modern
⊖ Lambeth North

Just to the north of Lambeth Bridge, on the south side of the Thames, join the riverside walk which begins as the Jubilee Walkway and follow it under its various different names, all the way to the Tate Modern at Bankside. The city's most imposing buildings, from Parliament to St. Paul's, unscroll along the opposite bank while people rollerblade past you. If you only have half a day in London, this is the way to use it.

LUCY HUGHES-HALLETT
Lucy Hughes-Hallett is an award-winning author and critic.

1

1.8   County Hall Restaurant

In the Marriott Hotel
Westminster Bridge Road SE1
020 7928 5200; www.londonmarriottcountyhall.co.uk
⊖ Lambeth North

🍴 The best view of the Houses of Parliament at sunset is
from across the river, from the County Hall Restaurant
of the Marriott Hotel, with its generous oak-lined spaces
left over from when this building was the London County
Council's grand floor. The entrance is equally grand,
being the old Council Members' entrance. Close-up, the
London Eye, my favourite Millennium structure, slowly
turns.

LADY STIRLING (MARY SHAND)
Lady Stirling is a furniture and interior designer.

1.9   The Millennium Wheel (London Eye)

2000, David Marks and Julia Barfield
Jubilee Gardens, next to County Hall SE1
0871 781 3000; www.londoneye.com
⊖ Waterloo

Is it art? Architecture? A feat of engineering? Who cares.
The Millennium Wheel—or the London Eye (so good they
named it twice)—is the most compelling spectacle on the
London skyline since the Crystal Palace caught fire. The
best way to see it is by accident—maybe innocently
glancing up from your tourist map as you step onto
Westminster Bridge, the whole sunlit upturned bicycle
wheel of it in the sky, the spokes just about turning as if
momentarily abandoned by a giant ten-year-old gone to
get his dad to fix the chain back on; or perhaps just an
arc's gleam of its hugeness curving over Hungerford
Bridge as you exit the Embankment Tube; or looming

sudden and impossibly tall as you round Jubilee Gardens, taking your eyes by surprise. Try not to laugh out loud.

And then look up at it from directly below, the thirty-two Brobdingnagian glass lozenges and steely white whatnots and cables and zigzagging girders, and then right up there—four hundred and fifty feet from the ground—those tiny faces at the windows, their features indistinct, looking down at you. And this is before you part with any money.

It may look like a fairground attraction, but the ride is not the point. The ascent, fittingly, is as slow as the turn of a century—no thrills, no spills, no one throwing up; the only sounds the hum of the air-conditioning and the clunk of jaws being dropped as you hit the summit. Apparently, on a clear day, you might spot St. Albans Cathedral, twenty-five miles away—though for most of us, the idea even of seeing Nelson's Column from Waterloo without the aid of an aeroplane seems fanciful enough. To those of us unused to skyscraping vistas, the panorama turns the familiar into something strange, like a trick from modern art—an East Enders river scything a bend into a London of Lego bridges, Dinky double-deckers, a Toytown Parliament, glassy waterfront blocks cut down to size, a paperweight St. Paul's, Hornby trains; the concrete hutches of the South Bank along to the Tate Modern and the Globe at Southwark—Shakespeare's "Wooden O." I wonder what he would have made of this metal one.

PHIL HOGAN
Phil Hogan is a novelist and a staff writer of The Observer.

A Summer Evening
☻ Waterloo

1.9   **The Millennium Wheel (London Eye)**
2000, David Marks and Julia Barfield
Jubilee Gardens, next to County Hall SE1
(see p. 17)
0871 781 3000; www.londoneye.com
☻ Waterloo

1.10   **Gourmet Pizza Company**
56 Upper Ground SE1
020 7928 3188

A ride on the London Eye and then a stroll upriver in
early evening in the summer. The river walk has become
a magnet for street entertainment, and personally my
biggest buzz was looking down on the fire-eaters from the
top of the wheel. A pizza at Gourmet Pizza Company in
Gabriel's Wharf is fun too.

KAREN WRIGHT
Karen Wright is the editor of Modern Painters and co-editor of the Penguin
Book of Art Writing.

1.11   **The Topolski Century**
1975–1989, Feliks Topolski
Hungerford Arches
150–152 Hungerford Arches, Concert Hall Approach SE1
020 7620 1275; www.topolskicentury.org.uk
☻ Waterloo

The Topolski Century, housed unpromisingly in a railway
arch on London's South Bank, is the city's only permanent
exhibition devoted to a single artwork. Vibrant and violent,
this expressionist collage chronicling the glories and
horrors of the twentieth century displays all the decadence and cruelty of a canvas by Dix. Part maze, part stage
set, pure art, it gains added drama from the trains rolling
towards Charing Cross Station overhead. Every visitor to

the National Theatre or Royal Festival Hall should allow time to experience Feliks Topolski's unique vision.

Michael Arditti

Michael Arditti is an award-winning novelist, short-story writer, and critic.

1.12 Royal National Theatre

1967–1977, Sir Denys Lasdun and Peter Softley

South Bank Centre SE1

020 7452 3000; www.nationaltheatre.org.uk

⊖ Waterloo, Southwark, or walk over the Hungerford Bridge from Embankment

RAIL Waterloo, Waterloo East, or walk over the Hungerford Bridge from Charing Cross

Go to the National Theatre. No need to buy a ticket. Theatre is all around you in Denys Lasdun's masterpiece of twentieth-century public architecture. To appreciate it properly you need to go alone. Buy a playscript from the bookshop, preferably Stoppard. Find a comfortable seat high up in the building giving you wonderful vistas down the Thames. Hear the distant hum of action, the clash of Shakespearean sword fights, from the auditoria. Watch the ebb and flow of people entering and exiting these grand convivial spaces. Patronize the bars and restaurants when the crowds vacate them. Spend a late afternoon there and stay on into the night.

Fiona MacCarthy

Fiona MacCarthy is a cultural historian and author of biographies of Eric Gill and William Morris.

1.13 Oxo Tower Brasserie

Oxo Tower Wharf, Barge House Street SE1

020 7803 3888; www.harveynichols.com

⊖ Southwark, or walk across the Millennium Bridge from the Mansion House station

🍴 Walking east along the Thames from the concrete brutalism of the South Bank Centre, I have a habit of visiting the unique contemporary retail design studios in the Oxo Tower and having a quick drink and a bite to eat at its panoramic brasserie. Despite the huge neon Oxo beacon that radiates from the tower, it is not the easiest place to find. Once you're there, though, the views from the eighth floor are spectacular, from St. Paul's, along the Thames, to the Houses of Parliament. What's more, you don't have to eat there to appreciate them. Although there is a restaurant, bar, and brasserie, there is also a free public viewing gallery.

ELLIOT BOYD

Elliot Boyd, a member of the Royal Institute of British Architects, is an architect practicing in London.

1.14 The Old Vic

103 The Cut, at Waterloo Road SE1
0844 871 7628; www.oldvictheatre.com
⊖ Waterloo

Behind a pleasant Victorian theatre façade is London's ghost-filled shrine to the history of modern English acting. Built in 1818 as the Royal Coburg and later renamed the Royal Victoria, this much-altered auditorium of nine hundred seats has been partially restored to its 1871 appearance. The Old Vic Company was England's de facto national theatre before there was a National Theatre. Under the early-twentieth-century management of Lilian Baylis, it became a world-renowned Shakespearean art theatre with a populist mission, producing in alignment with Sadler's Wells (drama at the Vic; ballet and opera at the Wells). Edmund Kean played this stage in 1824, to be followed by virtually every great English actor of the next hundred and fifty years. Laurence Olivier, John Gielgud, Ralph Richardson, Sybil Thorndike, Alec Guinness, Peggy Ashcroft, Edith Evans, all the Redgraves, and so many more were based here, among the great and near-great actors of their time. The National Theatre of Great Britain was formally launched at the Old Vic in 1963, led first by Olivier, and then by Peter Hall, and remained until its South Bank building was completed in 1976. Whatever happens at any given performance today, on this stage and within these walls one inhales the spirit of legends.

ROBERT MARX
Robert Marx is an essayist on theatre and opera.

BANKSIDE

1.15   Tate Modern

2000, Herzog and de Meuron
53 Bankside SE1
020 7887 8888; www.tate.org.uk
Southwark, or walk across the Millennium Bridge from the Mansion House station
The Tate Boat runs every forty minutes along the Thames between Tate Britain and Tate Modern; www.tate.org.uk/tatetotate.

The Tate Modern is one of the city's least-kept secrets. Ever since it opened at Bankside, in May 2000, Londoners have been bragging about it almost nonstop. And it really is spectacular: Swiss architects Herzog and de Meuron have converted, with grandeur and elegance, a post-war power station designed by Sir Giles Gilbert Scott, the man responsible for, amongst other things, the classic red telephone box.

The idea behind the new museum was to create enough space to house the Tate Gallery's extensive collection (most of its British art is still on show at the original Tate, on Millbank), but the experience remains a predominantly architectural one. The entrance to the main turbine hall is breathtaking, with interior detailing so beautiful that the art often seems a secondary decoration. The escalators, the wood panels on the stairs, or the glowing boxes of light are more likely to attract attention. It's also worth knowing that the bookshop is one of the best in the city for art and photography, and that you should be certain not to leave the building without taking in the view from the café at the top: St. Paul's Cathedral looms large across the river, and all of London seems to spread out before you.

GABY WOOD

Gaby Wood is a journalist and critic.

1.16 Shakespeare's Globe Theatre

1997, Theo Crosby
21 New Globe Walk SE1
020 7902 1400; www.shakespeares-globe.org
London Bridge, or walk across the Millennium Bridge from the Mansion House station

Fact: theatre is better in London. Don't argue. It's true. They take it more seriously, young people go, and despite the protestations from artists that it is underfunded, the government gives the institutions buckets of money. The most astonishing theatrical experience takes place at the Globe on the South Bank. No one knows exactly what Shakespeare's original playhouse, the "Wooden O," looked like, but this building, completed in 1997 and based on academic research, is one suggestion. What initially seemed to the cognoscenti (or "luvvies," as they're called over here) a potentially Disneyfied experience has proven the opposite. To hear an actor deliver a soliloquy directly to the groundlings from a bare stage with only the sun for illumination redefines Shakespeare; in fact, it redefines theatre in general. It almost makes any theatrical innovation since 1595 seem obsolete and twee. Who needs scenery, lighting, helicopters, when you can connect, one on one, with the most glorious poetry ever written? Granted, not every actor is great, not every production is flawless, but, as a rule, these are life-changing experiences. Especially for a theatregoer.

GLEN ROVEN
Glen Roven, four-time Emmy winner, has performed with orchestras around the world.

1.17 Monmouth Coffee Company

27 Monmouth Street WC2 (also 2 Park Street SE1)
0872 148 1409; www.monmouthcoffee.co.uk
⊖ Covent Garden

🍽 Good coffee in London is more common than ever. Recently the city has seen a succession of new cafés run by Australians and New Zealanders, usually cool young men making espressos with the intensity and interest in hardware that their sort used to bring to demonstrating stereos. The Monmouth Coffee Company is different: founded in the late 1970s, in the earliest days of the modern British food boom, there are still hippie traces in the woodsy decor of its two cafés, and the people brewing the coffee tend to be a bit more relaxed. The coffees, though, are up to the best modern standards, sometimes subtly fruity or chocolaty, and always strong—this is not Starbucks. Tables are communal and often tiny: expect to share. But you may find yourself opposite a resting actor or a coffee professional who's taking notes.

ANDY BECKETT
Andy Beckett is a feature writer for The Guardian and the author of When the Lights Went Out: Britain in the Seventies.

1.18 # Red Cross Garden

1887
50 Redcross Way SE1
020 7403 3393; www.bost.org.uk
⊖ Borough

When the London volume of *City Secrets* first appeared, Red Cross Garden was simply a footnote in the history of Victorian social reform. Yet the reformer Octavia Hill's 1880s transformation of a polluted industrial site has been a particularly personal enterprise. The little corner of Southwark demonstrated, on a single site, Hill's belief that the urban poor deserved decent housing (hence the surviving dollhouse-sized row of half-timbered Red Cross cottages), indoor activities in the now inaccessible Red Cross Hall and outdoor recreation, their "outdoor sitting room," the garden itself. With its winding paths, pond and fountain, seats, bandstand, pergola, and generous planting, it was very much a Victorian front room, and so used with pride and pleasure. By the 1990s, when I first saw it, the garden as such had vanished. All that remained was a grim, fenced-off pancake of blue-black tarmac with a couple of stunted urchin trees sitting in puddles of sour earth. Then along came the Bankside Open Spaces Trust, which heroically secured the large grants necessary to restore the little garden and, just as important, to maintain it for the future. In 2006, Red Cross Garden reopened, and once again it is as pretty and well-used a public garden as anyone could hope to find still embedded in a resolutely functional urban landscape.

GILLIAN DARLEY

Gillian Darley is co-author with Andrew Saint of The Chronicles of London, a historical anthology of London. Her most recent book is My Vesuvius.

BERMONDSEY

River Running
Thames Clippers to Bankside Pier
0870 781 5049; www.thamesclippers.com

`1.19` ### Borough Market
www.boroughmarket.org.uk

Neal's Yard Dairy
6 Park Street SE1
020 7367 0799; www.nealsyarddairy.co.uk
Closed Sundays.

De Gustibus
4 Southwark Street SE1
020 7407 3625; www.degustibus.co.uk

Artisan Foods
Borough High Street SE1
In the Green Market area
Open Thursday to Saturday.

`1.20` ### Southwark Cathedral
On the south side of the Thames, close to London Bridge
020 7367 6700; www.cathedral.southwark.anglican.org

I have a particular passion for boats, and so scudding about on London's river taxis brings me great joy. For one thing, the Thames Clippers—in truth, sleek, roomy catamarans—are really fast, and they depart from major piers about every twenty minutes. The commute from Victoria Embankment to Canary Wharf takes almost no time; if you're travelling on a Friday or Saturday, when Borough Market is open, disembark at Bankside Pier for a perambulation through one of the world's great open-air emporiums. Bring a tote with you and fill it with farm-house cheeses from Neal's Yard, a loaf of bread from De

Gustibus, and pastries from Artisan Foods, then eat a picnic lunch on a bench outside Southwark Cathedral, a pretty grand pile that manages to be more intimate—almost cosy, in fact—when compared to St. Paul's. Shakespeare buried his brother Edmund here in 1607, Lancelot Andrewes, co-author of the King James Version of the Bible, was laid to rest by the high altar in 1626, and a decade later, the Czech artist Wenceslas Hollar drew his iconic *Long View of London from Bankside* from a priory tower. Thames Clippers also provides service between Tate Britain (Millbank Pier) and Tate Modern (Bankside Pier), with a stop in-between at the London Eye. Download the free Thames Clippers iPhone app to make your river-running even easier.

JANE LEAR
Jane Lear is a food and travel writer.

Early Morning in Bermondsey

1.21 **Bermondsey Market (the New Caledonian)**
Long Lane and Bermondsey Street SE1
Open Fridays, 5 a.m. to 2 p.m.
⊖ Borough
RAIL London Bridge

1.22 **Rosie's**
125 Jamaica Road SE16
020 7231 0691
⊖ Bermondsey

1.23 **Design Museum**
Shad Thames SE1
020 7403 6933; www.designmuseum.org
⊖ London Bridge
RAIL London Bridge

🏛 Every Friday morning in the once disreputable section of Bermondsey, an antique market takes place. (If your cab driver is an old-timer, he may know it not as the Bermondsey Market but as the New Caledonian, since it descends from the pre-war market from that road in Islington.) Bermondsey has been a literary location for novelists from Dickens to Penelope Fitzgerald. It seemed to upset the writer Charles Kingsley: "Oh God! People having no water to drink but the water of the common sewer which stagnates full of dead fish, cats and dogs." Travelers need not worry—the water has been cleaned up, but much of the louche charm of the area remains. Stalls for the antique (flea) market open as early as 3 a.m. and vanish by mid-afternoon. Treasures include World War II memorabilia, costumes, the occasional piece of English pewter, crockery, jewellery—all the detritus of a layered and fluctuating island society, and all, we're assured by the vendors, at rock-bottom prices.

🍴 Include lunch at Rosie's; the savings will go a long way toward financing a splurge at the Ivy or the Square. Rosie seats you at communal tables, cheek to cheek with the teamsters, stall-keepers, and patrons pulled in by the sales. Platters of fish and chips are passed from the kitchen over the packed tables, bottles of vinegar follow, and you leave dyspeptic, perhaps in time to consider a last memento—that moustache cup or Macallan water pitcher or Royal Fusiliers's sabre.

After the market has closed, stroll the promenade at Butler's Wharf from London Bridge for a wonderful view of the city traffic on the Thames, or walk the Shad Thames beyond Tower Bridge (used as the backdrop for David Lynch's *The Elephant Man*), and drop in on the Design Museum. A serendipitous day.

BRUCE DUCKER

Bruce Ducker's novels include Lead Us Not into Penn Station and Dizzying Heights.

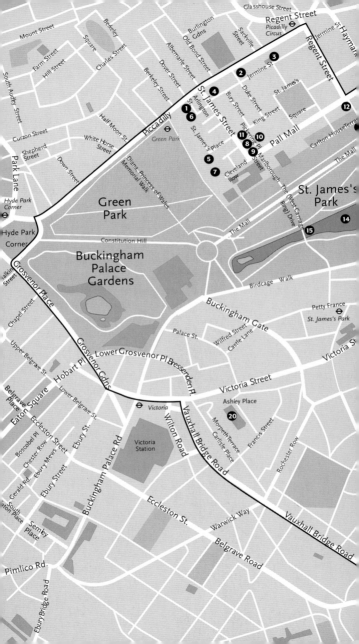

CHAPTER 2
St. James's,
Westminster
& Whitehall

1   The Ritz 🍽
2   Fortnum & Mason 🍽🎁
3   St. James's Church
4   Jermyn Street Shops 🎁
5   Spencer House
6   Wimborne House (William
    Kent House)
7   Bridgewater House
8   The Texas Legation
9   Berry Bros. & Rudd 🎁
10 Pickering Place
11 The Avenue Restaurant 🍽
12 The Athenaeum Club
13 Giro's Grave
14 St. James's Park Lake
15 The Blue Bridge
16 The Horse Guards
17 Banqueting House
18 Cabinet War Rooms
19 Westminster Walk
20 Westminster Cathedral

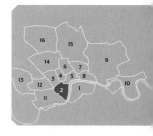

St. James's, Westminster & Whitehall

ST. JAMES'S

Afternoon Tea

2.1 **The Ritz**
1906, Mewes and Davis
150 Piccadilly W1
020 7493 8181; www.theritzlondon.com
⊖ Green Park

2.2 **Fortnum & Mason**
181 Piccadilly W1
020 7734 8040; www.fortnumandmason.com
⊖ Piccadilly Circus or Green Park

🍽 If you long to feel like a member of Britain's royal family, the most proximate equivalent might be tea at The Ritz.

Enter the hotel, where the doors are opened by waistcoated men who politely tip their hats. Up the stairs, in the gilded pink and gold tea room, a waiter eyes you for the briefest moment, then seats you at a tiny table and enquires if you require High Tea.

Soon, piled onto your small table is a three-tiered silver tray. There are triangles of ham, salmon, and egg-and-watercress sandwiches, then a plate full of warm scones, served with clotted cream and strawberry jam, best eaten when the cream and the jam are blended together into a fine pink paste. On the top level of the silver tray, a plate full of coiffed meringues and multi-coloured pastries (which actually look better than they taste) capture the flavour of this beautiful room, in which well-dressed men and women contentedly sip and nibble.

🏛 🍴   An alternative: after shopping for a few small items to take home as gifts at Fortnum & Mason (Major Grey Fresh Mango Chutney, Fortnum's Beer Mustard, something from the plethora of teas and jams on offer), find your way to St. James's Restaurant in the rear of the store, where High Tea is served every afternoon.

Either way, drink plentiful amounts of tea and emerge later into what will almost definitely be a grey and rainy afternoon, to stroll around Green Park.

LEXY BLOOM

Lexy Bloom is a senior editor at Vintage and Anchor Books.

2.3 St. James's Church

1676–1684, Christopher Wren
197 Piccadilly W1
020 7734 4511; www.st-james-piccadilly.org
⊖ Piccadilly Circus or Green Park

Font

Late 17th century, Grinling Gibbons

Consecrated in 1684, rebuilt after World War II, St. James's is an elegant space, and an active church with frequent concerts. The charming marble font with a sculpted frieze of Adam and Eve is thought to be a work of Gibbons, who certainly executed the astonishing limewood garlands of flowers, fruit, and game. William Blake was christened here, presumably at this font, and curiously enough was later famous for sitting in his garden with his wife, naked, and telling friends that they were playing Adam and Eve.

JEREMY MUSSON

Jeremy Musson is an architectural historian.

2.4 Jermyn Street Shops

Jermyn Street W1

☻ Green Park or Piccadilly Circus

🏛 The colours and objects in the shop windows in Jermyn
Street have remained, over the decades, a feast to behold.
THEODORE K. RABB
Theodore K. Rabb is Emeritus Professor of History at Princeton.

2.5 Spencer House

1756–1766, John Vardy and James Stuart
27 St. James's Place SW1
020 7499 8620; www.spencerhouse.co.uk

☻ Green Park

An enjoyable short walk across Green Park will lead you
to Spencer House, one of the rarest survivors of the
grand noble houses commissioned by the great families
of the eighteenth century. The house in St. James's Place
is still owned by the family of the late Diana, Princess of
Wales, and recently has been impeccably and lovingly
restored by Lord Rothschild. A must for those interested
in the most sophisticated aristocratic tastes of the mid-
eighteenth century and the results of restoration at the
highest level.

The house was originally built between 1756 and 1766
by the first Earl and Countess Spencer, after they had
eloped during his coming-of-age party; the Spencers
uncompromisingly employed the best craftsmen and
architects of their day. Designed for lavish entertaining,
the house contains some of the most perfect and earliest
neoclassical interiors and furniture in England. The
magnificent parade of ground-floor rooms, still used
during the week, culminates in the stunning green and
gilded Palm Room, designed by John Vardy, whilst

upstairs the series of glittering salons by James "Athenian" Stuart command fine views of the park.

JEREMY GARFIELD-DAVIES
Jeremy Garfield-Davies is an architectural and art historian.

High Society

2.5 **Spencer House**
1756–1766, John Vardy and James Stuart
27 St. James's Place SW1
(see p. 34)
020 7499 8620; www.spencerhouse.co.uk
⊖ Green Park

2.6 **Wimborne House (William Kent House)**
1740s, William Kent
22 Arlington Street SW1
020 7300 2233; www.theritzlondon.com/about/wkent.asp
⊖ Green Park

2.7 **Bridgewater House**
1840–1854, original house redesigned by Sir Charles Barry
14 Cleveland Row W2
Not open to the public.
⊖ Green Park

12.1 **Kensington Palace Gardens**
020 7298 2141; www.royalparks.org.uk
⊖ Notting Hill Gate

No other European city so cynically destroys its historic architecture. Even so, the widespread demolition of Georgian Mayfair in the course of the twentieth century is a mystery which still causes pain. The noblest mansions of Piccadilly and Park Lane, of Grosvenor Square and Berkeley Square, were pulled down within living memory in a ghastly alliance of British philistinism and commerce. Spencer House is the finest and best-known survivor, restored and opened to the public by Lord Rothschild,

who acquired it on a long lease from the Spencer family.
Wimborne House is now part of the Ritz next door,
adding its English eighteenth-century William Kent
interiors to the hotel's gorgeous Edwardian Louis Seize.
The post-Georgian Bridgewater House, Sir Charles
Barry's huge stone palazzo overlooking the Green Park,
survives as the most secretive great home in London—
what does go on there? But the sublime atmosphere of
pre-1914 *richesse* can now really only be found in one
London street, Kensington Palace Gardens, a late arrival
to the society map, put up in the middle of the nineteenth
century, adjacent to Kensington Palace. This uninter-
rupted flow of magnificence in mature gardens exerts a
quiet and very potent grandeur.

DUNCAN FALLOWELL

Duncan Fallowell is an author and cultural commentator. His books include
Going As Far As I Can: The Ultimate Travel Book.

London's Horses

In 1900, London streets were jammed with omnibuses,
hansoms, vans, wagons, and growlers—all pulled by some
of the three hundred thousand horses that lived and
worked in the city.

A century later the horses have disappeared, except
for a few used by the police, the army on ceremonial
occasions, and riders in Hyde Park. But their past importance is reflected in an enormous number of equestrian
statues in London. Do not expect historical or anatomical
accuracy. Opposite Big Ben a pair of over-large fiery
animals threatens to overturn the rebellious British Queen
Boadiccea (or more accurately Boudicca) in her exotic
and historically inaccurate chariot (Thomas Thornycroft,
1850s). Does any other city have a statue to someone who
destroyed it? On the other side of Parliament, by St.

Margaret Street, Richard the Lionheart—one of England's more useless kings—is magnificently mounted on a spirited charger (Carlo Marochetti, 1861), a contrast to Field Marshall Earl Haigh's wooden rocking horse (Alfred Hardiman, 1937) on Whitehall or Edward VII's apparently drunken mount at Waterloo Place (Bertram Mackennal, 1922).

In Trafalgar Square, dominated by Nelson's Column and traffic, it is easy to overlook the superb little equestrian statue of Charles I by Hubert Le Sueur (1633; see p. 90). Like so many of its breed, it was influenced by the Marcus Aurelius prototype in Rome. And tucked anonymously away, at the junction of Piccadilly and Dover Street, is perhaps the finest equestrian statue, the mythical horse and rider by Elizabeth Frink (1974).

And the horse that beat them all? Whistlejacket, whose portrait, by George Stubbs (1762), hangs in the National Gallery.

DAVID MILES
David Miles is the Chief Archaeologist of English Heritage.

2.8 The Texas Legation

3 St. James's Street SW1

⊖ Green Park

Texas is an integral part of the United States of America. However, following its liberation from Mexico in 1836, it was an independent country until it entered the Union in 1845. It included parts of present-day New Mexico, Oklahoma, Kansas, Colorado, and Wyoming. Anxious to foster support for his fledgling nation, President Sam Houston opened diplomatic missions in London, Paris, and Washington, D.C. The Legation in London, which functioned from 1842 to 1845, was on the first floor of 3 St. James's Street, a stone's throw from St. James's Palace.

At the mouth of the alley leading to the delightful Pickering Place, on the side wall of Berry Bros. & Rudd, the wine merchants and erstwhile landlords of the Texans, is a brass plaque embellished with a Lone Star, which was erected by the now defunct Anglo-Texan Society to commemorate this little-known slice of history. It was unveiled in 1963 by the Governor of Texas, Price Daniel, Sr.

PETER HORROCKS
Peter Horrocks, a barrister, is a freeman of the City of London. He is a former Chairman of the Sherlock Holmes Society of London.

2.9 Berry Bros. & Rudd

Established in 1698
3 St. James's Street SW1
020 7396 9600; www.bbr.com

⊖ Green Park

▥ The most gracious shopping experience in London without doubt is a visit to Berry Bros. & Rudd, wine and spirit merchants to the Queen and the Prince of Wales, who have carried on business at their sublime lopsided premises since the seventeenth century. There is no finer place to buy a bottle of claret than in this unchanging shop, with its creaking uncovered floorboards, collection of ancient bottles, large set of beam scales, and the courteous service of yesteryear.

PETER HORROCKS
Peter Horrocks, a barrister, is a freeman of the City of London. He is a former Chairman of the Sherlock Holmes Society of London.

Famed for selling and sourcing the best wines, particularly claret, Berry Brothers gives equal attention to a highly rare case of Château Latour as it does to a single bottle of their famed Cutty Sark whisky. Behind the green-shuttered façade, the Victorian clerks' desks stand on the ancient undulating floor, whilst on the scattered Georgian chairs clients quietly discuss their next purchase with the highly knowledgeable staff.

A huge old coffee scale, on which most of fashionable London has been weighed since the eighteenth century, still hangs in the shop, beside framed telegrams that include one gravely reporting the loss of a consignment of wine aboard the *Titanic*. Once their clients may have included Napoleon, countless European monarchs, and famous historical figures; now they could equally include pop stars and shrewd dot-com millionaires.

Below the shop lie the cavernous cellars, rumoured to link with St. James's Palace by a lost tunnel, which now also play host to dinners and tastings for both private and corporate clients.

JEREMY GARFIELD-DAVIES
Jeremy Garfield-Davies is an architectural and art historian.

2.10 Pickering Place

Enter 5 St. James's Street to find the sundial, which is behind 7 St. James's Street SW1

⊖ Green Park

I love the sequence of spaces, materials, surfaces, and textures in this short detour in the walk from Pall Mall to Piccadilly. As you go up St. James's Street, pass the Georgian shopfront of Berry Brothers (see above); follow its gnarled paintwork through a little alley that opens up into a microcosm of Georgian townscape. Only about twelve metres square, paved in stone, and surrounded on three sides by four-storey brick buildings—with a sundial at its centre—there it is. No one would let you build it now—not enough light, too much overlooking—but it works. A charming outdoor room. Then back to

St. James's Street, and up the hill, and past more organic paintwork on the hat shop. A magical experience.

EDWARD BURD
Edward Burd, an architect, was for thirty years a partner at Hunt Thompson Associates, where he worked primarily on conservation and social housing projects.

2.11 The Avenue Restaurant and Bar

7–9 St. James's Street SW1
020 7321 2111; www.theavenue-restaurant.co.uk
⊖ Green Park

Rick Mather's exciting essay in spacey urban chic, ultra-modern but perfectly at home in a traditional part of town, and fit for a Martian duke. Just to walk past it at night is to be involved in strange theatre, or some kind of installation, playing to the street yet aloof from it. The food is pretty good, too.

DUNCAN FALLOWELL
Duncan Fallowell is an author and cultural commentator. His books include Going As Far As I Can: The Ultimate Travel Book.

2.12 The Athenaeum Club

1830
107 Pall Mall SW1
020 7930 4843; www.athenaeumclub.co.uk
⊖ Charing Cross

F. E. Smith, later the first Earl of Birkenhead, used to pause here every day on his way home from the House of Commons, to urinate. After some months the porter asked if he was a member.

"Member?" the Earl said. "Do you mean this is a club, as well?"

BRIAN MASTERS
Brian Masters writes about crime and art. He is also an authority on gorillas and dukes.

2.13 Giro's Grave

Carlton House Terrace SW1
Under a tree, on the left of the top of the steps leading to the
Duke of York Column.
⊖ Charing Cross or Piccadilly Circus

Hyde Park has its evocative dog cemetery near Victoria
Gate, but rather odder is the grave of Giro, a terrier
belonging to Leopold von Hoesch, German ambassador
in London from 1932 to 1936. It is situated just a few paces
from the top of the Duke of York's Steps, on what used to
be part of the front garden of 9 Carlton House Terrace.
The German Embassy occupied numbers 7, 8, and 9 until
the start of the Second World War, when it was taken over
by the Foreign Office. The dog was accidentally electro-
cuted by an exposed wire in 1934, and the epitaph on his
headstone reads:

> "GIRO"
> EIN TREUER BEGLEITER! [A FAITHFUL COMPANION!]
> LONDON IM FEBRUAR 1934.
> HOESCH.

Von Hoesch himself died in office on April 10, 1936, and,
remarkably, his swastika-draped coffin was accorded a
full diplomatic funeral procession up the Mall, escorted
by the Grenadier Guards, together with a nineteen-gun
salute in St. James's Park.

PETER HORROCKS
*Peter Horrocks, a barrister, is a freeman of the City of London. He is a former
Chairman of the Sherlock Holmes Society of London.*

2.14 St. James's Park Lake

St. James's Park SW1
www.royalparks.org.uk

St. James's Park

After a long day visiting museums, my favorite place to
unwind is by the lake in St. James's Park. The many
beautiful and unusual aquatic birds offer a visual
delight—especially for a New Yorker like me who is used
to Central Park's pigeons. The lake offers not only great
bird-watching but also wonderful people-watching, as a
broad cross section of tourists and Londoners walk by.

NADINE ORENSTEIN
*Nadine Orenstein is Curator in charge of Dutch, Flemish, and German Old
Master prints in the Metropolitan Museum of Art.*

2.15 The Blue Bridge

*1957, Eric Bedford. Built to replace the original suspension bridge
(1857) by Rendell and Co.*
In the centre of St. James's Park. The closest entrance is off
Marlborough Road to the north, or Queen Anne's Gate to the south.

Stand in the middle of the footbridge that crosses St.
James's Park Lake and look east at the prospect away from
Buckingham Palace. Rising up beyond the water crowded
with ducks, swans, and herons and fringed by weeping
willows are the grey turrets, minarets, and rooftops of a
cluster of imposing white buildings. These are various
offices of the government that line Whitehall, but the
view is strikingly un-British. I always imagine it to be a
vast tsar's palace in St. Petersburg, or a snapshot of
Disneyland. It's a magical and romantic vista, crowned by
the upper half of the London Eye.

NICK WYKE
*Nick Wyke is a journalist at The Times and has recently devised a foodies'
walking tour of Belgravia in London.*

WESTMINSTER & WHITEHALL

2.16 The Horse Guards

1753, William Kent
Horse Guards Road SW1

⊖ Westminster

The west front of this massive building indicates the
grandeur of the place, but the centre block court on the
east illustrates its refinement. It takes time for the eyes
to adjust. What are those projections over the side arches?
Hogarth published a cartoon of the royal coachman
having his head knocked off passing under the "too small"
centre arch. However, it is really part of a careful
proportioning system. While you are there, you should
visit the Banqueting House, by Inigo Jones, next door.

ROBERT LIVESEY

*Robert Livesey is an architect and a professor at the Knowlton School of
Architecture at The Ohio State University.*

2.17 Banqueting House

1622, Inigo Jones
41 Whitehall SW1
020 3166 6154; www.hrp.org.uk
Check the website for hours, as the Banqueting House is often closed
for private functions.

⊖ Charing Cross or Embankment

The most important and most unassuming building in
Whitehall is Inigo Jones's Banqueting House. A building
externally hard to distinguish from the cold façades of
government ministries, it is passed daily by thousands of
tourists but is one of the hidden delights of Westminster.
The interior is, at first sight, indigestible but it contains

the fabulous ceiling by Rubens and the perfect Palladian proportions of Inigo Jones.

SIMON THURLEY
Simon Thurley is Chief Executive of English Heritage and was formerly Director of the Museum of London.

2.18 Cabinet War Rooms

Clive Steps, King Charles Street SW1
020 7930 6961; www.iwm.org.uk
⊖ Westminster

In a corner of Horse Guards Parade opposite St. James's Park, you can walk through a small door surrounded by sandbags and into the underground warren of rooms from which the British government ran the war when Hitler was dropping bombs on London.

Nowhere is more evocative of the old world in which the fortunes of war were tracked by coloured pins on faded maps. The pins are still there, stuck forever onto what was left of Europe when the lights were turned out on them for the last time, and the door was locked, three months after VE Day.

Thirty-five years later it was reopened to the public. Years that had seen the liquidation of the British Empire had left magically unscathed the rooms from which Churchill had fought to preserve it. The typing pool, the dormitories, the cabinet room, Churchill's own bed-room—everything breathes the tobacco-stained, down-at-heel heroism of our finest hour.

SIR NICHOLAS HYTNER
Sir Nicholas Hytner is the artistic director of London's National Theatre.

London's Cabinet War Rooms and adjoining Churchill Museum—both components of the larger British Imperial War Museum—stand out among the world's best examples of their type. The War Rooms (also called the Churchill

War Rooms and Churchill Bunker), in the former subterranean headquarters of the World War II–era British High Command, aren't only among the world's few publicly accessible military bunkers but are also linked to a warren of tunnels under the streets of Whitehall that is as extensive as it is little known.

The Cabinet War Rooms lie beneath the British Treasury Building, a (relatively small) part of a larger buried complex with some two hundred rooms, protected in places by more than fifteen feet of reinforced concrete whose corrugated steel cladding (to deflect bomb blasts) is visible in portions of the bunkers' roofs. Even today, some bunker sections remain in active use below the buildings that comprise the New Public Offices between Parliament and 10 Downing Street. The entrance to the complex, its roof topped by sandbags, lies at the foot of Clive Steps, a short stairway near the end of King Charles Street in the purlieus of St. James's Park, bearing a statue of sometimes renowned, sometimes reviled, Clive of India.

Visitors soon come to an area called the Dock. This was the main operational centre and sleeping quarters for low-level staffers including clerks, typists, orderlies, and cooks who kept the complex running throughout the war years. Rows of coat pegs, blocks of lockers, and framed art—including a photo-portrait of Winnie and a relief map of Malaya and Singapore—decorate the cream-coloured walls, the paint barely concealing the underlying brick and mortar. Signs posted outside some rooms, such as those reading "P.M.'s Typists," "P.M.'s Detectives," and "P.M.'s Dining Room," indicate the purposes they originally served.

These rooms, and the larger operational spaces deeper within, have been opened to view by glass partitions. All are Spartan enclosures, equipped with a bare minimum of creature comforts, as befitted the sombre years that endured the Battle of Britain and the London Blitz. The barracks décor also applies to Clementine Churchill's room. Churchill's devoted wife, Clemmie, was a frequent leaning-post to a sometimes faltering Prime Minister, and was rarely absent in times of crisis. As in U.S. factories where Rosie the Riveter filled gaps on production lines vacated by men fighting overseas, so, too, women in Britain made up a sizeable portion of regular staff, serving as typists, radio operators, and general functionaries.

The greatest attractions of the Cabinet War Rooms are its operational spaces. The Chiefs of Staff Conference Room and the Cabinet Room are among the most iconic, the former for its walls lined on three sides with strategic maps, including a Mercator projection on the right made of sections carefully pieced together to form a geographic composite centred on Russia, Eurasia, and the Indian subcontinent, beside a framed portrait of King George VI in full military regalia. However, it's the wall-length map on the left that catches the attention—it bears a hand-drawn cartoon of Adolf Hitler perched beneath the heading "North Sea," launching a salute westward in a curious sitting posture that makes a "V" for victory of the caricature's splayed legs. This was drawn in an idle moment by none other than Churchill himself, otherwise occupied artistically with watercolour painting at Chartwell, his country estate. Most rooms, by the way, include mannequins in lifelike poses that seem almost real in the dim bunker lightning.

Whatever else they gather from the Cabinet War Rooms, visitors of a literary bent may take away the impression of having rattled through something of an

Orwellian Ministry of Peace out of the novel *1984*. A tenebrous atmosphere that seems the product of more than mere claustrophobia invests the stark corridors. As awesome an experience a visit to the War Rooms can be, it's a relief to return to street level again. Churchill may have felt something similar; his memoirs, published as the six-volume *History of the Second World War*, record that the P.M. often preferred his offices in the Admiralty and 10 Downing Street, even at the height of the London Blitz, to the relative safety of the buried complex.

A post-visit stroll through nearby St. James's Park or along the adjacent Horse Guards Road is highly recommended after touring the subterranean confines of the Cabinet War Rooms, as is a pint of Guinness at any of Whitehall's excellent pubs, for reasons similar to Bogie's quip in *Casablanca* that alcohol "sort of takes the sting out of being occupied."

DAVID ALEXANDER

David Alexander is an author of fiction and nonfiction. His most recent book is The Building: A Biography of the Pentagon.

Architecture by Underground

The Jubilee Line Extension from Westminster Station to North Greenwich Station

The best architectural legacy of the millennium year was the Jubilee Line extension to the Underground, opened in December 1999 and still a fine advertisement for modern British architecture. A tour of inspection of all eleven stations, commissioned from British architectural stars, provides an unexpected thrill of a day out. Get on at Michael Hopkins's Westminster, a superbly engineered exercise in high-tech. Get off at all the stations until you reach North Greenwich. The greatest spectacle is at Canary Wharf, where Norman Foster's station, 313 meters in length, ellipsoid in its plan, admits radiant shafts of light deep into the station cavity. Escalators soar heavenward. Is this the nearest we now get to viewing a Gothic cathedral for the first time?

FIONA MACCARTHY
Fiona MacCarthy is a cultural historian and author of biographies of Eric Gill and William Morris.

JUBILEE LINE EXTENSION: Westminster Station, Hopkins Architects; Waterloo Station, Nicholas Grimshaw and Partners; Southwark Station, Richard MacCormac, MJP Architects; London Bridge Station, Roland Paoletti, JLE Architects; Bermondsey Station, Ian Ritchie Architects; Canada Water Station, Eva Jiricná, drum by Buro Happold; Canary Wharf Station, Foster and Partners; North Greenwich Station, Alsop, Lyall, and Störmer; Canning Town Station, Troughton McAslan; West Ham Station, Van Heyningen & Haward; Stratford Station, Troughton McAslan

2.19 Westminster Walk

⊖ Westminster

The tranquil backstreets of Westminster (Barton, Cowley, and Lord North Street) are lined with splendid Georgian houses, built for artisans, that have grown crooked with age. The original street signs are engraved in stone tablets and dated 1722. If you look closely, a fading arrow and the letter "S" can be seen on the ground-level façade of some of the houses, indicating the presence of underground World War II bomb shelters. At the end of Lord North Street looms the rare Baroque grandeur of St. John's in Smith Square. Discovering these beautifully preserved streets—most of which are still residential—is made all the more exciting by their being just a stone's throw from such tourist standards as Westminster Abbey and the Houses of Parliament.

NICK WYKE
Nick Wyke is a journalist at The Times and has recently devised a foodies' walking tour of Belgravia in London.

2.20 **Westminster Cathedral**

1892–1903, John Francis Bentley
Ashley Place SW1
020 7798 9055; www.westminstercathedral.org.uk

⊖ Victoria or Westminster

John Francis Bentley's master work. The cathedral
contains the exquisite reliefs of the fourteen
Stations of the Cross by English sculptor Eric Gill,
the anarchist typographer.

AL ORENSANZ

*Al Orensanz is a sociologist and semiologist, and the director of the Angel
Orensanz Foundation in New York.*

CHAPTER 3
Mayfair

1 Oxford Street 🍴🍷
2 Claridge's 🍴🍷🛏
3 Fenwick 🍴🍷
4 Browns 🍴🍷
5 Charbonnel et Walker 🍴🍷
6 The Royal Academy of Arts
7 Faraday Museum
8 Austin Reed
9 G. Heywood Hill Ltd. 🍴🍷
10 Shepherd Market 🍴🍷🛏
11 Farm Street Church
12 Home of Benedict Arnold
13 The Wallace Collection

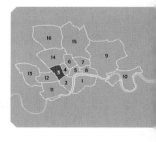

Mayfair

3.1 A Walk Along Oxford Street
Between Marble Arch and Tottenham Court Road WC1

⊖ Marble Arch or Tottenham Court Road

Plans drawn up in 1972 to transform Oxford Street into a
"tree-lined paradise" must have fallen down the back of
somebody's sofa, because the busiest street in Britain can
still, on occasion, make you lose the will to live—mainly in
the run-up to Christmas, when bright-eyed shoppers spill
out of the ground at Oxford Circus and congeal in a fog of
bus fumes and freshly roasted caramel nuts, while the
Metropolitan police attempt crowd control with
loudspeakers.

Still, pleasure and pain have always been what Oxford
Street does best. Nineteen-year-old Thomas De Quincey
bought his first dose of opium here one rainy autumn
Sunday in 1804, and never forgave the "stony-hearted
stepmother" of a place. This is a Roman road: the sun sets
at the Selfridges end and bounces straight off Centre
Point, a 1960s skyscraper unloved by millions, to the east.
It was in this neighbourhood that condemned prisoners
from Newgate got tanked up before the final mile of their
lives, west towards Tyburn gallows by Marble Arch. Little
club-footed Lord Byron was born at 16 Holles Street, now
the John Lewis department store. Look up here and you'll
see a sculpture that Barbara Hepworth made in 1962, an
attempt to give a sense of moving "in air and water." She
lived in St. Ives, though, not WC1.

In its day, Oxford Street was more than a place to find
a cheap Rolex watch. The Salvation Army at Regent Hall
(No. 275) occupies the site of an old ice rink. HMV's
flagship store (No. 150) used to be the Princess's Theatre,

where world-famous tenors competed in decibels. Masquerades drew beautiful people to the Pantheon (No. 173), with its stunning rotunda modelled on Hagia Sophia in Istanbul; it opened in 1772 and burnt down twenty years later. Now all you'll find here is Marks & Spencer. These days it's left to a Greek-Cypriot fiddle player outside Debenhams (or just across the road) to put on a bit of a show. Nick Leonidas (b. 1940), blinded by yellow fever as a child, has busked here since 1981; his hours are 9:30 a.m. to 4:45 p.m., Monday, and Wednesday to Saturday, in all weathers.

CAROL MCDAID

Carol McDaid is an editor and journalist for The Observer.

Bond Street Couture

⊖ Bond Street

3.2 Claridge's
55 Brook Street W1
020 7629 8860; www.claridges.co.uk

3.3 Fenwick
63 New Bond Street W1
020 7629 9161; www.fenwick.co.uk

3.4 Browns
23–27 South Molton Street W1
020 7514 0016; www.brownsfashion.com

3.5 Charbonnel et Walker
The Royal Arcade
28 Old Bond Street W1
020 7491 0939; www.charbonnel.co.uk

Ever since the mid-nineteenth century, Bond Street has been the epicentre of fashionable shopping. Beau Brummell took regular strolls here so that smart society could admire his clothes. Now the typical Bond Street shopper is more likely to check in at Claridge's hotel nearby, and wend her perfumed way to Michaeljohn on Albemarle Street, where she'll have a haircut or a spa treatment before submitting to the strain of purchasing that Versace dress or Cartier ring.

You don't have to be quite so at home here, though, to admire the view. On the main drag, big name fashion houses jostle for position: Prada, Hermès, Donna Karan, Armani, Calvin Klein, Nicole Farhi, Louis Vuitton. In general, the more recent the arrival, the larger the shop. But this competitive scene is not all there is. Bond Street has tributaries that open out onto other worlds. Savile Row is still the home of royally appointed tailors, and a new guard, of brighter shirts and hipper suits, have set up shop across the street. The arcades (Royal Arcade off Bond Street and Burlington Arcade off Burlington Street) have the hushed, old-world charm of nineteenth-century Paris, while Cork Street, a few paces to the East, is lined with galleries, and forms the heart of the contemporary art world.

At the north end of Bond Street is Fenwick, a department store slightly more modest than Harvey Nichols, and opposite it, a few yards down Brook Street, is the mouth of South Molton Street. South Molton Street, famous for Browns, the cutting-edge clothing emporium that can make or break a young designer's career, is also the handiest place to stop for coffee. But if you happen to find yourself at the Piccadilly end of Bond Street, choose a few chocolates from Charbonnel et Walker, and eat them while gazing into the windows of Tiffany's next door. Breakfast has never been better.

GABY WOOD

Gaby Wood is a journalist and critic.

3.2 **Claridge's Bar**
55 Brook Street W1
020 7629 8860; www.claridges.co.uk
⊖ Bond Street

🍴🏛 Walk to Old Bond Street, familiar from smash and grab
movies, to buy stiletto boots from Gina Shoes (9 Old
Bond Street). Have a chocolate martini in Claridge's bar.
If I were meeting God for a cocktail, I'd take him to this
Art Deco paradise.

CAROLE MORIN
Carole Morin's books include Lampshades, Dead Glamorous, *and* Penniless
in Park Lane.

Underground Design

The London Underground is a must for an architectural
detective. As London is built on clay, it was possible to
burrow and connect every corner of the city and suburbs.
There are nineteenth- and twentieth-century survivals
everywhere, with arcaded embankments, cast iron
columns, wooden platform canopies and furniture, glass
and metal light fittings.

At Baker Street, the Edwardian panelling is as good as
in an ocean liner. At Aldgate East, there are embossed
creamware 1950s tiles; at Covent Garden glazed brick
arches the colour of toffee and canary yellow bands. They
are della Robbia blue at Knightsbridge. Arnos Grove has a
complete 1930s station. Piccadilly Circus another, opened
in 1928, and circular. Hammersmith is almost completely
1950s. At Tottenham Court Road there are mosaic murals
by Eduardo Paolozzi (1984) and at Canary Wharf Norman
Foster's beautiful station (1999). And everywhere there is
Edward Johnston's sans serif lettering, the red, white, and
blue symbol, and the coloured map which is both a work

of art and very clear. Nearly everything needs cleaning
and mending, of course, but don't be put off by that.

DAVID MLINARIC
*David Mlinaric, now retired, was a partner at Mlinaric, Henry, and
Zervudachi, an interior design and decoration company. He has worked
on various museums and heritage sites, including the National Gallery
and the Royal Opera House.*

3.6 The Royal Academy of Arts

Burlington House
Piccadilly W1
020 7300 8000; www.royalacademy.org.uk
⊖ Piccadilly Circus or Green Park

The back of the Royal Academy (used to be the front of
the Museum of Mankind). I see its inspiring statues of
great thinkers from my office window. David Hume
stands opposite our company's boardroom, reminding
the board of the fallibility of "watertight" principles.

MARJORIE M. SCARDINO
*Marjorie M. Scardino is Chief Executive of Pearson PLC, owners of Pearson
Education, the Financial Times Group, and the Penguin Group.*

Sackler Galleries
1989–1991, Foster & Partners

In London, it seems that everyone has an opinion about
architecture—even Prince Charles, who set off a debate
about traditional versus modern styles when he said
that a proposed extension to the National Gallery would
be "like a carbuncle on the face of a much-loved and
elegant friend."

The best arguments, however, are in deed, not words,
and the best argument for modernism is the lovely jewel
of an intervention for the Royal Academy by Sir Norman
Foster. Here, a glass stair and a glass elevator have been
inserted in the narrow gap formed between the two
buildings that make up the Royal Academy. On one side is

the original garden façade of the 1666 house (converted in the eighteenth century by Lord Burlington), now revealed for the first time in over a hundred years, and on the other is the façade of the Victorian galleries. The stair and elevator, beautiful free-standing objects in their own right, lead to a glazed reception hall incorporating the parapet of the original façade. From here one enters the former Diploma Galleries, which were added above Burlington House in Victorian times. These rooms have been completely renovated, replete with new barrel-vaulted ceilings, and house the changing exhibitions.

This carefully detailed and thoroughly modern upstart manages to simultaneously assert itself while remaining completely respectful of its elders. As a bonus, in the glazed atrium there is a permanent installation of Michelangelo's *Taddei Tondo*. One can only imagine Michelangelo, himself no stranger to breaking the rules, looking down with a smile at being shown here.

ROBERT KAHN

Robert Kahn is founder and principal of the award-winning firm Robert Kahn Architect, based in New York. He is also the creator and series editor of the City Secrets series.

3.7   Faraday Museum

In the Royal Institution of Great Britain
21 Albemarle Street W1
020 7409 2992; www.rigb.org
⊖ Green Park

A compact museum of Faraday memorabilia. In the nineteenth century, Michael Faraday was a pioneer of the uses of electricity. Here in the museum you will find the world's first electric motor (the springboard of the transport industry), the world's first induction ring (the basis of the world's power supply), and the very first sample of benzene to be isolated (and hence the basis of the world's chemical industry). There is nowhere else in London where so much of technological importance has sprung from such a small area.

P. W. ATKINS

P. W. Atkins was Professor of Chemistry at Oxford University until his retirement. He is the author of many widely used textbooks, and books on science for the general public.

3.8 Austin Reed Barber Shop

1930s, Joseph Emberton
103 Regent Street W1
020 7734 6789; www.austinreed.co.uk
⊖ Oxford Circus

The chrome and marble interior of this Art Deco barber shop has an austere glamour that is given a frivolous edge by an extraordinary twisting light fixture. It looks like the set of a Hollywood musical, and has survived remarkably intact, tucked away in the basement. The architect, Joseph Emberton, was also responsible for Simpsons Piccadilly (now Waterstone's, 203–206 Picadilly), and the HMV building on Oxford Street, as well as the exhibition buildings at Olympia and the Casino building on Blackpool Pleasure Beach—and the Royal Corinthian Yacht Club, which was featured in the first edition (but not the second) of *The International Style* (H. R. Hitchcock and P. Johnson).

ANDREW BALLANTYNE

Andrew Ballantyne has written about a wide range of topics in architectural history and theory. He is Professor of Architecture at Newcastle University.

3.9 G. Heywood Hill Ltd.

10 Curzon Street W1
020 7629 0647; www.heywoodhill.com
⊖ Green Park

🕮 This wonderful bookshop, idiosyncratic and full of character, is in many ways more like a cluttered private house than a shop; founded in 1936 by Heywood Hill, it earned a reputation as a rendezvous for leading figures in society and the literary world. It narrowly escaped closure during the Second World War, when Nancy Mitford and a loyal band of helpers were largely responsible for keeping it going; a plaque at the entrance recalls her efforts. The shop specialises in literature and books on history, architecture, biography, and travel, and it has a fine selection for children. It stocks old, new, and antiquarian titles, and its staff is the best informed and most obliging in London. What one sees today owes a great deal to John Saumarez Smith, who was managing director for thirty-four years, until his retirement in 2008. The ambience of the shop survived refurbishment in 1990, a process which has so often stripped old premises of their charm, and today, books are still piled high on every available surface and sometimes on the floor.

PETER HORROCKS

Peter Horrocks, a barrister, is a freeman of the City of London. He is a former Chairman of the Sherlock Holmes Society of London.

3.10 Shepherd Market

Located between Shepherd and Curzon Streets W1
www.shepherdmarket.co.uk

⊖ Green Park

Shepherd Market is bounded by Piccadilly and Curzon Street. I first saw it during World War II, when available ladies patrolled its streets, keeping up the raffish tradition of the eighteenth-century May Fair (which gave its name to the surrounding area). Both the May Fair and the ladies are gone now, although, in the early 1950s, when I took my wife there for the first time, she remarked, "Isn't it interesting that the dress shops have their models walking back and forth outside in front of them." Today, there are a variety of ethnic restaurants, pubs, and small shops; it's good for a snack or a meal almost any time of day or night.

KENNETH SEEMAN GINIGER
Kenneth Seeman Giniger is a book publisher, editor, and anthologist.

3.11 Farm Street Church

1849, Joseph James Scoles
114 Mount Street W1
020 7493 7811; www.farmstreet.org.uk
⊖ Bond Street

This is the Jesuit church where Graham Greene frequently confessed adultery. Despite its association with famous Catholic converts, the ornate church contains a mysterious spiritual silence alongside its glamour. Popular for Sunday mass with Mayfair diplomats, it is usually empty on weekdays. Light a candle, then eat coconut ice cream in the adjoining Mount Street gardens.

CAROLE MORIN
Carole Morin's books include Lampshades, Dead Glamorous, and Penniless in Park Lane.

MARYLEBONE

3.12 The Home of Benedict Arnold

62 Gloucester Place W1
Not open to the public.
⊖ Baker Street

The home of Benedict Arnold at 62 Gloucester Place in Marylebone is one of London's most ironic sites for American visitors. Arnold masterminded the defeat of the British military in New England, but became disillusioned with American politics. As commander at West Point, he switched sides and escaped to London, thereby becoming the American Revolution's most infamous traitor. But the plaque on his house reads, "Major General Benedict Arnold, American patriot, resided here from 1796 until his death, June 14, 1801." Could Arnold, universally defamed throughout American history, have been an "American patriot"? If so, how does history get told, and from what perspective? A walk past this historic marker by the American playwright Richard Nelson led to his drama, *The General from America*, starring the great British actor Corin Redgrave, whose performance received much acclaim in both England and the U.S.

ROBERT MARX

Robert Marx is an essayist on theatre and opera.

3.13 The Wallace Collection

In the Hertford House
Manchester Square W1
020 7563 9500; www.wallacecollection.org
⊖ Bond Street

The Wallace Collection has the reputation of being a repository of l'ancien régime at its most self-indulgent. Indeed it is crammed with Sèvres and Boulle and ormolu, the dimpled flesh of Boucher and the costly gleam of Titian and Velázquez and Rembrandt, lovely Watteaus, a remarkable collection from the golden age of Dutch painting and choice offerings in more specialised fields, armour, majolica, and mid-nineteenth-century French academic art. All housed in Lord Hertford's and Sir Richard Wallace's skilfully refurbished mansion, offering now a tranquil covered courtyard. Happily (or sadly!) you will not find crowds. This is London's Frick Collection. When will there be concerts in the courtyard on Sundays?

PETER CARSON

Peter Carson was formerly Editor-in-Chief at Penguin. Now semi-retired, he works as an editor for Profile Books and translates from Russian.

If you want a refuge from the maelstrom of Oxford Street, walk north past Selfridge's and across Manchester Square to the Wallace Collection. There you will be delighted by the delicate paintings of Boucher and Fragonard and the rather less delicate portrait of *The Laughing Cavalier*, splendidly displayed in a historic house full of eighteenth-century French furniture. In the courtyard, now roofed over to provide a light and spacious restaurant, you can meet friends or lunch over a newspaper.

DAME JENNIFER JENKINS

Dame Jennifer Jenkins is President of the Ancient Monuments and formerly Chair of the National Trust, the Consumers Association, and the Historic Buildings Council for England.

CHAPTER 4
Soho & Fiztrovia

1. Denmark Street
2. French Protestant Church
3. House of St. Barnabas
4. Manette House
5. Kettners
6. Maison Bertaux
7. Notre Dame de France
8. The Phoenix Theatre Bar
9. Princi
10. Andrew Edmunds
11. Bar Italia
12. Air Street
13. Royal Institute of British Architects
14. BBC Broadcasting House
15. The Goldbeater's Building
16. Back to Basics
17. Contemporary Applied Arts
18. Charlotte Street Hotel
19. Hat Factory
20. Bradley's
21. Costa Dorada

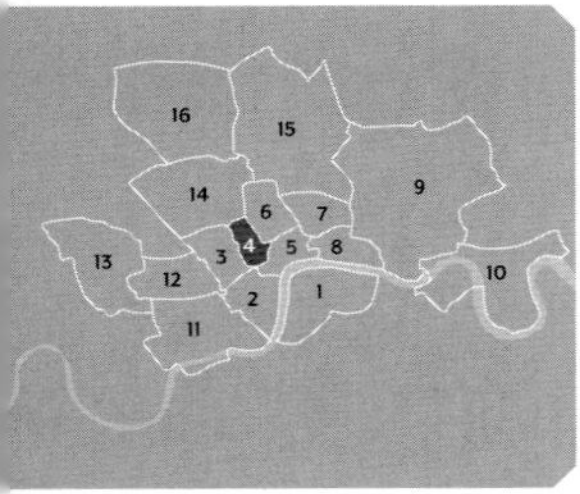

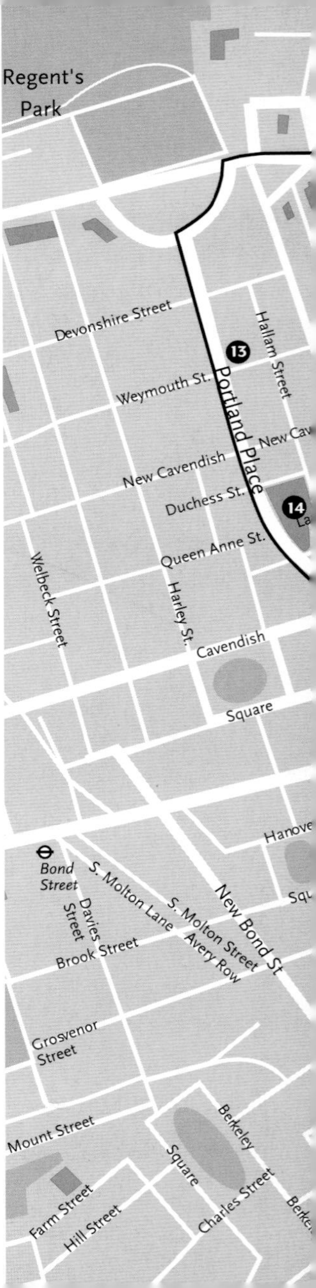

Soho & Fitzrovia

SOHO

4.1 Denmark Street
Between Charing Cross Road and St. Giles High Street WC2
⊖ Tottenham Court Road or Leicester Square

If rock and roll was one of the twentieth century's greatest contributions to Western culture, then Denmark Street's place in the grand scheme of history has been criminally underplayed—perhaps because it can hardly claim to be one of London's most respectable thoroughfares. A grubby afterthought of a street attaching its one-way obstinacy to Charing Cross Road's bookish charms, its permanently unswept pavements seem to have the knack of attracting only Soho's more insalubrious denizens. London's Tin Pan Alley it may be but Highway 61 it's not, and the Kinks' "Denmark Street" isn't exactly an ode to be proud of. However, there can't be many streets that the fields of oceanography, contemporary art, and rock and roll all owe debts to. Only the numerous guitar shops clumsily cranking out a perpetual loop of amateur Led Zeppelin renditions give any clue as to this seedy dog-leg of a street's past.

In the sixties (that Never-Never Land of my parents' youth), the Rolling Stones had their office here, Orange Amplifiers traded off The Who's patronage, and Bob Dylan played the 12 Bar Club—an endearingly shabby folk venue along Denmark Place, a tiny alleyway by Andy's Guitars. In the seventies, David Bowie frequented a long-gone café on the south side of the street, Elton John churned out a few hits, and a back room at number 6 gained anti-establishment credibility as the Sex Pistols' rehearsal space.

So next time you marvel at the Mall, or drink in the grandeur of St. Paul's, spare a thought for poor old Denmark Street. Like Janis Joplin, it may not be much to look at, but boy, it's got soul.

DAN FOX

Dan Fox is senior editor of Frieze magazine. He is also a writer, filmmaker, and musician.

The French Connection

⊖ Tottenham Court Road or Leicester Square

4.2 **French Protestant Church**
1893, Aston Webb
8–9 Soho Square W1
020 7437 5311; www.egliseprotestantelondres.org.uk

4.3 **House of St. Barnabas**
1 Greek Street W1
020 7437 1894; www.hosb.org.uk

4.4 **Manette House**
Manette Street, across from the Goldbeater's Arm W1

4.5 **Kettners**
29 Romilly Street W1
020 7734 6112; www.kettners.com

4.6 **Maison Bertaux**
28 Greek Street W1
020 7437 6007; www.maisonbertaux.com

4.7 **Notre Dame de France**
1865, Louis-Auguste Boileau; 1953–1955, rebuilt by Hector O. Corfiato
5 Leicester Place WC2
020 7437 9363; www.notredamechurch.co.uk

Greek Street (named after a Restoration Greek church) was taken over by the French in the 1690s. The influence of those Huguenot refugees still gives the place a French flavour. In the northwest corner of Soho Square is the

French Protestant Church, a deep red Flemish Gothic building designed by Aston Webb, who also gave us the façades of the V & A and Buckingham Palace. On the opposite corner at the top of Greek Street stands the House of St. Barnabas, birthplace of the Gothic horror author William Beckford, who received piano lessons from Mozart here. Since 1861 it has been House of Charity for Homeless Women, and is mentioned in Dickens's *A Tale of Two Cities*. Further down Greek Street, if you duck through the arch at the Pillars of Hercules pub, you will enter Manette Street, named in 1895 after Doctor Manette from the same book, and see the house where the Manettes might have lived (the wall opposite it still sports a replica of the goldbeater's sign described in the novel).

🍽 If you're thirsty, nip into Oscar Wilde's favourite restaurant, Kettners (founded in 1868 by Napoleon III's chef), for a quick glass of champagne, or the oldest French
🍽 patisserie in London, Maison Bertaux (founded by Communards in 1871), for a coffee and the best *chocolat religieuse* you will taste outside Paris. Maison Bertaux is run by the eccentric actress Michele Wade who, on July 14th, occasionally performs a *tableau vivant* of the French Revolution in the street outside, complete with a guillotine, *tricolores*, and a carefully arranged glimpse of nipple.

Dash across Shaftesbury Avenue, through Chinatown, and into Leicester Place to Notre Dame de France, London's French Catholic church. Built on the grounds of the former panorama, a vast circular oil painting created by Robert Barker in 1793, the building was converted into a church in 1865, much of which was destroyed by bombs during World War II, but was again rebuilt after the war. It still contains Barker's ninety-foot diameter circular plan, and inside there are frescoes painted by Jean Cocteau in 1960.

FIDELIS MORGAN

Fidelis Morgan, writer and actor, is the author of a mystery series set in London.

4.8 The Phoenix Theatre Bar

111 Charing Cross Road WC2

020 7836 1077; www.phoenixartistclub.com

⊖ Leicester Square or Tottenham Court Road

🍴 Below the Phoenix Theatre on Charing Cross Road is the Phoenix Artist Club, a drinking den covered in decades' worth of headshots, playbills, and some of the best bad paintings in the capital.

Presided over by Maurice, rarely seen without a brightly brocaded waistcoat, you're as likely to hear your favourite show tunes as you are songs from musicals long forgotten. It's also one of the few places in the West End where actors can actually afford a round, and possibly the only place one can find beer mats (ostensibly for smoking breaks) that read, "I'm out with a fag."

TRAVIS ELBOROUGH

Travis Elborough is the author of The Bus We Loved: London's Affair with the Routemaster and Wish You Were Here: England on Sea.

4.9 Princi

135 Wardour Street W1

020 7478 8888; www.princi.co.uk

⊖ Tottenham Court Road or Oxford Circus

🍴 When Princi opened a few years ago, in the middle of the financial crisis, it seemed a little too good to be true. A huge, expensively decorated café, complete with indoor fountain and fancy cutlery, serving properly made Italian pastries, pizza, pasta, coffee, and alcohol almost round the clock, and at strikingly low prices: such affordable, grown-up pleasures were out of place in expensive but still slightly shabby central London. Princi would surely go bust in six months. It hasn't, but it has got much busier, so avoid weekend evenings and lunchtimes. Instead, go mid-morning or mid-afternoon during the week; spread out your newspaper on one of the smooth, stone-topped communal tables, make sure there are no advertising or fashion people holding a loud impromptu meeting within earshot, and see if you can manage something from every section of the menu. Then stagger outside and try to imagine you're in Milan. The illusion may last as long as thirty seconds.

ANDY BECKETT
Andy Beckett is a feature writer for The Guardian and the author of When the Lights Went Out: Britain in the Seventies.

4.10   Andrew Edmunds

46 Lexington Street W1
020 7437 8594
⊖ Oxford Circus or Piccadilly Circus

🎁 🍴 What I liked about Soho when I lived there as a child was its sense of secrecy and history. There are few remaining places in Soho now which give me this sensation, but one that still does is the shop in Lexington Street run by, and called, Andrew Edmunds (who also owns the excellent restaurant of the same name next door). The shop sells eighteenth-century prints, including English satirical prints, which I have always loved. The building is wonderful too—a panelled Georgian townhouse.

MARK SLADEN
Mark Sladen is a curator and writer based in London.

4.11 **Bar Italia**

22 Frith Street W1

020 7437 4520; www.baritaliasoho.co.uk

Tottenham Court Road or Leicester Square

In his laboratory in a room above what is now this café, John Logie Baird transmitted the first television pictures. Using a mechanical scanner made from a hatbox mounted on a coffin lid, Baird watched as the screen on his "televisor" flickered to reveal the outline of a ventriloquist's dummy (no human had been brave enough to volunteer to be transported across the airwaves); Baird rushed downstairs to tell the world. Now, you can sip your espresso and watch the mixed-media executives and film PRs go by.

TIM ADAMS

Tim Adams is a staff writer at The Observer, where he was formerly Literary Editor.

4.12 **Air Street**

From Glasshouse Street to Piccadilly W1

Piccadilly Circus

The weight and mass of the huge stone arches which loom over the two short halves of Air Street darken the mood, oppress the pedestrian, and heighten the drama of emerging into the elegance first of the sweeping curve of Regent Street and then of the pompous parade of Piccadilly.

One of the misconceptions about London is that it lacks grandeur. Walk from the crowded streets of Soho down the vaulted tunnel of Air Street and this notion will be dispelled. London excels in the juxtaposition of extreme opposites, and the contrast between the dirty, dense streets of Soho and the Beaux Arts bombast of the West End is accentuated by this grand alley. The Brobdingnagian scale of the arches, the deep shadows

of the rustication, and the intense downward pressure
of the weighty stone seem to derive from the brooding
prison fantasies of Piranesi. The only glimpse of the sky is
carefully measured through a colonnade which sits atop
the arches, creating an unattainable upper level.

Incredibly, the architecture dates from as late as 1923,
when Regent Street was rebuilt in its current grand
incarnation. Obliquely opposite in Piccadilly you can see
one of London's finest storefronts in the Waterstone's
store (203–206 Piccadilly), a smooth-faced work of
modernism of great clarity which was completed only a
little more than a decade after the massive arches of Air
Street yet seems to belong to a different world. Air Street
acts like a breach in the city walls, a monumental gateway
from the genteel world of West End shopping into the
dark, Dickensian world of Soho's back streets. Be careful
of the piles of black rubbish bags which appear at these
city gates during the night, an indication of Air Street's
status as the seedy service underbelly of West End
grandeur and a stark reminder that this is an unsanitized,
if monumental, alley in a big city.

EDWIN HEATHCOTE
Architect Edwin Heathcote is the Architecture and Design critic of the Financial Times, co-founder of the door handle manufacturer Izé, and an author.

FITZROVIA

4.13 Royal Institute of British Architects

1934, Grey Wornum
66 Portland Place W1
020 7580 5533; www.architecture.com
⊖ Regent's Park or Great Portland Street

The RIBA is a classic example of a thirties building
commissioned by architects for architects. Its architect,

Grey Wornum, a progressive traditionalist, won the job in open competition in 1932. The symmetrical simplicity of its exterior belies an astonishing openness inside: do walk up to the second floor and look down at the imaginative handling of the staircases and the transparency of the glass screens. The quality and craftsmanship of its applied decoration and sculpture, all of which symbolises architecture and the building trades, make it the most interesting piece of art of the inter-war period in London.

MARGARET RICHARDSON

Margaret Richardson is a Council member of the National Trust, the Society of Antiquaries, and the Hon. Curator of Architecture at the Royal Academy.

4

4.14 BBC Broadcasting House

1932, G. Val Myers
Portland Place W1
020 7765 4422; www.bbc.co.uk
For tour schedule, call 0370 901 1227. Reservations are required.
⊖ Regent's Park or Great Portland Street

A temple to Lord Reith's aspirations for the BBC. It's curved like a great ship, the prow facing into London.

But it reminds me of something else as well. In the 1560s, the Flemish painter Pieter Bruegel the Elder did two paintings of the Tower of Babel, a structure weirdly like Broadcasting House. According to Genesis, God prevented the completion of the tower by causing everyone to speak in mutually incomprehensible languages. This seems very apt for the babel of voices which have emanated from the BBC over the years. Once you've seen the similarity, you can't forget it. And it's a marvellous building.

VICTORIA GLENDINNING

Victoria Glendinning is a prize-winning biographer and journalist.

A Film Buff's Stroll

For thirty years I worked at Broadcasting House near Oxford Circus, and lived first on the west side of Hampstead Heath, then on the east side, and would often walk the three miles home via Camden Town. The first journey is the one Sherlock Holmes and Dr. Watson took from Oxford Street to Hampstead in *The Adventure of Charles Augustus Milverton* to burgle the home of the "king of all blackmailers," who lived at a Gothic mansion on the corner of East Heath Road and Well Road. They subsequently fled from the house, zigzagging across the Heath to emerge presumably on the Highgate Road and catch a cab back to Baker Street.

The second journey is the one walked by the intrepid Richard Hannay in John Buchan's classic conspiracy thriller *The Three Hostages*, just after World War I, following the first clue that leads him from Oxford Circus via Camden Town to Gospel Oak at the Heath's southeast corner. His walk takes him past the apartment block at 122 Portland Place from which Hannay would later escape, disguised as a milkman, in Hitchcock's *The 39 Steps*.

The most sublime Hitchcock image from the 1930s is of the unattended horse-drawn milk-float in Park Crescent. You can get to Camden Town by the Nash Terraces of Regent's Park's Outer Circle or Albany Street, from the top of which, at the White House, the Soviet spy Gordon Lonsdale ran his espionage ring in the 1960s. Camden Town is where the nine-year-old Charles Dickens lived in Bayham Street, as well as being the home of the Cratchit family in *A Christmas Carol* and the inner-city area transformed by the coming of the railways in *Dombey and Son*. At Parkway, Camden Town, is Palmer's Pet Store, above which the Communist leader Bennett lived in Graham Greene's *It's a Battlefield*. (The black-and-white shopfront remains intact but inside is now a fashionable café, Yumchaa.)

Going North by the Holmes or the Hannay route takes you through George Orwell territory—in the mid-1930s he lived in Warwick Mansions, Pond Street, 77 Parliament Hill, and 50 Lawford Road, Kentish Town, and worked at a bookshop called Booklover's Corner (immortalised in *Keep the Aspidistra Flying*) in South End Green, as recorded by a plaque on the corner. At Gospel Oak you'll reach Gordon House Road, along which a psychopathic hitman drives on his way to a killing on the opening page of Ruth Rendell's *The Lake of Darkness*. Cross over to the Heath and climb to the top of Parliament Hill, where D. H. Lawrence and Frieda watched zeppelins bombing London in World War I, as described in *Kangaroo*.

PHILIP FRENCH

Philip French is The Observer's film critic, author of Westerns, and co-editor of The Faber Book of Movie Verse.

4.15 The Goldbeater's Building

1919, Ernest H. Abbott
54–60 Whitfield Street w1
⊖ Warren Street or Goodge Street

The area called Fitzrovia, to the north of Oxford Street and west of Tottenham Court Road, is famous for its early-twentieth-century artists and writers—Augustus John, Walter Sickert, Wyndham Lewis, George Orwell, and many others. Little note is made of the area's interesting industries, but one of these was the production of gold leaf.

George Manning Whiley was a goldbeater and since 1896 had worked in Whitfield Street. He grew wealthy and commissioned an interesting building, now called the Goldbeater's Building, from an architect by the name of

Ernest H. Abbott, about whom almost nothing is known. The façade has decorative capitals that incorporate tools of the goldbeaters' trade. The building was completed in 1919 and has passed through many hands since Whiley's day. Local residents have fought against its demolition but only the façade was saved.

MICHELE FIELD
Michele Field is a writer on food issues and on the materials environment.

4.16 Back to Basics

21a Foley Street W1
020 7436 2181; www.backtobasics.uk.com
⊖ Oxford Circus or Goodge Street

⊗ This is an unpretentious fish restaurant, located in a lively pocket of bars and restaurants which are less well-known than those on Charlotte Street. In the summer, tables outside quickly fill with BBC lunchers. Gypsy bands come serenading and a colony of seagulls living inexplicably in the area create the illusion of a harbour nearby. The food is always deliciously fresh. There are no great tourist sites in Fitzrovia, but it's a good place to head after exploring Bloomsbury or to get away from shopping crowds.

OPHELIA FIELD
Ophelia Field is a biographer, journalist, and policy analyst in the field of refugees and human rights.

Specialty Shops

11.20 Egg

36 Kinnerton Street SW1
(see p. 212)
020 7235 9315; www.eggtrading.eu
Closed Sundays and Mondays.
⊖ Knightsbridge

16.18 Livingstone Studio
36 New End Square NW3
020 7431 6311
⊖ Hampstead

4.17 Contemporary Applied Arts
2 Percy Street W1
020 7436 2344; www.caa.org.uk
⊖ Goodge Street

4

4.18 Charlotte Street Hotel
15–17 Charlotte Street W1
020 7907 4000; www.firmdalehotels.com
⊖ Goodge Street

🎁 There are some shops which are almost art galleries, and if you come only to look, you look with a different eye than when you look at priceless (or unpriced) pieces in a museum. Egg in South Kensington and Livingstone Studio in Hampstead are two such shops, but my favorite is Contemporary Applied Arts in Fitzrovia. This "shop" has seven seasons each year, each season six or seven weeks long. Everything on the two floors changes with each season, much as it would in a commercial art gallery. There is background to read for each object, as in a museum—so you buy a provenance, no matter how practical the teapot or how "everyday" the earrings. And you can buy postcards showing what you might have acquired if money or space were no object.

Contemporary Applied Arts is at the bottom end of Charlotte Street on the corner with Percy. This is media central, with CNN and Pearson and dozens of film and television companies within sight of one another. After a visit to Contemporary Applied Arts, enjoy a drink at the
🍴 Charlotte Street Hotel, a building which once housed London's biggest supplier of dentists' chairs and

drills—and opened in 2000 as a gentlemanly hub (as opposed to gentleman's club) for the arts and media.

MICHELE FIELD

Michele Field is a writer on food issues and on the materials environment.

4.19 Hat Factory

105 Oxford Street W1

⊖ Goodge Street

Maddening to cross the traffic of Oxford Street at any time, but if you are stuck outside the HMV shop or nearby, walk with your back to the Marble Arch end, to Newman Street which crosses Oxford Street to become Great Chapel Street on the south side. The block on this corner was built in 1887 as a hat factory for Henry Heath, whose name is majestically lettered on the workers' entrance round the back, on Hollen Street. At 105 Oxford Street, the central facia is decorated by four carved figures associated with the hat trade. Designed by Benjamin Creswick, a protégé of Ruskin, they are visible high against the skyline, and include a delightful stone beaver, contemplating a jump down onto the roof, or wagging its paddle in disapproval when observed by a tipsy eye.

GEOFFREY ELBORN

Geoffrey Elborn, a biographer and critic, has written about lives of Edith Sitwell and Francis Stuart.

Hanway Street

Off Oxford Street, north of Soho Square W1

✆ Tottenham Court Road

4.20 Bradley's

42–44 Hanway Street

020 7636 0359

4.21 Costa Dorada

47–55 Hanway Street

020 7631 5117; www.costadoradarestaurant.co.uk

5.10 Oasis

32 Endell Street

020 7831 1804; www.camden.gov.uk

🍴🐠 London can be a hard home: sink or swim, it says. If you're sinking, then the best way to drown is to head for Hanway Street, the side alley that connects the east of Oxford Street to Tottenham Court Road.

Start off in the basement of Bradley's for Guinness, tapas, and London's finest jukebox: it boasts the theme tune to *The White Horses*, and several Elvis rarities. After-hours, move on to Costa Dorada: five quid in after nine on a Friday and Saturday, dogged flamenco dancing, more tapas and room to stretch out and argue.

And if you're swimming? Make straight for Oasis, the outdoor swimming pool at the end of Shaftesbury Avenue.

MIRANDA SAWYER

Miranda Sawyer is a journalist and broadcaster.

CHAPTER 5
Trafalgar Square, Covent Garden & Holborn

1   The National Gallery
2   National Portrait Gallery
3   St. Martin-in-the-Fields Church
4   Post Office
5   Statue of King Charles I
6   Lyceum Theatre
7   Theatre Royal, Drury Lane
8   The Criterion Theatre
9   Sir John Soane's Museum
10 Oasis (see p. 79)
11 The Hunterian Museum
12 The Royal Opera House ¶♀
13 Somerset House
14 The Adelphi
15 Royal Society of Arts
16 Gordon's Wine Bar ¶♀
17 Lincoln's Inn
18 Gray's Inn
19 Inner Temple
20 Middle Temple
21 Middle Temple Hall
22 Temple Church
23 C. Hoare and Co.
24 Prince Henry's Room

Trafalgar Square, Covent Garden & Holborn

TRAFALGAR SQUARE

5.1 The National Gallery

Trafalgar Square WC2
020 7747 2885; www.nationalgallery.org.uk
⊖ Charing Cross

Perhaps the most visited building in London, but not to be omitted for that reason. It is the world's most magisterial collection of European painting. Less rubbish than in either the Uffizi or the Louvre. The Sainsbury Wing (disliked by modernist architects but decorated in convincing reproduction of Florentine pietra santa) houses an unequalled collection of Italian art—from early Sienese to Mannerism. Most user-friendly, visible gallery in Europe.
PETER PORTER
Peter Porter is a poet.

Supper at Emmaus
1600–1601, Caravaggio

No visit to London would be complete without a climb up the grand central staircase of the National Gallery, and a brief wander through stately rooms and glass doorways to the heart of the Baroque, and to Caravaggio.

To stand in front of this painting is to enter an ordinary home in Rome around the year 1600. The torn clothes and the simple food, table, and chairs bring that very different world to immediate and vivid life. But this is no ordinary home. The drama as the apostles suddenly recognize the resurrected Jesus leaps out of the painting.

One spreads his arms wide, almost reaching out of the canvas; the other grips the arms of his chair, about to rise in amazement. As you look, the textures and the colours that Caravaggio has created—the wood, the meat, the cloth, the muted green and brown—gradually bring the scene into recognizable reality. You leave, aware once again, of the possibility of the miraculous amidst everyday life.

<small>THEODORE K. RABB</small>
Theodore K. Rabb is Emeritus Professor of History at Princeton.

The Arnolfini Portrait
1434, Jan van Eyck

A trip to London should certainly include a pilgrimage to Jan van Eyck's *The Arnolfini Portrait* in the galleries of early Netherlandish paintings at the National Gallery. I am always surprised by this jewel of a painting's small size and intense colours, since the image was imprinted in my brain long ago through an in-depth elucidation of the painting before a projection of a large black-and-white glass slide by Howard McP. Davis at Columbia University.

Scholars dispute the function of the painting and the possible meanings of the shoes, the dog, the orange on the windowsill, and even the identity of the couple, but I would venture that few would argue about the chills that can be sent down your spine by the inscription "Johannes de eyck fuit hic 1434" ("Jan van Eyck was here 1434") on the back wall and the tiny reflection of the artist himself at this event in the mirror.

<small>NADINE ORENSTEIN</small>
Nadine Orenstein is Curator in charge of Dutch, Flemish, and German Old Master prints in the Metropolitan Museum of Art.

Museum Trails

Visiting museums with children, an activity that so often takes on the character of a forced march, is most enjoyable in London, where all of the major galleries—and many of the small ones—provide a particularly British item called "trails." For Americans unfamiliar with the term, these are simple guides through the museums especially geared to children. Available at the front desk, they are usually free (and never more than a few pence). At best, they provide the excitement of a treasure hunt; at the very least, they point parents in the direction of pieces in the collection most likely to appeal to children.

Over the years, our family has devised our own trails of artworks in three favorite museums: the British Museum, the National Gallery, and the National Portrait Gallery.

6.11 The British Museum

Great Russell Street WC1
020 7323 8000; www.britishmuseum.org
(see p. 121)
⊖ Tottenham Court Road

The crowds are overwhelming, but it's worth soldiering through to view the Mildenhall Treasure. Beforehand, be sure to read Roald Dahl's riveting account of the discovery of this Roman silver—the greatest treasure ever found in the British Isles—by a farmer plowing his field in Suffolk in 1942, and of the treachery that ensued. In addition, don't miss the greatest surviving set of medieval chessmen. Most enthralling of all, however, is the Lindow Man: the body of a murdered prehistoric man discovered under a peat bog and now enhanced by a hologram which lends an unearthly glimmer. His body dates back to the Iron Age—mid-first century C.E.—and he was found in

1985 in Lindow Moss, Cheshire, England. He's affectionately called Pete Marsh, and we've found it nearly impossible to tear ourselves away from him in less than twenty minutes.

5.1 **The National Gallery**
Trafalgar Square WC2
020 7747 2885; www.nationalgallery.org.uk
(see p. 82)
⊖ Charing Cross

5

While not particularly bloodthirsty in real life, our children nonetheless have never tired of visiting *Perseus Turning Phineas and His Followers to Stone*, by Luca Giordano (1680); *Belshazzar's Feast*, by Rembrandt (1635), with its terrifying judgement in Hebrew, "You have been weighed in the balances and have been found wanting"; and the endlessly alluring *Samson and Delilah*, by Peter Paul Rubens (1609).

If parents can recount the stories behind the paintings, following a Biblical trail is another way to wend your way through the galleries. Here are some dramatic moments: *The Agony in the Garden*, by Andrea Mantegna (1460); *The Stigmatisation of Saint Francis*, part of *The Life of Saint Francis*, by Sassetta (1437–1444); *Christ Driving the Traders from the Temple*, by El Greco (1600); *Saint Jerome in a Rocky Landscape*, attributed to Joachim Patinir (1515–1524); *Joseph with Jacob in Egypt*, by Jacopo Pontormo (1518); *The Raising of Lazarus*, by Sebastiano del Piombo (1517–1519); *Christ Washing the Feet of His Disciples*, by Jacopo Tintoretto (c. 1556); *The Supper at Emmaus*, by Caravaggio (1601), with the teetering fruit basket about to fall onto the floor of the National Gallery; *Christ Before the High Priest*, by Gerrit van Honthorst (1617); and *The Finding of Moses*, by Nicolas Poussin (1651).

A warning note: we've always found *A Grotesque Old Woman*, attributed to Quinten Massys (1525–1530), much too creepy, especially for the six and unders.

5.2 National Portrait Gallery
2 St. Martin's Place WC2
020 7306 0055; www.npg.org.uk
(see p. 89)
⊖ Charing Cross

One way to enjoy this lovely, moving collection is to purchase select postcards in the gift shop beforehand, then hand them to the children and ask them to find the corresponding paintings. (Ask the children not to turn over the postcard and read the subject's name before finding it.) Younger children will be charmed to discover Beatrix Potter, J. R. R. Tolkien, and A. A. Milne and Christopher Robin Milne with Winnie the Pooh. Another great conversation piece is the portrait of Edward VI, the little prince who ascended to the throne at age nine and was immortalized in Mark Twain's *The Prince and the Pauper*. No child will fail to be moved by the story of the prince who changed places with a poor boy just for a trial, but whose life might have changed permanently, were it not for the deep faith of the one, and the sincere honesty of the other.

Older children will be intrigued by the portraits of Charles Dickens, the Brontës, Charles Darwin, Lord Byron, Elton John, Paul McCartney, and a host of others.

Angela Hederman
Angela Hederman is editor and publisher at The Little Bookroom in New York.

Trafalgar Square Afternoon
⊖ Charing Cross

5.3 **St. Martin-in-the-Fields Church**
1682–1754
Trafalgar Square WC2
020 7766 1100; www.stmartin-in-the-fields.org

5.4 **Post Office**
24–28 William IV Street WC2

5

5.2 **National Portrait Gallery**
2 St. Martin's Place WC2
020 7306 0055; www.npg.org.uk

Everyone has heard recordings of music performed by the Academy of St. Martin-in-the-Fields. In London, you have a chance to visit the actual church and hear a free performance. (Recitals are offered several afternoons a week and donations are at the visitor's discretion—check a daily paper for performers and times.) Afterwards, be certain to go downstairs to the crypt, where you will walk over marked graves as you buy an inexpensive but tasty lunch at the Café in the Crypt. On some days at the back of the church a small open-air market is held, where jewellery, posters, and other quirky items are sold. Near the church (on the same street, leading into Charing Cross Road) is a post office where you can buy stamps—and not just for mailing cards home, either. British stamps honour authors and events, and are wonderfully handsome. A set can be framed. (I have the four stamps commemorating comic poet Edward Lear, each with a reproduction of one of his drawings and a line or two of his text, hanging over my writing desk.) And finally, cross the street and go into possibly the most interesting museum in all of London or England—the National Portrait Gallery. Here are portraits, some formal, some caricatures, some photographs and even sculptures of the most significant people in British history: royalty, rock stars, writers, actors, sports figures, and prime ministers. This small area can keep you occupied, entertained, and fed for at least half a day.

JOHANNA HURWITZ
Johanna Hurwitz is the award-winning author of seventy popular children's books.

A Giant's Wedding

Halfway through the writing of my novel about the Canadian giantess Anna Swan, I found myself on the steps of St. Martin-in-the-Fields, imagining her June wedding in 1871 to her giant American husband at one of London's most loved churches. I stood on the grand neoclassical portico looking out through its three-storey columns at Trafalgar Square, dwarfed as she must have been by St. Martin's vast scale. Still, feeling small would have been a pleasure for my giantess, who stood seven foot six in her stockinged feet, weighed 413 pounds, and tried all her life to exemplify the virtues of a thoughtful Victorian lady.

Although she exhibited with P. T. Barnum in New York during the 1860s, she read widely and dressed in the style of the time, which meant following the fashions in *Godey's Lady's Book*. Her Victorian dresses were so voluminous that she is said, on one occasion, to have knocked a man off his chair entering a drawing room. Despite her best efforts, Anna's extraordinary female body remained a challenge to Victorian notions of femininity and a caricature of her own aspirations for respectability.

Both Anna and her groom, Martin Van Buren Bates, were interested in history, so it's possible that they knew that St. Martin-in-the-Fields dates back to 1222, when the monks of Westminster pastured their animals and grew their fruits and vegetables in Covent Garden. But the giants probably chose the cathedral, which was rebuilt in 1722–1724 by the architect James Gibbs, primarily because it was in London's theatre district. It was also close to their new home, an apartment on 45 Craven Street.

The wedding at St. Martin's was an auspicious London event, staged with the blessing of Queen Victoria, who had asked the couple to appear before her on June 2nd at Buckingham Palace. The Queen, who stood only four feet seven inches herself, was so delighted with the pair, sometimes known as "the love couple," that she gave Anna a cluster diamond ring and Martin a giant watch and chain.

The crowd outside St. Martin's after the wedding was so large that the police had problems clearing a path for the wedding party as it left for 45 Craven Street. A reporter from London's *Daily Telegraph* politely referred to the groom's panic after he dropped the ring during the ceremony in this way: "A giant may get used to being eight feet, but marrying an eight foot woman while idlers gawk is enough to flummox any old cock. . . ."

Whether Anna truly felt satisfied with herself is hard to say. She died in 1888 at the age of forty-four, worn down by gravity, like most giants, and by the hardship of her last birth labour. But for me St. Martin's remains the place where she stepped so happily into her married life.

SUSAN SWAN

Susan Swan's books include What Casanova Told Me *and* The Wives of Bath.

5.2 National Portrait Gallery

2 St. Martin's Place WC2

020 7845 4600; www.npg.org.uk

⊖ Charing Cross

I recommend the Portrait Gallery, especially, after its brilliant redesign by Dixon Jones, the architects who refurbished the Royal Opera House. From the top-floor

¶ restaurant, the Portrait Café, is my favourite view of the Houses of Parliament; after seeing that I am ready to go back for another look at the sinister Tudor portraits, situated in a small, dimly lit gallery which effectively conveys the tense and secretive atmosphere of the era.

LADY STIRLING (MARY SHAND)
Lady Stirling is a furniture and interior designer.

5.5 Statue of King Charles I

1633, Hubert Le Sueur
Trafalgar Square WC2
⊖ Charing Cross

The statue of Charles I is arguably the finest, most striking, and most evocative of all London statues. However, very few of the thousands who pass it every day pause to admire it on its island site, let alone know of its long and colourful history. It is the work of Hubert Le Sueur and dates from 1633. It was not erected in its present location until about 1675, having been sold under Cromwell to a brazier who, with a shrewd eye to later financial advantage, buried it until the Restoration though he was ordered to destroy it. The statue predates Trafalgar Square itself by some hundred and fifty years and is one of the oldest remaining features of this part of London. It is prominent in one of the earliest known photographs of London, taken in 1838, when the statue was already two hundred years old. During the Second World War it was removed, and upon its return in 1947 it was given a new sword to replace the original, which had disappeared in 1867. Each year on January 30th at 11 a.m., a wreath-laying takes place at the statue to commemorate the execution of the King on that day in 1649.

PETER HORROCKS
Peter Horrocks, a barrister, is a freeman of the City of London. He is a former Chairman of the Sherlock Holmes Society of London.

COVENT GARDEN

London Theatre Architecture

5.6 **Lyceum Theatre**
1834, façade and portico by Samuel Beazley
12 Wellington Street WC2
020 7420 8100; www.lyceumtheatrelondon.org.uk
⊖ Covent Garden or Charing Cross

5

5.7 **Theatre Royal, Drury Lane**
1812, Benjamin Dean Wyatt
Catherine Street WC2
0844 412 2955; www.reallyuseful.com
⊖ Covent Garden

5.8 **The Criterion Theatre**
1873, Thomas Verity
218–223 Piccadilly W1
0870 060 2313; www.criterion-theatre.co.uk
⊖ Piccadilly Circus or Leicester Square

No city in the world has a greater concentration of nineteenth- and early-twentieth-century theatre buildings than London. Far more than in the side streets of Times Square in New York, a walk through London's West End is an experience in thrilling theatrical architecture. From the gorgeous columned façade of the Lyceum to the arcades of Drury Lane (Catherine Street) to the underground Criterion (where one enters from street level above the second balcony, then descends via lushly mirrored Victorian tiled stairwells towards prime seating further down), these buildings show remarkably little repetition in character. Distinct personalities of brick, plaster, and theatre history abound. Nearly all the theatres have survived as mix-and-match designs altered by different management across two centuries. (The

Drury Lane's lobby is from 1811, the façade from the 1820s, and its auditorium from 1922. Some Drury Lane foundation stones probably date back to the theatre's original structure of 1663.) Wonderful theatre buildings can be found throughout London, but the West End "Theatreland" district remains its core along Shaftsbury Avenue, Charing Cross Road, St. Martin's Lane, Haymarket, the Strand, and dozens of side streets. Look up as you walk. See a play. Enjoy.

ROBERT MARX

Robert Marx is an essayist on theatre and opera.

5.9   Sir John Soane's Museum

1792–1824, Sir John Soane
13 Lincoln's Inn Fields WC2
020 7405 2107; www.soane.org

⊖   Holborn

Sir John Soane's Museum is still probably the least known museum in London. Even though its three contiguous townhouses are crammed with fine art and artifacts—Turners, William Hogarth's most famous work, A Rake's Progress, bronze sculptures, antique cork architectural models, and Regency décor—the museum at 13 Lincoln's Inn Fields, bequeathed to the nation by the architect John Soane upon his death in 1837, attracts only a hundred thousand visitors a year.

This may change: The museum has launched a program called "Opening Up the Soane," making a series of "lost" interiors, including his bedroom and bath, accessible to the public for the first time since the architect's death. The director, Tim Knox, former head of the National Trust, has written a new book on the museum, and it includes splendid photographs by Derry Moore; there is a new study centre where scholars can examine the ten thousand

Robert Adam drawings in the collection; and a conservation lab is currently under construction.

Soane was a bricklayer's son who apprenticed with architects. He became such an accomplished draftsman that he won the Prix de Rome, a three-year scholarship to study in the Italian capital. He eventually became the architect of the Bank of England, and wealthy enough to collect everything from contemporary paintings to an Egyptian sarcophagus. (He was a shopaholic on the level of Andy Warhol.) He continually re-arranged the rooms in his house, adding yellow-glass skylights, and creating mysterious spaces that still delight visitors. For decades he taught architecture students from the Royal Academy in his atelier, which partly explains the wealth of architectural models and plaster casts.

Considered a classicist, Soane was actually a "proto-modernist," interested in stripping down Beaux Art idioms. To this day, he remains popular with architects of every stripe: neoclassicists, modernists, post-modernists, and even the avant-garde (Frank Gehry, Jean Nouvel, Zaha Hadid). Many artists (including Anish Kapoor) say they find inspiration in the idiosyncratic museum and visit it often. Now, with the "opening up," it's time for the general public to appreciate the special appeal of Sir John Soane's enduring vision.

WENDY MOONAN

Wendy Moonan covers architecture, fine arts, and the decorative arts for Veranda and Elle Decor, as well as for several websites.

"Oranges and Lemons"

The bells of the medieval church towers of London mark out its topography. Even now, despite cars, sirens, and cell phones, the peal of bells on a quiet Sunday morning ring from different corners of the city, one after the

other. The importance of parish churches was broadcast
in their bells—the more bells of different tones, and the
more skilful the bell ringers, the more powerful the
parish. In London there was a famous children's song that
gave words to the peals of bells. It has many different
versions, but the first one recorded is from 1744:

> Two sticks and apple,
> Ring the bells at Whitechapel,
> Old Father Bald Pate,
> Ring the bells at Aldgate,
> Maids in white aprons,
> Ring the bells at St. Catherine's,
> Oranges and lemons,
> Ring the bells at St. Clement's,
> When will you pay me?
> Ring the bells at the Old Bailey,
> When I am rich!
> Ring the bells at Fleetditch,
> When will that be?
> Ring the bells at Stepney,
> When I am old,
> Ring the bells at St. Paul's.

Some of the churches are very easy to identify: St.
Paul's, of course, and St. Aldgate. St. Martin's may be
St. Martin's Lane, in the City, apparently a zone of money-
lenders. The Old Bailey, a prison, did not have a bell, but
St. Sepulchre-without-Newgate was opposite it. St.
Clement's may be St. Clement Danes, on the Strand, or St.
Clement Eastcheap, both of which were close to the river
docks where ships unloaded goods, including imported
fruit. St. Clement Danes today rings the tune of the rhyme.

What I like about this rhyme is that it reminds us
about the way that church bells were beacons of

neighborhoods in old cities. To be Cockney was to be born within the sound of Bow's Bells (St. Mary le Bow), and that as well as other church peals made communities within the vast city. You hardly had to believe in the teachings of the Church to hear your neighborhood's church bells, by which people started and ended their day, each with a slightly different little song.

CAROLINE GOODSON

Caroline Goodson is an archaeologist and historian.

5

5.11 The Hunterian Museum

Founded in 1813
The Royal College of Surgeons
35–43 Lincoln's Inn Fields WC2
020 7405 3474; www.rcseng.ac.uk
⊖ Holborn

It's easy to understand why the selection of postcards this museum offers is so unrepresentative. Most of the things John Hunter, eighteenth-century surgeon and comparative anatomist, preserved and collected are far too disturbing for postcards; jar upon jar of human or animal organs in alcohol or formaldehyde, early wax models of dissections, the wasted bones of someone who suffered from osteosclerosis, a mummified hand. The contrast between the quiet orderliness of the place and the nature of some of the exhibits is one of the things that makes this collection so strangely compelling. And the pathos: the row of foetal skeletons, ranging from the first little wispy gathering at three months, through to the complete nine-month version, or the skeleton of the poor Irish Giant, who, having regretted his short career as a marketable freak, vainly sought to avoid the anatomists by asking to be buried at sea. But he is still on show, more than two hundred years later.

RUTH PAVEY

Ruth Pavey writes for national publications on contemporary fiction, crafts, and horticulture.

5.12 The Royal Opera House

The façade, foyer, and auditorium date from 1858;
1996–2000, reconstruction by Dixon Jones
Covent Garden WC2
020 7240 1200; www.roh.org.uk
⊖ Covent Garden

Floral Hall

1999, Dixon Jones

Even if you are not attending a performance in the main
theatre, go early evening for a drink in the spectacular
Floral Hall. Because of political sensitivities and the
lottery of funding, architects Jeremy Dixon and Ed Jones
almost grew old waiting for their plans for the expansion
and refurbishment of the crumbling House to take shape.
There is, then, a sense of celebration—and relief—as you
take the wonderful extravagant great glass escalator
through the vast crystal conservatory. At the top, in a
Starck-like bar you can view the early Opera crowd dining
below, or take in an unusual sweep of London skyline—
including, apparently standing out on the balcony,
Nelson on top of his column.

Tim Adams
Tim Adams is a staff writer at The Observer, where he was formerly
Literary Editor.

5.13 Somerset House

1776; 1998, fountains by Dixon Jones
Strand WC2
020 7845 4600; www.somersethouse.org.uk
⊖ Temple, Embankment, or Charing Cross

Robert Burton gave us a cure for melancholy: "Be not
solitary, be not idle." Now we have another one: go to the
Fountain Court of Somerset House at dusk.

Duncan Fallowell
Duncan Fallowell is an author and cultural commentator. His books include
Going As Far As I Can: The Ultimate Travel Book.

Somerset House has an elegantly restored cobbled courtyard and fountains by Dixon Jones enhancing the architecture. The Gilbert Collection and Hermitage Treasures and, of course, the Courtauld Institute Gallery are a treasure trove. The courtyard provides direct access to Waterloo Bridge, and there's an attractive outside café for tea on a warm day, with views along and across the Thames.

LADY STIRLING (MARY SHAND)
Lady Stirling is a furniture and interior designer.

5

The Adam Brothers

5.14 **The Adelphi**
1768–1774, Robert Adam
Strand WC2
Not open to the public.
Embankment or Charing Cross

5.15 **Royal Society of Arts (RSA)**
1772, Robert Adam
8 John Adam Street WC2
020 7930 5115; www.thersa.org
Not open to the public.
Charing Cross

Robert Adam's Adelphi (Greek for the "brothers," that is, Robert, James, John, and William) was built between 1768 and 1774, aided by a lottery in 1774.

It runs between the Thames and the Strand, and, though largely demolished in 1936, is a fine statement about Georgian urban architecture. The grandest is that for the Royal Society of Arts building, by Adam in 1772. His source lay in the quarters of Paris; it followed a graduated social structure, with the grandest houses in the Royal Terrace (now rebuilt) facing the river. A system of underground streets and passageways—a utilitarian labyrinth—supported, in every sense, the smart society above. Robert and James Adam lived in Royal Terrace from 1773 to 1778, as did the great actor David Garrick, from 1772 to 1775. Robert Adam moved in 1776 to the end house beside the river at 9 Robert Street, which survives and is shown in the engraving of the entire scheme of July 1768.

A. A. TAIT

A. A. Tait, a professor of art history at the University of Glasgow, is the author of two books on Robert Adam, the architect, and on landscape architecture.

5.16   **Gordon's Wine Bar**

Established in 1890

47 Villiers Street WC2

020 7930 1408; www.gordonswinebar.com

⊖ Embankment or Charing Cross

⊪ At the foot of Villiers Street, off the Strand, sits Gordon's, the oldest wine bar in London. A basement entered by neck-breakingly narrow stairs, this fine and squalid place also debouches a few awkward steps on to a shadowy alley where I loll, tumbler of *fino* in hand, with my back to gardens on the Thames embankment. In the summer, live jazz beats the traffic out of the air, and as I look up from the page of a paperback I feel intimately surrounded not only by the eighteenth century—at an angle I can glimpse Buckingham Street—but by modern business online in glimmering low-level offices, by a country summer breezing over my head, and by New Orleans stomping into our metropolis. If you get your moment right (the sherry's always there, with its savour of Spain), it's one of not so very many places in London where you have the delicious illusion of the whole world coming your way.

DAVID HUGHES

The late David Hughes was an award-wining crime writer. He published eleven novels, among them The Pork Butcher and The Little Book.

I love this place for its triumphant seediness, among so much that is brash and new and smart. The façade is so unassuming that you can pass it without seeing it. Downstairs, half the tables are in candlelit darkness under black, damp arches. The rest of the cellar is hung with prints and posters dating from the 1940s and 1950s. The walls are scabby, the furniture and fittings ancient, and I can't think how it's allowed to remain open! It's always buzzing and the wines are excellent.

VICTORIA GLENDINNING

Victoria Glendinning is a prize-winning biographer and journalist.

HOLBORN

The Inns of Court
Built between the 14th and 20th centuries

5.17 **Lincoln's Inn**
Southeast corner of Lincoln's Inn Fields at Serle Street WC2
020 7405 1393; www.lincolnsinn.org.uk
⊖ Chancery Lane

5.18 **Gray's Inn**
8 South Square WC1
020 7458 7800; www.graysinn.info
⊖ Chancery Lane

5.19 **Inner Temple**
Crown Office Row, King's Bench Walk EC4
020 7797 8250; www.innertemple.org.uk
⊖ Temple

5.20 **Middle Temple**
Middle Temple Lane EC4
020 7427 4800; wwww.middletemple.org.uk
⊖ Temple

5.22 ## Temple Church

Fleet Street EC4

www.templechurch.com

⊖ Temple

Weave your way through the Inns of Court, from Grays
Inn down to the river, not forgetting the Temple church
and the stone knights or King's Bench Walk. This is the
closest anyone will ever get to the atmosphere of late
seventeenth- and eighteenth-century London, but
beware, every gate—but one—closes at the weekends.

GILLIAN DARLEY

Gillian Darley is co-author, with Andrew Saint, of The Chronicles of London, a
historical anthology of London. Her other books include biographies of Sir
John Soane, Octavia Hill, and John Evelyn.

5.21 # Middle Temple Hall

1562–1573

Middle Temple Lane EC4

020 7427 4800; www.middletemple.org.uk

⊖ Temple

The only building surviving from Shakespeare's time
where it is known that one of his plays had its first night:
Twelfth Night, on February 2, 1602. With its magnificent
double hammer-beam roof, its only rival when it was
constructed between 1562 and 1573 was Westminster Hall
(1097). Many talented young poets and playwrights,
including John Webster, John Ford, and John Marston,
were students at the Middle Temple and would have
dined and argued legal niceties in the Hall. It was a
monument to the success of the legal profession. Its
function is unchanged today.

GILES DE LA MARE

Giles de la Mare is the chairman of Giles de la Mare Publishers.

5.23 C. Hoare and Co.

Current building dates to early 1820s; bank established in 1672

37 Fleet Street EC4

020 7353 4523; www.hoaresbank.co.uk

Blackfriars

Messrs. C. Hoare and Co., the oldest bank in Britain, older than the Bank of England, has been owned and run by the Hoare family for nearly four hundred years at 37 Fleet Street. The counters are still of human dimension, behind which real people sit, the messengers and doormen wear top hats, and there is a museum upstairs. It defies the modern age.

BRIAN MASTERS

Brian Masters writes about crime and art. He is also an authority on gorillas and dukes.

5.24 Prince Henry's Room

17 Fleet Street EC4,

www.cityof london.gov.uk

Blackfriars

In 1610, the Inner Temple Gate and the house above it were rebuilt. Despite alterations and refurbishments over the centuries, it is one of the few remaining timber-framed buildings in London, housing some equally remarkable survivals in its interior.

Part of the new building of 1610 continued in use as a tavern under the sign "The Prince's Arms," and the splendid first-floor room (now known, misleadingly, as "Prince Henry's Room") contains Jacobean oak panelling on its west wall, the rest of the panelling being of eighteenth-century pine; stained glass windows commemorating the rescue of the building from demolition in 1906 by London County Council; and a wonderful lime plaster ceiling, typical of London decorative plasterwork of 1610. The layout of the enriched ribs of the ceiling is unique among recorded examples, but many of the motifs, cast from wooden moulds, could have been seen in contemporary London houses. At the centre of the ceiling, in a star-shaped field, the Prince of Wales's feathers are flanked by the initials "P. H."

Prince Henry (1594–1612) was James I's eldest son and the most popular member of the royal family. His creation as Prince of Wales in 1610 was an occasion of great public celebration. Even if the earlier inn on the site had not been called "The Prince's Arms," it was an appropriate moment for a citizen who did not himself bear arms to mark his loyalty and devotion by displaying the Prince's initials and badge of feather so prominently.

CLAIRE GAPPER

Claire Gapper is an architectural historian.

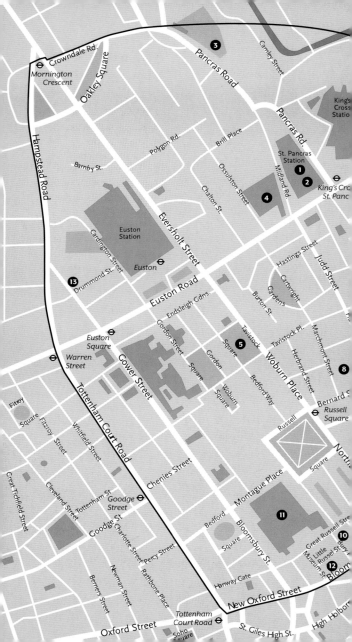

CHAPTER 6
Bloomsbury

1   The Barlow Shed
2   Midland Grand Hotel
3   St. Pancras Old Church
4   The British Library
5   Gandhi Memorial
6   St. George's Gardens
7   The Foundling Museum
8   The Brunswick Centre
9   Coram's Fields
10 London Review Bookshop 🍴
11 The British Museum (see p. 84)
12 St. George's Bloomsbury
13 Ravi Shankar Restaurant 🍴

Bloomsbury

Old St. Pancras

🚇 King's Cross St. Pancras

6.1 The Barlow Shed

1863–1867, W. H. Barlow and R. M. Ordish
St. Pancras International
Euston Road, between Midland and Pancras Roads NW1
www.stpancras.com

6.2 Midland Grand Hotel

1868–1876, Sir George Gilbert Scott
Euston Road, between Midland and Pancras Roads NW1

6.3 St. Pancras Old Church and Gardens

Pancras Road NW1

Echoes of Britain's railway age can be discerned at any of London's great stations (the grim bunker of Euston is an exception), but for Gothic grandeur and industrial muscle, none compare to St. Pancras. The ornate red brick façade of Sir Gilbert Scott's Midland Grand Hotel, topped with its cluster of fantastical spires and bustling chimneys, remains one of London's most popular landmarks. Its lofty spirit jeers at the squat, soulless form of the British Library opposite, and, after years of neglect, its sweeping staircases and ironwork traceries are being restored to their former glory.

Opinion remains divided about the refurbishment of William Barlow's station as the Eurostar terminus, whose concrete platform extension jars with the original station, but you can still marvel at its vast iron arch, and at the ornate reconstructed clock. Below, the space that housed the vaults where Burton-on-Trent beer was once stored is now a shopping mall.

The redevelopment of the hundred and twenty-five acres behind the station and its less imposing neighbour King's Cross remains bitterly contested. Several of the area's iconic gasometers and the Victorian tenements of Stanley Buildings—both the star of innumerable films, from *The Ladykillers* to *High Hopes*—have been demolished. Other relics of the nineteenth century await a similar fate.

Leave the Eurostar behind, wander up Hampstead Road, and you'll find St. Pancras Old Church, named after a fourth-century martyr and allegedly one of London's most ancient holy sites. The medieval church was restored almost beyond salvation by Victorian do-gooders, though inside remains a jumble of seventeenth- and eighteenth-century monuments and a sixth-century altar stone retrieved from the churchyard during the 1847 alterations. Best of all is the churchyard itself, the Gardens, where a whiff of pre-industrial London still lingers, albeit overshadowed by the terminus to the south and the gloomy red brick Hospital of Tropical Diseases to the north.

St. Pancras church has a long and troubled history. Sited in fields outside of London, it was described in 1593 by the map publisher John Norden as "all alone as utterly forsaken," with its environs "visited by thieves." Later the parish church became notorious as a place for no-questions-asked marriages and as the resting place for both criminals and exiled French aristocrats. In Dickens's *A Tale of Two Cities*, a spy's body is interred there, only to be later retrieved for the dissection labs by body snatchers.

Shadowy associations persisted into the railway age. Forging the Midland line required levelling the tightly packed medieval burial ground, and a scandal arose when early passengers espied bones and skulls poking out from the trackside. The architect charged with the reburial sent his assistant, a young Thomas Hardy, to relocate the remains, as well as the gravestones, many of which still swirl dramatically around the churchyard's plane trees. Hardy later wrote about the experience:

> We late lamented, resting here,
> Are mixed to human jam,
> And each to each exclaims in fear,
> "I know not which I am."

St. Pancras Gardens have other literary and artistic associations. Here the poet Shelley first met his future wife, Mary Godwin, while she attended the grave of her mother. The composer Johann Christian Bach is buried here, lost in Hardy's "human jam." Thomas Chatterton used to frequent the place, and W. B. Yeats, who lived in nearby Woburn Walk, surely visited. The Beatles definitely did, on their "Mad Day Out" photo session of July 1968— the Fabs were captured posing alongside the local population (see the centrefolds of the so-called Red and Blue compilations) and peering through the Gardens' hollyhocks.

Somewhere below, along with the uncharted dead, lies the buried Fleet River, its passage from Hampstead's heights to the Thames (via Fleet Street) now contained entirely in an iron pipe. Of the "spa and wells" of old St. Pancras, there is no sign.

NEIL SPENCER

Neil Spencer is a journalist, writing mainly for The Observer. He co-wrote the script for Bollywood Queen.

6.4 The British Library

1999, Sir Colin St. John Wilson & Partners
96 Euston Road NW1
0843 208 1144; www.bl.uk
⊖ King's Cross St. Pancras

The British are good at renovating or restoring old buildings, but less good at building new ones. The exception is the unashamedly modern British Library by Sir Colin St. John Wilson at St. Pancras. The outside is not to everyone's taste, but stand in the piazza off Euston Road by the Paolozzi statue of Newton and look towards the Gothic extravaganza of St. Pancras Station. Inside the library, you'll find the finest public space created in the United Kingdom in the late twentieth century, filled with works by living British artists: a Kitaj tapestry, a Woodrow sculpture, and a Patrick Hughes picture. There are incomparable exhibition galleries with the Magna Carta, Beatles manuscripts, and more. All free.

JOHN M. ASHWORTH

John M. Ashworth has been the Chairman of the British Library Board, the Director of the London School of Economics, and the government's chief scientist. In 2008 he received a knighthood for public service.

Seating yourself in Humanities II, seat No. 3189 or 3183 (whichever is available), then staring into the space in front of you at about forty-five degrees and upwards provides you with one of the clearest and most peaceful spaces in London. Use ear plugs if you feel there's too much noise from laptop keyboard activity behind you, or too much map-rustling from the mezzanine above. Take out about twenty centimeters of books (through randomly selecting a keyword on the library computer index) which you must stack unread on the table in front of you. Then begin concentrating on the spectacular light

6

changes within the space upwards and ahead of you—
4 p.m. to 7 p.m. should be ideal.

ADAM CHODZKO
Adam Chodzko is a multimedia artist.

Epitaph for a Library

Yesterday I received proof that my cosy and beloved
London refuge would be irrevocably confiscated from me.

I entered the Reading Room of the Library, in the heart
of the British Museum, and instead of the usual warm
atmosphere I was greeted with a distressing spectacle: half
of the vast shelves surrounding the room had been
emptied, and in place of the elegant rows of thousands of
bound books, I saw discolored wood, some of it stained
with what seemed to be cobwebs. I don't think I've felt
such a sense of betrayal since my mother took me, upon
turning five years old, to the La Salle School of Cochabamba
and abandoned me in Brother Justinian's classroom.

I came to this place for the first time thirty-two years
ago, newly arrived in London, to read books by Edmund
Wilson, whose essay about the evolution of socialism—*To
the Finland Station*—had touched me. Before I could notice
the richness of its collection—about nine million volumes—
I was dazzled by the beauty of the main Reading Room,
covered by those shelves smelling of leather and paper and
submerged in a blue light that discreetly descended upon
her from the incredible dome built by Sidney Smirke in
1857, the largest in the world next to that of the Pantheon
in Rome, which exceeds it only by two feet in diameter.
Since I was accustomed to working in impersonal and
uncomfortable libraries, like that of Paris—always so
crowded that during the exams period you had to stand in
line in the Place de la Bourse for an hour before it opened

to be admitted—I couldn't believe that this one, besides being so beautiful, was so comfortable, so quiet and hospitable, with its fluffy seats and long tables where you could spread out your notebooks, index cards, and high stacks of books without cramping your neighbors.

It was here old Marx had spent a good part of his life, according to Wilson, and where in the sixties his desk was still preserved to the right of the entrance, but which in the mid-eighties disappeared with all the desks in that row in order to make room for computers.

Without exaggeration, I can say that I have spent four or five afternoons a week in the Reading Room of the British Library during all of my stays in London over three decades, and that here I have been extremely happy, more so than in any other place in the world. Here, lulled by the quiet hum of the carts that hand out their orders to each reader, and calmed by the intimate security that no phone nor bell would ring, and no visitor would drop by, I would prepare my literature classes when I taught at Queen Mary College and at King's College; here I've written letters, articles, essays, plays, and a half dozen novels. And here I've read hundreds of books, thanks to which I've learned almost everything I know. But mostly in this place I've fantasized and dreamt about the great thinkers, of the formidable illusionists, of the masters of fiction.

I became used to working in the library since my university days, and in every place I have lived, I have been able to continue doing so, such that my memories of the countries and cities are in good measure shaped by the images and anecdotes that I retain of their libraries. The old big house of San Marcos had a dense and colonial air and the books exhaled a light dust that made one sneeze. In the National Library, on Abancay Avenue, the schoolchildren made an infernal noise, as did the monitors, who would shush them (or emulate them, rather) with shrill whistles. In the National Club, where I worked, I read an entire erotic collection, *Les Maîtres de l'Amour*, directed, introduced, and translated by Guillaume Apollinaire. In the freezing National Library of Madrid, toward the end of the fifties, you had to wear a coat so as not to get sick, but I went there every afternoon to read the novels of chivalry. The library in Paris was so uncomfortable it surpassed all the others: if you accidentally moved your arm away from your body, you would elbow your neighbor in the ribs. There, one afternoon, I raised my eyes from a crazy book, about crazy people, *Les Enfants du Limon* by Raymond Queneau, and I came face to face with Simone de Beauvoir, who was sitting right in front of me, writing furiously.

The greatest surprise I had with regard to libraries was with an erudite Chilean in charge of the acquisition of Spanish American books in the Library of Congress in Washington. In 1965 I asked him what the criteria was for acquiring books and he responded: "Very easy. We buy all the books that are published." This was also the millionaire policy of the formidable library at Harvard, where one had to go alone to search for a book following a complicated itinerary traced by the computer, which acted as a receptionist. In the semester I spent there I never managed to orient myself in that labyrinth, I never could read what I wanted, I just wandered through the belly of the bibliographic whale, but I can't complain because I made some wonderful finds, such as the memoirs of Herzen—a Russian liberal—and *The Octopus* by Frank Norris.

One snowy afternoon in the library at Princeton, while taking advantage of the carelessness of my neighbor, I spied a book he was reading and found a quote about the cult of Dionysus in Ancient Greece, which led me to completely change the novel I was writing and attempt an

Andean, modern re-creation of that classic myth about irrational forces and divine intoxication. In the New York Public Library, the most efficient of all—you don't need a membership, the books you need are brought to you in minutes—and with the hardest seats, it was impossible to work for more than a few hours straight unless you brought a small pillow to protect your tailbone.

I have nice memories of all these libraries and several others, but none of them, alone or separately, was able to help, stimulate, and serve me as well as the Reading Room. Of the innumerable episodes with which I could illustrate this statement, I chose this one: to have found in its archives the most obscure little magazine that the Dominican priests of the Amazonian mission published there, in those remote lands, half a century ago, and that are one of the scarce testimonies about the Machiguengas, their myths, their legends, their customs, their language. I was desperately asking my friends from Lima that they find and photocopy them—I needed the material for a novel—and it turns out the complete collection was there, in the British Library, at my disposal.

When in 1978 the Labour Party announced that, due to a lack of space, a new library would be built and the Reading Room would be returned to the British Museum, a cold shiver ran through my spine. But I figured that, given the poor state of the British economy then, the costly project would take probably more than the years I had left in life to materialize. However, in the 1980s things started to get better in the United Kingdom and the new building, constructed in a neighborhood known above all for its ruffians and prostitutes, St. Pancras, began to grow and show its horrendous brick face and prison-like grates. The historian Hugh Thomas formed a committee to try to convince the authorities that, although the British Library was moving to the new space, they should preserve the Reading Room of the British Museum. I was one of its members and I wrote letters and signed manifestos that were completely pointless, because the British Museum was determined to recapture what de jure belonged to it, and its influence and arguments prevailed over our own.

Now, all is lost. The books have already been taken to St. Pancras and although in theory this Reading Room will remain open until mid-October and a month later the Humanities Room will open in its place, this one has already begun to die, slowly, since they ripped out the soul which gave it life, the books, and they left a large empty shell. Those few sentimentalists of us left will continue coming here until the last day, just as one accompanies a loved one in their last days of agony, in order to be with them until the final death rattle. But nothing will be the same these months, neither the hushed hustle and bustle of days gone by, nor that comfortable sensation with which one could read, research, take notes and write, possessed by a curious state of mind, that of having escaped the wheel of time, of having consented to that concave space of blue light and to that timelessness of the life of books, and that of ideas and of the admirable fantasies incarnated in them.

Of course, in the nearly twenty years it's taken to be built, the St. Pancras Library has turned out too small and will be unable to house all of its collections, which will be dispersed in different storage spaces strewn throughout London. And the defects and deficiencies that seem to afflict it have caused the *Times Literary Supplement* to describe it as "The British Library or The Great Disaster." I, of course, have not visited it and when I pass by I look at the brave prostitutes on the sidewalks, and not at its rocky and bloody walls, reminiscent of banks, barracks, or electrical plants, not of intellectual endeavors. I, of course, will not step foot inside until I have no choice, and will continue proclaiming until my death that, by replacing that beloved place with this horror, a shameful crime has been committed—and one that is quite explicable. After all, aren't these the same people who sent poor Oscar Wilde to jail and who banned Joyce's *Ulysses* and Lawrence's *Lady Chatterley's Lover*?

MARIO VARGAS LLOSA
Mario Vargas Llosa, the Peruvian writer and politician, is author of The Time of the Hero, The War of the End of the World, and The Bad Girl, among other novels. In 1990 Vargas Llosa ran for the Peruvian presidency. In 2010, he received the Nobel Prize in literature.

Written in London, June 1997; translated by Paula Bloom.

EDITOR'S NOTE: The Reading Room at the British Museum has been restored since Mario Vargas Llosa wrote this essay in 1997. It now houses a modern information centre, the Walter and Leonore Annenberg Centre, and a collection of twenty-five thousand books, catalogues and other printed material, which focused on the world cultures represented in the Museum.

6.5 Gandhi Memorial

1968, Fredda Brilliant
Tavistock Square WC1

⊖ Euston
LO Euston

When I'm stressed out in Bloomsbury—it can happen—a good place to realign the energies is with this bronze Mahatma. He's just sitting there on top of the stone plinth that always seems to have fresh flower offerings. The traffic and all that noise become the background and the memorial gives you back to yourself with gentleness and strength.

ANTONY GORMLEY
Sculptor Antony Gormley's work has been exhibited worldwide. His large-scale installations include Angel of the North (in Gateshead) and Another Place (in Liverpool).

6.6   St. George's Gardens

1713, originally a burial ground; 1885, opened as a public garden
Handel Street wc1
020 7974 1693; www.friendsofstgeorgesgardens.org.uk and
www.camden.gov.uk
⊖   Russell Square

From 1713 to about 1850, St. George's Gardens was a burial
ground attached to the church of St. George the Martyr,
Queen's Square, and also for St. George, Bloomsbury. In
1884, it reopened as a public garden designed by William
Holmes. It was always a pleasure to walk from Sidmouth
Street to Handel Street under big plane trees, past graves
and the terracotta muse who stood alone in a flower bed.
A period of neglect spoiled the Gardens for a while, and
the muse had her hand broken off. Around that time, the
Friends of St. George's Gardens formed to restore the
grounds. Today there is interesting planting, the muse
has her hand back, and St. George's Day is marked with
celebrations.

Ruth Pavey
*Ruth Pavey writes for national publications on contemporary fiction, crafts,
and horticulture.*

6.7   The Foundling Museum

*1741, Theodore Jacobsen (original building); 1938, J. M. Sheppard (current
building)*
40 Brunswick Square wc1
020 7841 3600; www.foundlingmuseum.org.uk
⊖   Russell Square or King's Cross St. Pancras

Thomas Coram, a rich sea captain, came back to London
from a voyage and was shocked to see so many beggars
and street urchins living rough in the midst of the city's
bustle and prosperity—children who were the predeces-
sors of Fagin's gang and *Les Misérables*. The Foundling
Hospital, near Coram Fields, which he founded in 1742,

now houses the Coram Foundation and its fine collection of paintings—put together originally by none other than William Hogarth. He was a friend of Coram's and painted the magnificent portrait of him. But the orphanage is worth a visit above all to see the poignant tokens the mothers left with their babies: buttons scratched with their names, scraps of ribbon, clipped coins, and poems.

MARINA WARNER

Marina Warner is a writer of fiction and cultural history, a curator, and an art critic.

6

Everything about this collection of eighteenth-century painting, sculpture, furniture, and memorabilia is extraordinary, from its origins to the fact that it is still together and still little known. It exists only because a retired sea captain, Thomas Coram, was so appalled by the state of London's neglected street children that he spent the rest of his life setting up The Foundling Hospital, and because he was so good at enthusing other people like Hogarth and Handel to help, that it became *the* fashionable cause. From 1750 Handel conducted annual performances of *The Messiah* in the Hospital Chapel. Roubiliac's terra cotta bust of him, and the keyboard of the organ he gave, form part of the collection, to which Hogarth, Ramsay, Reynolds, and Gainsborough all contributed. When women handed over their babies to the care of the hospital they often attached tokens to identify them, in case changed circumstances should ever allow them to reclaim their lost children. This did occasionally happen, but the display of unreclaimed pins, chains, ribbons, hearts, coins, and other items speaks poignantly of the more usual outcome.

RUTH PAVEY

Ruth Pavey writes for national publications on contemporary fiction, crafts, and horticulture.

6.8   The Brunswick Centre

1967–1972, Patrick Hodgkinson
Marchmont Street WC1
www.brunswick.co.uk

The Renoir Cinema

In the Brunswick Centre
Brunswick Square
020 7837 8402; www.curzoncinemas.com
⊖ Russell Square

With its huge concrete frame, elevated walkways, and stepped ranks of apartments, the Brunswick Centre has the look of some strange Alvar Aalto–inspired space station. Variously loved and scorned, this extraordinary modernist estate was built in 1972 as an experiment in low-rise, high-density housing in an oft-neglected corner of Bloomsbury. A recent refurbishment has seen the water-stained concrete painted a blazing white—something the Brunswick's architect, Patrick Hodgkinson, had first proposed—and though an influx of chain stores and cafés has turned the ground floor into a somewhat bland shopping precinct, the new paint job is a triumph. Early on a fine summer evening, take a moment to look upwards and marvel at how the building cascades against a bright blue sky. Later, wander across the plaza to visit the Brunswick's original picture house, the Renoir Cinema (previously the Bloomsbury Cinema). At first glance it will appear as nothing more than a small, black-framed glass box standing within the shadow of the Brunswick's concrete frame and looking out onto the green space of Coram's Fields. Venture downstairs, however, and you'll find one of the city's best art-house programmes, showing the work of established auteurs alongside new-world cinema talent. A tiny but well-stocked bar is a pleasant extra, but as you walk outside the location that really completes this cinematic experience and lets you feel that the film's still playing. Finish the evening by strolling around the corner and along the edge of Coram's Fields to the pubs and restaurants on Lamb's Conduit street.

HELEN GORDON

Helen Gordon is a journalist, editor, and the author of Landfall.

6.9 Coram's Fields

93 Guilford Street WC1
020 7837 6138; www.coramsfields.org
⊖ Russell Square

6

Visiting London with young children can be difficult. The traffic, the appalling public transport, and the hostile restaurant staff can all add up to an extremely trying experience. Yet there are a few oases, even in central London. One of these is Coram's Fields: a lovely children's park five minutes' walk east of Russell Square. The entrance is on Guilford Street, where a sign on an iron gate states, with a gentle ironic twist, "No adults unaccompanied by children."

The park was originally part of a foundling hospital, built in the early eighteenth century by the philanthropist Thomas Coram. You enter to find an unexpectedly large expanse of green, dotted with majestic plane trees and flanked on either side by rows of miniature Palladian columns. It's easy to imagine that you've entered the grounds of an eighteenth-century estate, save for the all-weather football pitch at the far end.

The park contains a variety of facilities for children: swings, monkey bars, and a range of other energy-sapping constructions. In addition, the park keeps animals, mostly chickens and sheep, which roam around an enclosed area, adding to the bucolic calm and amusing

the children no end. For very young children there is
the "under fives club," where parents can get a cup of
tea or coffee and the kids can play with one another and
an impressive variety of toys. The professional carers
on site are charming and helpful, and there are clean
changing facilities. Once you've explored the fields take
a walk down Lamb's Conduit, straight out the gate at
the south end of the park and across Guilford Street at
the Zebra Crossing. There are some interesting shops
and a number of very good cafés on this street, as well
as one of the best-preserved and best-run pubs in central
London, appropriately known as the Lamb (94 Lamb's
Conduit, 020 7405 0713).

RICHARD NOBLE
*Richard Noble writes about political philosophy from the eighteenth century to
the present and the contemporary visual arts.*

6.10 London Review Bookshop

14 Bury Place WC1
020 7269 9030; www.lrbshop.co.uk
⊖ Holborn

Bookshop windows tell all. Here on Bury Street they lay
out their wares with devilish skill: a handful of recently
reviewed titles and others with links—in subject matter,
author, or more oblique connections—to new books or
matters of the moment. With that enticing stall, the LRB
Bookshop can't fail but to ensnare the bookish passerby.
Inside is a well-lit and quiet book-lined room, a bit like
the perfect library (if only!), with books—again cleverly
arranged by association—on several tables and more,
much more, below stairs. By now you have the feeling
that someone here knows your mind better than you do;
these are the very books you'd been planning to read! Thi
oasis has quiet corners to stand and browse, places to sit,

a cupboard of first editions, and, presiding discreetly over it all, a helpful and knowledgeable staff. Spoil yourself (at modest cost) in their café next door, a shrine to excellence in baking and fine teas, and your day will have been made. Then come back another evening to hear writers talk, or to meet fellow readers on a late opening. The shop's dimensions may be modest but its ambitions are considerable.

GILLIAN DARLEY

Gillian Darley is co-author, with Andrew Saint, of The Chronicles of London, a historical anthology of London. Her most recent book is My Vesuvius.

6

6.11 The British Museum

1823–1852, Sir Robert Smirke, among others
Great Russell Street WC1
020 7323 8000; www.britishmuseum.org
⊖ Tottenham Court Road

"A foggy day in London town . . .
I viewed the morning with alarm,
The British Museum had lost its charm . . ."
—Ira Gershwin

These lyrics from "A Foggy Day" have to be among the most ironic in popular music: nobody could ever find the severely imposing British Museum charming under any circumstances. In the peace following the Napoleonic period, Britain commissioned Smirke to design the massive neoclassical pile to house the collections of art and antiquities bequeathed to the nation in the late eighteenth and early nineteenth centuries. Fragments of the Temple of Artemis at Ephesus, one of the canonical Seven Wonders of the World, are displayed in Room 3. Over the years numerous other architects, most recently Norman Foster, have made improvements and alterations.

At night the orange sodium floodlights render the refined
Ionic façade wildly Asiatic and pagan.

PETER J. HOLLIDAY
*Peter J. Holliday is Professor of Art and Classical Archaeology at California
State University in Long Beach.*

Though obviously a standard attraction for most tourists,
the British Museum is my favorite because of its enormous collections, covering over two and a half miles of
galleries! The Greek, Roman, Egyptian, and Near Eastern
collections are among the finest in the world—appropriate for the oldest public museum in the world. Among its
other superb collections are the great "treasures" of the
migration period and illuminated manuscripts, the Asian
art collection, and the Mexican and pre-Columbian art
gallery. It would take days to discover all of its treasures,
not to mention to visit its always excellent temporary and
visiting exhibitions.

SUSAN SILBERBERG-PIERCE
*Susan Silberberg-Pierce is a classical art historian and photographer of ancient
sites.*

The Great Court

A must is Norman Foster's Great Court, hidden away
inside the British Museum. The old Reading Room is
restored to its former glory in the centre. All is transformed, sparkling under the ingenious doughnut glazed
roof: intricate shadows criss-cross the cream stone
façades of the court when the sun is out.

The museum has become much more accessible: a joy,
especially when remembering previous labyrinthine
routes when working on British Museum installations.

LADY STIRLING (MARY SHAND)
Lady Stirling is a furniture and interior designer.

6.12 **St. George's Bloomsbury**

1718–1720, Nicholas Hawksmoor
Bloomsbury Way WC1
020 7405 3044; www.stgeorgesbloomsbury.org.uk
☰ Holborn

Conceived in 1716 and finished in 1731, St. George's Bloomsbury has recently been magnificently restored with a bequest from the Paul Mellon Estate, a grant from the Heritage Lottery Fund, and other gifts. (God bless the Fund—it is doing amazing things for British culture.) St. George's now radiates its English Baroque brilliance. Most noticeably it is a steeple church swallowed by a classical temple, a play on church and state. The temple follows the site axis from south to north. The church respects the west–east liturgical axis. Church and temple differences are played out in multiple ways—vertical vs. horizontal, thick pier vs. spindly columns, compressed vs. extended, to name just a few. Although church and temple differences are recorded on the surfaces of the central hall, they both share the cubic volume. Note the overlay of the temple form on the nave and side aisles in the ceiling moldings. Also not to be missed are the Palladian window and recess in the clerestory. In addition to reiterating a church section, they are a sop to the English Classicists of the time. And in case we did not know the difference between the English Baroque and the Palladians, there are the over-scaled keystones most easily seen on the north elevation, and the hugely exaggerated steeple with its base, triumphal arch, treasury, stepped pyramid (complete with lion and unicorn), sacrificial altar, and statue of George I in Roman garb. Although the tower is recorded as being derived from the tomb of Mausolus at Halicarnassus, it is at once a pile, a denser version of the sacred way at Delphi, and beads on a string. Hawksmoor is a pro. There is something for everyone in this assemblage.

ROBERT LIVESEY
Robert Livesey is an architect and a professor at the Knowlton School of Architecture at The Ohio State University.

The neighbouring buildings are so close to the site that one can easily miss Hawksmoor's magnificent Portland stone Corinthian portico and steeple on this busy street. It has some of the grandeur of Rome, even of the portico of the Pantheon. It is of course smaller, as this is London, and eighteenth-century High Baroque. The design of the stepped steeple is based on Pliny's description of the Mausoleum of Halicarnassus (353 B.C.E.). It is topped by more Corinthian columns and a statue of George I as St. George, but in Roman dress, as one can see in Hogarth's engraving *Gin Lane*.

Inside, the central space is nearly square, balanced, symmetrical, grand but plain, as was thought to befit the reformed English Church. There are carved brown oak fittings, moulded plasterwork, an altarpiece niche with cherubs and clouds in marquetry. (Imagine drawing, let alone making, this.) Otherwise stone—white and gold.

DAVID MLINARIC
David Mlinaric, now retired, was a partner at Mlinaric, Henry, and Zervudachi, an interior design and decoration company. He has worked on various museums and heritage sights, including the National Gallery and the Royal Opera House.

14.13 ## Ravi Shankar Restaurant

133 Drummond Street NW1
020 7388 6458

Euston Square or Euston

LO Euston

In a little grid of streets my side of the Euston Road, there is an entire little village devoted to South Indian vegetarian restaurants. My favourite is the Ravi Shankar Restaurant, opposite the Islamic Book Centre. Many Muslims live or work in the area and there is a mosque one street away from the restaurant. I love the food, particularly the *bhel puri*, a dish made apparently of spicy rice crispies and yogurt, and it has the additional advantage of being extremely cheap. I also like the area, which is an oasis of calm marooned between the Euston Road and Camden.

LUCRETIA STEWART

Lucretia Stewart is the author of Tiger Bam: Travels in Laos, Vietnam and Cambodia; The Weather Prophet: A Caribbean Journey; and Making Love.

CHAPTER 7
Clerkenwell

1 Carnevale ♨♟

2 Bunhill Fields

3 St. John ♨♟

4 Jerusalem Tavern (see p. 147)

5 Marx Memorial Library

6 International Magic 🎁

7 Finsbury Health Centre

8 Spa Green Estate

9 Old Finsbury Town Hall

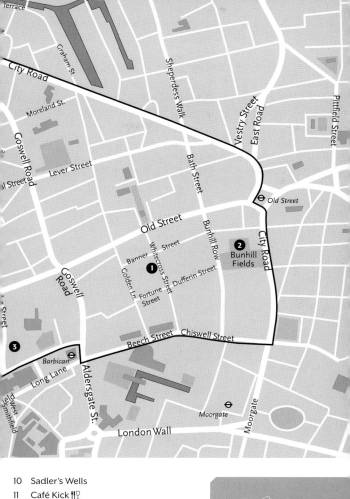

10   Sadler's Wells

11   Café Kick

12   Church of the Holy
       Redeemer

13   Quality Chop House

14   Moro

15   Wilmington Square

16   "Plum Pudding Steps"

Clerkenwell

A Saturday Afternoon

7.1   **Carnevale**
135 Whitecross Street EC1
020 7250 3452; www.carnevalerestaurant.co.uk
⊖   Old Street or Barbican

7.2   **Bunhill Fields**
(see below)
⊖   Old Street

An ideal Saturday afternoon: a stroll through the City of London—virtually a ghost town on this day of the week and preceded or followed by a visit to Carnevale, the vegetarian restaurant and deli in Whitecross Street. If the weather is fine, buy a take-out from the deli and proceed to Bunhill Fields, three minutes' walk away, a fine historic graveyard containing the tombs of Bunyan, Thomas Strothard, and William Blake. Enjoy your picnic on the central lawns, listening to numerous species of birds but few humans. Otherwise, indulge in a delicious meal in Carnevale's restaurant—a treat is in store!

IMOGEN MAGNUS
Imogen Magnus has worked as a theatre designer and costume designer for films and television. She now writes on historic gardens and teaches.

7.2   **Bunhill Fields**
Burial ground from the mid-16th century until it closed in 1854; 1867, opened as a public park
Off City Road, entrance on Bunhill Row EC1
City Gardens Office: 020 7374 4127; www.cityoflondon.gov.uk
Check website for opening hours for the enclosed areas, or call the

City Gardens Office to arrange for the gates to be opened.
⊖ Old Street

There are more people buried here than the current
population of Southampton (England, that is), partly due
to the fact of it having been a plague pit. In 1708 the
Calvinist mystics the Camisards gathered here to wait for
their leader, Dr. Emms, to rise from the dead five months
after his interment. Dr. Emms disappointed them. But
here, too, are the great Non-Conformists: John Wesley,
who lived across the road and whose ghost is still said to
visit his grave, Daniel Defoe (1731), John Bunyan (1688),
and William Blake (1827), whose gravestone is often
decorated by pebbles, in the Jewish tradition, and cut
flowers, in the English tradition.

7

Tumbledown memorials and full-grown London
plane trees give the place a Gothic air, a mysterious
escape from the heaving throb of the City and its financial
pulse that surrounds this green remnant. You can still
feel the old town here, beneath your feet; even the paths
are made from old gravestones. My parish priest regards
this place as his personal garden. He is not the only
black-garbed figure to haunt its dark green lawns. Take a
copy of Peter Ackroyd's *Blake* or his novel *Hawksmoor* and
contemplate the launch, in 1796, of Vincenzo Lunardi's
hot-air balloon from the neighbouring Artillery Fields,
his miraculous ascent giving, for the first time, a view of
London from the sky.

PHILIP HOARE
*Philip Hoare's books include biographies of Stephen Tennant and Noël
Coward; Wilde's Last Stand; and England's Lost Eden.*

7.3 St. John

26 St. John Street EC1
020 7251 0848; www.stjohnrestaurant.co.uk
⊖ Farringdon

¶ Run by Fergus Henderson, the space is an old smoke-house adjacent to Smithfield Market, and the food is very British (the sign is a pig, indicating "nose to tail eating"). Excellent.
LADY STIRLING (MARY SHAND)
Lady Stirling is a furniture and interior designer.

7.5 Marx Memorial Library

1737
37a Clerkenwell Green EC1
020 7253 1485; www.marx-memorial-library.org
Check website for hours and guided tours.
⊖ Farringdon

London is home to a good many libraries, but few have the radical lineage and charm of the Marx Memorial Library. Centred on the partly pedestrianised Clerkenwell Green, the library is located in what is referred to locally as Marx House, a Grade II-listed eighteenth-century building that serves as a vessel for a microcosmic social history of London, housing in turn a charity school and various small workshops and storefronts before becoming a public house and coffee rooms in the last quarter of the nineteenth century. These were in effect workmen's clubs, where one could read the seditious and blasphemous literature long produced and distributed in and around the Green.

The building was frequented by Eleanor Marx and was a home to radical reform clubs supported by John Stuart Mill; with the financial support of William Morris, the Twentieth Century Press took over its lease in 1892. The

TCP produced many of the earliest English editions of the works of Marx and Engels, and during his London exile, Lenin edited *Iskra*, the newspaper of Russian Social Democracy, from an office lent to him by the press. The library has preserved this office as the Lenin Room. Other than some original well-worn Lenin-lino, the library boasts a large fresco, painted by Jack Hastings in 1935 shortly after the library was founded, that depicts a heroic worker of the future overturning the economic chaos of the present. A charity supported by independent subscriptions, the Marx Memorial Library lends books which contain ideas that still deserve a wider circulation.

JOHN SLYCE

John Slyce writes on contemporary art and culture.

7

7.6 International Magic

89 Clerkenwell Road EC1

020 7405 7324; www.internationalmagic.com

⊖ Chancery Lane or Farringdon

If you have ever wondered where in London you might be able to obtain a wand that turns into a bunch of flowers, or a set of steel rings that defy the normal laws of physics by slotting in and out of one another, then International Magic is the emporium for you. Even if you haven't, go anyway. It is a kind of tiny *wunderkammer* of all things magical—and that's definitely magical with a "c," as opposed to your Aleister Crowley/Anton LaVey magickal with a "k," hexes and sex-with-goats stuff. Even if you fail to be impressed by the selection of tricks, or by the collection of photographs on its walls of heavily eyelinered prestidigitators of yesteryear coaxing doves from thin air or rabbits from hats, it serves free tea and coffee. It was founded by the magician Ron MacMillan nearly sixty years ago (a shot of Ron, resplendent in white tie and dinner jacket, has pride of place in the store), and his late wife, Teresa; MacMillan remains on hand to greet regulars and welcome newcomers. The shop derives its name from the fact that in the 1950s Macmillan was in a double act with the legendary Ali Bongo; the pair, in those days, performed a language-barrier-breaking silent show that was extremely popular in Germany.

TRAVIS ELBOROUGH

Travis Elborough is the author of The Bus We Loved: London's Affair with the Routemaster and Wish You Were Here: England on Sea.

Walking in Finsbury

Stroll begins at Angel station

⊖ Angel

7.7 **Finsbury Health Centre**
1938, Berthold Lubetkin
17 Pine Street EC1

7.8 **Spa Green Estate**
1950, Berthold Lubetkin
St. John Street EC1

7.9 **The Old Finsbury Town Hall**
1895, Evans Vaughan
The Urdang Academy
Rosebery Avenue EC1
020 7713 7710; www.theurdangacademy.com

7.10 **Sadler's Wells**
Rosebery Avenue EC1
020 7863 8198; www.sadlerswells.com
(see p. 134)

7.11 **Café Kick**
43 Exmouth Market EC1
020 7837 8077; www.cafekick.co.uk

7.12 Church Our Most Holy Redeemer
1887, J. D. Sedding
24 Exmouth Market EC1
020 7837 1861; www.holyredeemer.co.uk

7.13 Quality Chop House
94 Farringdon Road EC1
020 7837 5093; www.qualitychophouse.co.uk

I never tire of the streets, parks, gardens, and squares off Rosebery Avenue. This is northwest Finsbury, a tiny Victorian borough between the City and the Angel, swallowed by Islington Council in the 1960s and now vanishing for good under the vigorous revival of its medieval name, Clerkenwell. Finsbury is a monument to both London's pride and its hands-on local govern-ment. "Nothing is too good for ordinary people," declared Berthold Lubetkin, Tbilisi-born architect of the luminous Finsbury Health Centre (1938) and the Spa Green Estate (1950), and the councillors agreed. They replaced the blitzed houses with Modernist flats and public gardens that have the fresh, open feel of 1950s West Berlin. Earlier, Finsbury Council treated itself to a voluptuous Town Hall (1895) which looks a bit like a pirate's galleon about to set sail in three different directions. (Inside, it's a Borgia movie.) Tiny old boroughs being no match for the imperatives of showbiz, this building is now home to a performing arts college, the Urdang Academy. You can also throw your own party there.

There are obvious grown-up reasons for walking the area: the pioneering Health Centre; the new Sadler's Wells Theatre, now one of the world's leading dance venues; and the irresistible London Metropolitan Archives. But these are bedded in the eccentric realities of daily London life: a rose garden, a tennis court, tarmac peeling to reveal old cobbles, a memorial angel of death, and a Portuguese footie bar where the 1950s have never ended and Benfica still rule the world. Flats and gardens have been seriously well restored in recent years: in May, blue Paulownia trees now flower above the combat-strength, vandal-resistant children's playground, and giant brooms foam like mimosa all June. One modest Starbucks aside, the pedestrianised working-class high street of Exmouth Market has fought off the feared invasion by multiples. In its place is a sociable culture of independent bookshops, cafés, restaurants, and bars, alongside the old pub, newsagents, ironmongers, betting shop, and tattoo parlour. The architectural star of the Market is J. D. Seddon's wonderful Church Our Most Holy Redeemer (1887)—Lombard Romanesque in banded London brick, spectacular lettering, proper campanile and all. Around the corner on boring Farringdon Road is the addictive Quality Chop House ("Progressive Working-Class Caterer"), where generations of journalists and designers have consumed cottage pie, salmon fishcakes, and corned beef hash. Return to the Angel via unchanged, late-Georgian Amwell Street and handsome Myddelton Square.

MICHAEL RATCLIFFE
Michael Ratcliffe has been Literary Editor and Chief Book Reviewer of The Times, and Theatre Critic of The Observer.

7.10 Sadler's Wells

Rosebery Avenue EC1
020 7863 8198; www.sadlerswells.com

⊖ Angel or Farringdon

Sadler's Wells' performance history dates back to 1683. The current theatre is the seventh built upon this Rosebery Avenue site, and a time capsule containing memorabilia from the prior buildings is buried beneath the centre stalls. It was here, in the years after World War II, that the Sadler's Wells ballet and opera companies transformed themselves into the majestic Royal Ballet (now at Covent Garden) and the adventurous English National Opera (based today at the Coliseum on St. Martin's Lane).

ROBERT MARX

Robert Marx is an essayist on theatre and opera.

7.14 ## Moro

34–36 Exmouth Market EC1
020 7833 8336; www.moro.co.uk
Ө Farringdon or Angel

7

Samuel Clark married Samantha Clarke, and the two chefs took a leisurely ramble through Spain and Morocco. They had ravenous appetites, as lovers do, and they ate everything in sight. When they returned to London they couldn't stop craving those flavours, and they began thinking about food in a whole new way. The result was Moro ("Moor"), the restaurant they opened in 1997. The instant you open the door, you are transported into an intensely fragrant, ornate Arab-Spanish world. The authentic, powerful food is based on recipes and cooking methods that have travelled through the centuries. Because the Clarks feel that cooking over live wood or real hardwood charcoal is integral to their shared vision, you'll find a big, wood-burning oven taking pride of place in the kitchen. And although their food is uncomplicated, it is far from crude. A whole sea bass, seasoned with lemon and fennel and roasted in that oven, is drizzled with pan juices and served with a chunky relish made of roughly chopped pistachios and garlic, given added mystery and allure by orange-flower water, lemon, and mint—flavours that have been entwined since antiquity.

Gleaming ruby-red seeds from pomegranates, long cultivated in Arabia, transform a rustic parsley-grain tabbouleh into a sumptuous side. The Clarks have a family now, and a second home in Spain, but they still eat everything in sight.

JANE LEAR
Jane Lear is a food and travel writer.

Moro is also steeped in Mediterranean culture, in particular, that of Andalucia, where the cuisines of southern Europe and North Africa create a delicious synthesis; last time I ate there I started with quail in flatbread with pistachio sauce, followed it with wood roasted *peri-peri* chicken with coriander rice and rocket salad, and concluded with fresh raspberries on a bed of Jerez cream.

As you eat you can watch the chefs at work in the open kitchen at the far end of the restaurant.

CLIVE SINCLAIR
Clive Sinclair is the author of novels including Blood Libels and Cosmetic Effects.

7.15 Wilmington Square

Finsbury WC1

⊖ King's Cross St. Pancras

Small municipal gardens and squares are often poorly conceived and managed, but here in Wilmington Square is an enjoyable piece of urban landscape design with its trees now reaching maturity. It provides a welcome respite to the noise and hardness of the heavily trafficked streets in this inner-city area. Its designers must have been part of the highly talented team of the now forgotten borough of Finsbury who created the best municipal housing in London.

ALAN BAXTER
Alan Baxter is the engineering designer of many new landmark buildings and is involved in the conservation of historic structures in London.

7.16 "Plum Pudding Steps"

Gwynne Place, off King's Road WC1

⊖ King's Cross St. Pancras

There aren't many steps in the streets of London. And this wide flight is a bridge between two eras, linking the raucous King's Cross Road to a quiet nineteenth-century square. Plum Pudding Steps, as they were called by children who played on them in the fifties, gave Arnold Bennett the setting for his novel of 1923, *Riceyman Steps*, which points out that "dreadful things were often witnessed in Clerkenwell." Then, small shops clustered around the steps: now they're hidden from the street by the huge and ugly arches of the 1970s Ryan Hotel.

SUSANNAH CLAPP

Susannah Clapp is Theatre Critic of The Observer.

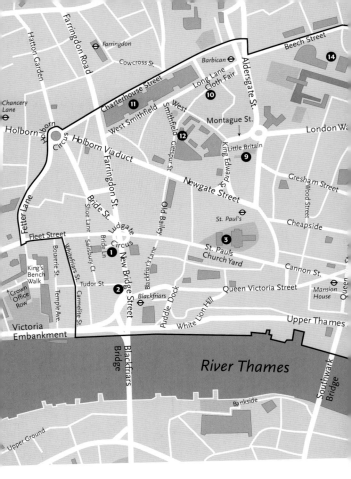

CHAPTER 8
The City

1 St. Bride Foundation
2 The Black Friar Pub 🍴
3 St. Paul's Cathedral
4 No. 1 Poultry 🍴
5 St. Stephen Walbrook
6 St. Mary Woolnoth
7 Bank of England Museum
8 Leadenhall Market 🍴

9   Postman's Park
10 St. Bartholomew-the-Great
    Church
11 Smithfield Market 🍴🎁🏛
12 St. Bartholomew's Hospital
13 St. Mary Abchurch
14 The Barbican Centre 🍴🎱

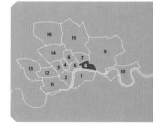

The City

8.1 St. Bride Foundation

14 Bride Lane EC4
The Library's reading room and archives are housed within the
St. Bride Institute building, in Bride Lane behind Fleet Street.
020 7353 4660; www.stbride.org

⊖   Blackfriars

Want to pore over a first edition of Samuel Johnson's
dictionary or learn about the "unpolished arts" (which,
needless to say, include taxidermy, funerals, food, and
rustic work)? Need a piece of lead type, in virtually any
size or font? You'll find them all at the St. Bride
Foundation. The lead type is stacked in cardboard boxes
with handwritten labels, such as "K–S (with alternative
capital N)." Some of the fonts are still sitting in cases
attached to old printing presses—with capital letters
appropriately in the upper cases, small letters in the
lower cases beneath.

The St. Bride Foundation, established in 1891 as the St.
Bride Institute to do nice things for the exploited print
workers of neighbouring Fleet Street, houses what may
be the biggest collection of typography, printing para-
phernalia, and related broadsheets, books, and papers in
the world. It is still a working library, but, in addition, it
once housed a public laundry (lately transformed into a
bar, complete with mangles and drying racks), public
baths (six second class and two first class), and a swimming pool. The pool is boarded over now, providing a
stage for professional actors at lunchtime, amateurs in
the evenings. Lawyers from the nearby Inns of Court
stride around giving PowerPoint presentations in the
stately rooms on the first floor. In the attic, there are yoga
classes for refugees from nearby office buildings.

A very long time ago, when there were still journalists in Fleet Street, I worked in a newsroom that overlooked the deeply eccentric Foundation, but I failed to unearth its charms. I stumbled upon them in 2009, when a group of young actors staged a run-around performance of *Broadsheet Ballads*, the adventures of rival lads-about-town, Tom and Jerry, inspired by early comic handbills in the library's collection. Part red brick, part glazed white tiles, part London Grey granite, the outside of the purpose-built institute mirrors the architectural chaos of the interior. There isn't a straight line or right angle in the place—even the doors are carved into curves in some rooms. At last count there were sixteen staircases, and more are discovered as old printing presses are shifted and box-rooms emptied.

A new director is trying to modernise the place without compromising its charm. That's a tall order. Catch it while you can.

ELIZABETH PISANI

Elizabeth Pisani worked as a foreign correspondent in Asia for several years before happening upon epidemiology and becoming an authority on HIV prevention. Her books include The Wisdom of Whores: Bureaucrats, Brothels, and the Business of AIDS.

8.2 ## The Black Friar Pub

174 Queen Victoria Street EC4
020 7236 5474
⊖ Blackfriars

Squeezed in between busy roads and a looming railway bridge on an awkward corner site by Blackfriars Bridge stands a completely undistinguished Victorian building. Subtle green mosaics and copper signs begin to hint that there may be a better world within.

The interior is an unbelievable collage of richly grained marbles, golden mosaics, and copper figures.

This is a temple to drinking. Taking inspiration from the friary which stood on this site, the architect, H. Fuller Clark, and the sculptors Henry Poole and Frederick Callcott, launched into a decorative frenzy based around a monastic theme. This is the diametric opposite of the Zen monastic aesthetic that has inspired the ubiquitous minimalism of London's fashion boutiques and top-end hotels; this is monastic maximalism. Art Nouveau and Arts and Crafts details are mixed in to stew with Byzantine and Olde English styles. Every surface is richly grained, decorated, or embellished. The pub is at its liveliest on weekday lunchtimes and just after work, when it is heaving with sweaty suits, while the grotto (carved out of a railway arch) boasts a smoky, booze-soaked atmosphere which could be distilled and sold as essence of London. In fact, this whole incredible interior, which was executed in the years between 1905 and 1921, is virtually a distillation of the density, cosiness, and womb-like comfort of the very notion of London pub-ness.

EDWIN HEATHCOTE

Architect Edwin Heathcote is the Architecture and Design critic of the Financial Times, co-founder of the door handle manufacturer Izé, and an author.

8.3 St. Paul's Cathedral

1675–1710, Sir Christopher Wren
Ludgate Hill EC4
020 7236 4128; www.stpauls.co.uk
St. Paul's or Mansion House

The Turner Monument

1851–1859, Patrick MacDowell
South Transept

St. Paul's is a great work of theatre in itself. I recommend attending either an evensong, to enjoy the choral music, or a Sunday Eucharist, for the procession. But the great moment of pathos for me is in the south transept, where among all the bemedalled and beweaponed generals and admirals stands a monument to the painter J. M. W. Turner in a frock coat, holding only a paintbrush.

JEREMY MUSSON

Jeremy Musson is an architectural historian.

Whispering Gallery

Secrets often come in whispers, so the Whispering Gallery of St. Paul's Cathedral must have overheard a few in its time. Now it's far too noisy to hear anything beyond the sound of security guards screaming at the parties of schoolchildren, and at tourists to stop taking photographs. Years ago there were no guards here at all, only guides, who would whisper the story of St. Paul's and its gallery straight along the curve of the great dome and into your own ear. One of London's biographers, H. V. Morton, describes climbing the 259 steps to the gallery and hearing a voice whispering to him. "I looked across to the other side of the gallery. The guide was whispering against the wall. His message came to me like a spirit voice from the Beyond: 'The diameter of the dome is a hundred and eight feet . . . '" From there it went on to tell the story of the dome and its design, as a kind of private confession of the building itself. There are still other ways for the voice to fall through the air of St. Paul's. In 1990, Russell Powell made the lowest indoor BASE jump in the world, by leaping from the Whispering Gallery with a parachute.

PAUL ELLIMAN

Paul Elliman is an artist and designer. He has exhibited at the Tate Modern and the New Museum in New York, among other places.

8.4 No. 1 Poultry

1997, James Stirling, Michael Wilford and Associates
1 Poultry EC2

⊖ Bank

DLR Bank

One of my favourite buildings is No. 1 Poultry, which was my husband Jim's [Sir James Stirling] penultimate building and his only one in the City of London. As the site was occupied by Mappin and Webb, a Grade II building, marathon court cases ensued, but a development, mainly offices, designed in the mid-eighties for Peter Palumbo, was at last completed in the nineties. The site itself is of great interest. Early Roman wooden buildings with stone extensions were uncovered; some had mosaic floors.

The restaurant at the top of the building (Le Coq d'Argent, 020 7395 5000; www.coqdargent.co.uk) is the Conran flagship in the City, and is usually full of young, energetic, and noisy City traders. But once you are at the top of the building and in the rotunda you could almost be in Italy. Through the gates, the formal parterre with its magnificent views over London (Lutyens's Midland Bank, the Mansion House and Hawksmoor's church) is stunning, the view spoilt only by brash new buildings (not sure whose, but not including Richard Rogers's) towards the river.

LADY STIRLING (MARY SHAND)
Lady Stirling is a furniture and interior designer.

8.5 St. Stephen Walbrook

1672–1680, restoration by Sir Christopher Wren
39 Walbrook EC4

⊖ Bank

DLR Bank

Londoners aren't supposed to have a favourite Starbucks, but I don't mind telling you mine. Not that I've even been in there, it's just that it occupies the southern corner of one of my favourite buildings in the city: Christopher Wren's restoration of St. Stephen Walbrook. First built in 1439, it was destroyed in the Great Fire of 1666; Wren worked on the small church from 1672 to 1680, and the dome is thought of as a prototype for the larger and much more famous version only a few hundred yards to the west, at St. Paul's Cathedral. St. Stephen Walbrook should be better known for its huge circular stone altar, designed by Henry Moore and installed in 1987, slap in the middle of the church like a well in a Venetian *campo*. A stranger and possibly stronger connection to voices beyond the church's dome is the black Bakelite 1950s GPO rotary telephone sitting inside a glass vitrine on a white plinth at the back of the church. This was the first telephone used by the Samaritans, the charity established by Dr. Chad Varah in 1953, while he was rector of St. Stephen's.

PAUL ELLIMAN

Paul Elliman is an artist and designer. He has exhibited at the Tate Modern and the New Museum in New York, among other places.

8

8.6 St. Mary Woolnoth

1716–1727, Nicholas Hawksmoor
Lombard Street EC3
020 7626 9701; www.london-city-churches.org.uk
⊖ Bank
DLR Bank

On the prow end of Lombard Street at Bank stands this curious, often overlooked masterpiece. Hawksmoor played with variations of the centralised church plan in his four churches as a response to urban context; at St. Mary the building is jammed on the site, but the Lombard Street elevation with "baroque and roll" windows turns elegantly to the front entrance, and the extraordinary front is stretched between the flank corners

by seemingly elastic stone rustication. Then across the
street into Sir James Stirling/Michael Wilford's referential
postmodern icon No. 1 Poultry (see p. 144). Climb to the
roof garden and look back down over St. Mary from a
perspective that Hawksmoor could only imagine.

ROBERT DYE

Robert Dye RIBA is an architect in private practice in London.

The Churches of London

Tramp the City with the paperback *London: The City
Churches* by Simon Bradley and Nikolaus Pevsner and see
as many of Wren's masterpieces (others too) as you have
stamina for. When flagging, follow your nose into
pubs—or the many excellent restaurants round
Smithfield, now one of London's centres of good eating.

PETER CARSON

*Peter Carson was formerly Editor-in-Chief at Penguin. Now semi-retired, he
works as an editor for Profile Books and translates from Russian.*

8.7 Bank of England Museum

1925–1934, Sir Herbert Baker; museum opened in 1988
Bartholomew Lane EC2
020 7601 5545; www.bankofengland.co.uk

⊖ Bank

DLR Bank

I love wandering around the City of London—and discovering its secret museums, like the wonderful Bank of
England Museum in Bartholomew Lane. It's free, and
fascinating—a comprehensive history of the Bank and
banking. Even if you think you're not interested in finance
you'll love it—it's history, politics, and sociology, too.

ERICA WAGNER

Erica Wagner is Literary Editor of The Times.

From Leadenhall to Jerusalem

⊖ Monument or Bank
DLR Bank

8.8 ## Leadenhall Market
1881, Sir Horace Jones
Whittington Avenue, off Gracechurch Street EC3
www.leadenhallmarket.co.uk

8.9 ## Postman's Park
King Edward Street EC1
(see p. 148)

8.10 ## St. Bartholomew-the-Great Church
1123; restoration, late 19th century, Sir Aston Webb
West Smithfield EC1
020 7606 5171; www.greatstbarts.com
⊖ Barbican

8.11 ## Smithfield Market
Charterhouse Street EC1
020 7332 3092; www.cityoflondon.gov.uk
Market open weekdays from 4 a.m. to 12 noon; building accessible
at all hours.

7.4 ## The Jerusalem Tavern
55 Britton Street EC1
022 7490 4281; www.stpetersbrewery.co.uk

🍽 Another magical city walk: coffee in the spectacular
Leadenhall Market, then a stroll to the Postman's Park,
near St. Paul's, where acts of valour are recorded on
a wall of tiles. Even greater spiritual uplift follows in a
walk to St. Bartholomew-the-Great Church, ancient
and beautiful and strangely friendly, then finally a walk
🍽 through Smithfield Market to the magic little pub the
Jerusalem Tavern for excellent beer.
DEBORAH MOGGACH
*Deborah Moggach is a writer of screenplays and novels, including These
Foolish Things and Tulip Fever.*

8.9   Postman's Park

In 1900, the churchyards of St. Botolph's, St. Leonard, and Christchurch Newgate Street were combined to create Postman's Park.

King Edward Street EC1

⊖ St. Paul's

Watts Memorial

1900, Ernest George

A minute away from St. Paul's Cathedral you can visit this tiny park during daylight hours. St. Botolph's Church next door is also worth a look.

I live nearby and discovered the park one day when I was walking my dog. The park is surrounded on all sides by buildings, which makes it feel like a special, enclosed little patch of green in the city. It's surprisingly quiet most of the day. It has a few gravestones of marginal interest, in that they're crammed up together in various parts of the park. It used to have a wonderful Michael Ayrton sculpture of a minotaur but a couple of years ago it was removed (having stood there since the 1970s) because it was deemed sacreligious or pagan by the church who presumably owns the land. It did have inordinately large genitals, I won't deny.

However, the most arresting aspect of Postman's Park is the Watts Memorial. G. F. Watts was a painter of considerable repute in the late nineteenth century; he was also a philanthropist. He observed that most urban memorials honour the famous or the celebrated and campaigned for every major city in England to have a memorial to ordinary people. Neither government nor town planners, it seems, were interested in the idea, so Watts paid for this memorial in London himself. There are no others to my knowledge.

It consists of a number of rather beautiful William Morris–style plaques beneath a wooden canopy. Each one commemorates a "heroic act of self-sacrifice: children who drowned saving the lives of other children, firemen, policemen, even a music hall artiste who burnt saving a fellow 'turn.'"

The tablets are strangely poignant in their verbal formality, and I find these words and the gesture of the memorial itself moving and sentimental in equal measures. That the memorial abuts a modern block of flats adds, for me, to its curiosity value. There is nothing else quite like it in London.

When I was writing my play *Closer*, I decided to send one of my characters to Postman's Park—indeed she took her name from one of the dead on Watts's memorial (Alice Ayres). I also set the last scene of the play in the park. After the production opened I received a letter from a member of the audience who had been inspired by the play to visit the park and the Watts Memorial. I was delighted. I hope it might delight you too.

PATRICK MARBER

Patrick Marber is a writer. His plays and screenplays include Dealer's Choice, Closer, Notes on a Scandal, and Don Juan in Soho.

8

8.10 St. Bartholomew-the-Great Church

1123; restoration, late 19th century, Sir Aston Webb
West Smithfield EC1
020 7606 5171; www.greatstbarts.com
⊖ Barbican

Between the Barbican and Smithfield Markets, both of which were entirely reconstructed after being devastated during the Blitz, a small corner of medieval London survives. The church of St. Bartholomew the Great was originally part of a monastery at a hospital (the hospital is still there, behind the great gates), said to have been founded in honor of the Apostle, after an Augustinian monk was miraculously cured of a fever. Much of what stands today was built in the early twelfth century, and the choir has the classic Norman interior of an aisle arcade, a triforium passageway, and clerestory windows. The heavy round piers and the round arches with rounded mouldings are perhaps not the most elegant of England's early Gothic, but they do reflect the internationalism of an architectural form that united much of England and Northern France in the early twelfth century; even this small monastic church in the City of London, unnoticed by royalty, bore the imprint of the new Norman way of building. The hospital survived the suppression of monasteries, the church became a parish church at the hospital and was cut down to about half of its original length, and part of the cloister was destroyed; you can follow the lines of the original cloister walls and the nave towards the post-war apartment block next to the small garden. The streets alongside the church preserve, in part, houses and shops of the eighteenth century.

CAROLINE GOODSON
Caroline Goodson is an archaeologist and historian.

Smithfield Market on a Sunday afternoon feels like London is having a hangover; the bars and restaurants are quiet, the meat market is empty, and the hospital (St. Bartholomew's, the oldest in London, founded in 1123) the same. There is a church in the northwestern corner— St. Bart's, featured in Hugh Grant's wedding to Duckface in *Four Weddings and a Funeral*, where you can stroll into an exquisite service. They are very welcoming to strangers, the choir is excellent, and the church a beautifully preserved example of a City parish church—one of the few to survive the Great Fire.

IAN KELLY
Ian Kelly is an actor and writer. His publications include Shakespeare Cinema.

8.11 # Smithfield Market

1868–1883, Sir Horace Jones; in 1962, Sir Thomas Bennett redesigned the Poultry House after the original was destroyed by fire in 1958
Charterhouse Street EC1
020 7332 3092; www.cityoflondon.gov.uk
Market open weekdays from 4 a.m. to 12 noon; building accessible at all hours.

⊖ Barbican

This is a splendid and spectacular piece of architecture which has two distinct lives. In the daytime it is a bustling meat market with huge trucks rumbling in and out. At night a different crowd arrives to eat at fashionable restaurant, Smith's of Smithfield (67–77 Charterhouse Street, 020 7251 7950; www.smithsofsmithfield.co.uk), and dance at one of the city's most famous dance music venues, Fabric (77a Charterhouse Street, 020 7336 8989; www.fabriclondon.com)—both right opposite the market. Fabulous views of the market and St. Paul's Cathedral from the top floor of Smith's.

LESLEY DOWNER
Lesley Downer is a writer. Her books include The Courtesan and the Samurai and The Last Concubine.

William Hogarth

8.12 # St. Bartholomew's Hospital

Staircase Hall, in the North Wing
West Smithfield EC1
020 7377 7000; www.bartsandthelondon.nhs.uk
The paintings can be viewed from St. Bartholomew's Hospital Museum. Check the website for hours, as they may vary.

⊖ Barbican

The Pool of Bethesda

1736, William Hogarth

The Good Samaritan
1737, William Hogarth

Although Hogarth is a very well-known artist and some of his most famous and characteristic "Modern Moral Subjects" can be seen in London at Tate Britain and Sir John Soane's Museum (see p. 92), these large and ambitious oil paintings show a much less well-known aspect of his work. They decorate the staircase walls of the architect James Gibbs's northern block at St. Bartholomew's Hospital, which was rebuilt in the mid-1730s. Hogarth appropriately depicts biblical subjects of healing: Christ at the pool of Bethesda and the Good Samaritan.

Hogarth was born next door to the hospital and his mother and sister were pensioners there; these pictures were painted by the artist free of charge when it looked likely that the commission might be given to one of the many foreign decorative painters working in England in the first half of the eighteenth century. Somewhat optimistically, Hogarth thought their public display would lead to a rash of commissions of this sort for churches and other public buildings.

BRIAN ALLEN
Brian Allen is Director of Studies at the Paul Mellon Centre for Studies in British Art in London and Adjunct Professor of History of Art at Yale University.

8.13 St. Mary Abchurch
1681–1686, Sir Christopher Wren
Abchurch Lane EC4
020 7626 0306; www.london-city-churches.org.uk
⊖ Bank or Monument
DLR Bank

Simply the warmest and sunniest, and in some ways the most Mediterranean, of all the Wren churches, red brick and homely on the outside, but a great painted dome on the inside, plus quantities of woodwork by Grinling Gibbons and others.

ROGER WOODLEY
Roger Woodley is the author of the London Blue Guide.

From Monument to Liverpool

 Θ Monument

Just follow your nose, ear, and eye from Monument to Liverpool Street station, taking as many twists and turns as you can via Lombard Street, Bishop's Gate, Finsbury Circus—churches, pubs, passages, gardens, monuments, citygoers at work and pleasure. Best done in the week but a certain ghostly splendour at weekend. Organ recitals at St. Magnus the Martyr, St. Botolph's, and many others.

This is real London.

PIERS PLOWRIGHT
Piers Plowright retired from BBC Radio in 1997 after thirty years as an award-winning producer.

B.14 The Barbican Centre

1982, Chamberlin, Powell, and Bon
Silk Street EC2
020 7588 3008; www.barbican.org.uk
Arts Centre: 020 7638 4141 or 020 7638 8891

Θ Barbican

Supper at the Barbican Centre—another modern architectural tour de force come back into fashion—followed by a play or concert. One of London's most exciting and imaginative cultural programmes—which also includes art exhibitions and film screenings—is found in London's most extraordinary inner city council estates.

JOHN M. ASHWORTH
John M. Ashworth has been the Chairman of the British Library Board, the Director of the London School of Economics, and the government's chief scientist.

CHAPTER 9
The East End & Hackney

1 19 Princelet Street Synagogue
2 Christ Church, Spitalfields
3 Spitalfields Market 🍴🍷
4 A. Gold 🎁
5 Dennis Severs' House
6 Blondie 🍴🍷
7 Absolute Vintage
8 Brick Lane Market
9 This Shop Rocks 🍴🍷
10 Beyond Retro 🍴🍷
11 Brick Lane Beigel Bake 🎁
12 Boundary Estate
13 Rochelle School Canteen 🍴🍷
14 Columbia Road Flower Market 🍴🍷🎁
15 White Cube 2
16 Geffrye Museum 🍴🍷
17 V&A Museum of Childhood
18 Spa London (see p. 242)
19 Trinity Green
20 Tayyabs 🍴🍷
21 Wilton's Music Hall
22 London Fields Lido
23 Broadway Market 🍴🍷🎁
24 Broadway Bookshop
25 Hackney City Farm
26 Fred Bare 🎁
27 Far Global 🎁
28 Jones Dairy 🍴🍷
29 Two Columbia Rd 🎁
30 No-One 🍴🍷
31 Atomica 🎁
32 Caravan 🎁
33 Albion 🍴🍷
34 Vyner Street
35 Victoria Park
36 Arcola Theatre (see p. 288)
37 Café Oto 🍴🍷
38 Ridley Road Market 🍴🍷🎁
39 The Narrow Way
40 Hackney Empire Theatre

THE EAST END & HACKNEY

9.1 ## 19 Princelet Street Synagogue

19 Princelet Street, off Brick Lane E1
020 7247 5352; www.19princeletstreet.org.uk
Open to the public several days a year.
Check website, or call to schedule a tour.

⊖ Aldgate East
LO Shoreditch High Street
RAIL Shoreditch High Street

Perhaps the most charismatic building in all of London, this fragile treasure in Spitalfields is a testament to generations of hope and faith. Originally a Protestant Huguenot weavers' house, it became a home to Jewish émigrés—fleeing pogroms and making their lives and their devotions in the East End—who created a secret synagogue stretching out over the back garden. A shabby, crumbling frontage gives no indication of the jewel within, and sadly today it is so parlous in its condition that its heavy old doors are rarely opened.

The Jewish folks who deemed this place holy have now left Spitalfields; in their place is a large Muslim community, and, as is fitting for this ever-changing area, there are now plans to turn 19 Princelet Street into Europe's first museum of immigration. For the moment, however, try to visit on one of the increasingly infrequent days when it is open to discover a place of serenity and spirituality, redolent with the prayers of ages, heavy with the sadness of passing, but radiant with the promise of moving on. This building is, for me, a wonderful monument to the transformative powers of migration and the transcendent beauty of human endeavour.

ROBERT ELMS
A native of London, Robert Elms is a broadcaster whose daily show on the BBC is a passionate song of praise for the city he loves.

9.2 Christ Church, Spitalfields

1714–1729, Nicholas Hawksmoor
Commercial Street E1
020 7247 7202; www.ccspitalfields.org
⊖ Aldgate East or Liverpool Street
LO Shoreditch High Street
RAIL Shoreditch High Street

When I first discovered this astonishing Baroque tour de force—by an architect whose name was almost forgotten—it was full of dust and broken pews, with water dripping through the ceiling and pigeons nesting in the nave. The churchyard was full of meths drinkers and was known locally as Itchy Park. Miraculously, though, Christ Church escaped collapse or demolition. A painstaking restoration took twenty-six years, from 1976 to 2002, under the eye of an architect with a wonderfully craftsman-like name: Red Mason. Thanks to him, Christ Church regained its bright, white, pristine beauty. You can regularly hear music performed within it. And it stands, like an angular, awkward, strange bird, in one of the oldest districts of London, with the City to one side and the heartland of London's Bangladeshi community behind. See it, and be amazed, and go on to discover Hawksmoor's other masterpieces, two more of them also in the East End: St. Anne's Limehouse (see p. 195), and St. George's in the East (Cannon Street Road E1).

PAUL BARKER
Paul Barker writes widely on social, cultural, and architectural issues.

Classic "piling it on." Start with a funky temple. Add a triumphal arch, a few volutes, a base, smaller base, and end the magic trick with a hanging handkerchief. Inside, the church has a Gothically proportioned space made with classical elements.

ROBERT LIVESEY
Robert Livesey is an architect and a professor at the Knowlton School of Architecture at The Ohio State University.

9

9.3 Spitalfields Market

Commercial Street, between Lamb and Brushfield Streets E1
020 7377 1496; www.visitspitalfields.com

⊖ Aldgate East or Liverpool Street
LO Shoreditch High Street
RAIL Shoreditch High Street

Not far from the commercial heart of London, the City, lies Spitalfields. This area was once a rich suburb populated by wealthy weavers and cloth merchants, many of whom translated their earnings into large and fashionable houses. Today it preserves, better than any other part of London, a feel for the eighteenth century. On a weekday go to Liverpool Street station and cross Bishopsgate into Spitalfields Market. On the far side is Christ Church, the parish church. From here, abandon yourself to the maze of ancient terraces, and afterwards choose a pub or bar in the market and relax. Visit Spitalfields Market itself on a Sunday when the full array of stalls and shops opens up. The site of a busy market since 1638, these days the focus is on interiors, fashion, and artisanal foods.

SIMON THURLEY

Simon Thurley is Chief Executive of English Heritage and was formerly Director of the Museum of London.

9.4 A. Gold

42 Brushfield Street E1
020 7247 2487

⊖ Liverpool Street
RAIL Liverpool Street

My current favourite weekend activity is bicycling to A. Gold, a small specialist grocer and wine merchant alongside Spitalfields Market, close to the City and Liverpool Street station. My route takes me through Brick Lane and the small side streets of this part of eighteenth-century London, now smartened up as if it were a piece of New England.

CHARLES SAUMAREZ SMITH

Charles Saumarez Smith is Secretary and Chief Executive of the Royal Academy of Arts.

9.5 Dennis Severs' House

1724; 1979–1999, interior, Dennis Severs

18 Folgate Street E1

020 7247 4013; www.dennissevershouse.co.uk

Tours only. Check website for schedule.

⊖ Liverpool Street

LO Shoreditch High Street

RAIL Shoreditch High Street

Dennis Severs' House is a museum of sorts, but also the very opposite of a museum. It's a Georgian terraced house tucked in a back street between Spitalfields Market and the City, restored in the styles of the eighteenth and nineteenth centuries by Californian artist Dennis Severs, who died in 1999. The best time to visit is a dark winter evening (you have to book a slot beforehand). A man in a black shirt and black trousers will open the door (you have to knock, there's no bell) and take £12 off you, in return for which you are allowed to walk around the house for forty-five minutes. The man will tell you that you have to do this in complete silence. There is no electric light in Dennis Severs' House, only candles and open fireplaces.

Stumbling from room to room, you feel not only like you are travelling back in time but like you have walked straight into a Dickens novel, or the Hogarth painting that hangs in one of the rooms. There are half-made mince pies on the kitchen table and spilt glasses of punch in the smoking room, and there's a real canary in the lounge. Occasionally, you can hear the haunting chime of clocks, the rattle of a horse-drawn carriage outside, and the creak of footsteps in the room next door; it's as if the people who used to live here are standing around the corner.

As with any good story, you feel like you've uncovered a secret by the time you get to the end, the last room in the house. On the top floor, eighteenth-century opulence gives way to shocking nineteenth-century poverty. The wallpaper is peeling off the damp walls, the bed linen is filthy, there's a stench of oysters and vinegar, and it's freezing cold. It comes as a shock when you realise the banisters have been burned for firewood: such was the completeness of Severs's operatic vision that he has planted the seeds of its own destruction inside it. As you walk into the cold winter night, you will try to touch the next automobile on the pavement just to see if it's real.

PHILIP OLTERMANN

Philip Oltermann is an editor at The Guardian. He is writing a book on Anglo-German meetings.

A Romantic Evening

DLR Bank to Wst India Quay

Possibly one of the most romantic evenings to be had in London begins by taking the Docklands Light Railway from Bank station. After the initial sci-fi departure into the open air, the bizarre mix of old, new, and barren that is Docklands opens up before you. Ideally, take the line as far as West India Quay and cross the Future Systems Bridge over to Canary Wharf. Canary Wharf by night almost lends plausibility to conspiracy theorists who suggest it is a beacon to aliens, falling as it does on several significant ley lines.

SHEZ 360

Artist Shezad Dawood has exhibited widely, including at the Tate and the Venice Biennale.

Brick Lane Fashion

www.visitbricklane.org

⊖ Aldgate East

LO Shoreditch High Street

RAIL Shoreditch High Street

9.6 ## Blondie

114–118 Commercial Street (Unit 2) E1
020 7247 0050

9.7 ## Absolute Vintage

15 Hanbury Street E1
020 7247 3883; www.absolutevintage.co.uk

9.8 ## Brick Lane Market

85 Brick Lane E1
020 7364 1717
Open Sundays from 8 a.m. to 2 p.m.

9.9 ## This Shop Rocks

135 Brick Lane E1
020 7739 7667

9.10 ## Beyond Retro

110–112 Cheshire Street E1
020 7613 3636; www.beyondretro.com

9

If shopping for vintage clothes is on the agenda, one need not look any further than London's Brick Lane for one-of-a-kind fashion finds. As a Mecca for fashion students and other trendy locals living in the area, it's a place where finding inspiration to curate your own look is a bonus, and the whole scene serves as a barometer to make sure your own style is in check—or perhaps not, as vintage fashion can assist in going against the grain.

The best time to visit Brick Lane is during the week, when the hubbub of tourists and the like is absent. Not only will you be able to sift through rails of clothing without the jab of an accidental elbow from fellow shoppers but you will also have first pick of freshly laid-out goods before the weekend crowd swarms into the area.

I suggest starting at Blondie, filled with premium pre-1950s vintage gear. Items are priced in the higher-priced "boutique" range, a stark contrast to its more affordable sister store, Absolute Vintage, located just around the corner. Absolute Vintage's warehouse space is filled with wonderful finds from the 1930s to the 1980s, but your first impression may be that its specialty is shoes.

Just one minute away on foot, one will step into Brick Lane, the home of many vintage shops—but the Brick Lane Market is where you need to be, provided you are in the area Friday to Sunday. The market has a colossal selection and is currently *the* hot spot to grab a good vintage bargain (but who knows for how long once the word spreads).

Heading north, your next destination should be This Shop Rocks, which stocks vintage garments such as 1950s tea dresses and pinafore gingham at boutique prices. No one said vintage has to be cheap, and this especially applies to the beautiful pieces sold here.

A detour off Brick Lane and down Cheshire Street is strongly recommended, as it is filled with vintage shops left and right, but the most appreciable of the lot has to be Beyond Retro. Containing thousands of vintage pieces, the Beyond Retro warehouse is the largest shop in the Brick Lane area and focuses on a huge range of styles from 1900 to 1990. The shop hosts frequent film and music events to help forge its rock-and-roll vibe, and perhaps explains why it holds cult status amongst dedicated fashionistas.

JOHN NOI
John Noi is the editor of Spektacle, a magazine of fashion, music, and design.

9.11 Brick Lane Beigel Bake

159 Brick Lane E1
020 7729 0616
⊖ Aldgate East
LO Shoreditch High Street
RAIL Shoreditch High Street

🍴 Publishing the secret haunts of your hometown seems an exercise in reckless bragging, trading the kudos of showing off your insider knowledge for the loss of your favourite café or quiet retreat. But the Brick Lane Beigel Bake, well . . . it's one of those city institutions that can barely be described as a secret anymore, yet for any visitor it still gives off that strange sense of satisfaction at having found a gem away from the beaten track. Open 24/7.
DAN FOX

Dan Fox is senior editor of Frieze magazine, as well as a writer, filmmaker, and musician.

9

9.12 Boundary Estate

1899, London County Council
The Boundary Estate is approximately bordered by Virginia Road at its north end, Swanfield Street at its east end, Old Nichol Street at its south end, and Boundary Street at its west end, with Arnold Circus in the centre.
www.boundaryestate.co.uk
LO Shoreditch High Street
RAIL Shoreditch High Street

Southeast of Shoreditch Church lies the Boundary Estate, a whole area of beautiful red brick Arts and Crafts tenement buildings that were built to replace the infamous Jago, the Victorian Hell's Kitchen of London. Streets lined with plane trees radiate out from Arnold Circus. The bandstand in the centre of the Circus sits on a mound made from the rubble of the nineteenth-century slums. Visit on a Sunday morning, when a two-minute walk north takes you to Columbia Road Flower Market (cappuccinos and exotic plants), or a two-minute walk south takes you to Brick Lane Market (stolen bikes and three-card tricks).

CORNELIA PARKER
Artist Cornelia Parker has had major solo exhibitions in London, Paris, and New York.

9.13 Rochelle School Canteen

Rochelle School
Arnold Circus E2
020 7729 5677; www.arnoldandhenderson.com
Open Monday to Friday, lunch only.
LO   Shoreditch High Street
RAIL Shoreditch High Street

From the street, the only sign that there might be somewhere to eat in this former primary school is the typewritten word "Canteen" next to one of the buzzers (the bottom-right-hand buzzer—the last one you would look at) outside the Boys' gate.

If you're lucky enough to hear the gate unlock (the Canteen is open only on weekday lunchtimes), when you step through, you'll see a beautiful lawn, wooden tables, chairs and benches in the sunshine, and a bike shed that has been converted into a restaurant. The school is now used for studio space, so there might be some well-dressed artists on their lunch break. The owners, Melanie Arnold and Margot Henderson, are married to Jon Spiter and chef Fergus Henderson, respectively, who started the renowned St. John restaurant, and Rochelle Canteen has many of the same impeccable qualities: nose-to-tail eating, with fresh ingredients and simple dishes. Everything on the menu is good, but I'm always drawn back to the purple sprouting broccoli with anchovy, their pies for two, and the chocolate pot.

JOE DUNTHORNE

Joe Dunthorne is the author of Submarine. He currently lives in London and is a striker for the England Writers' Football Team.

9.14   Columbia Road Flower Market

Columbia Road E5
Sunday morning only.
www.columbiaroad.info

LO   Hoxton

RAIL Hoxton

My favourite place is ephemeral. It comes into being on Sunday mornings, at the moment the trucks wake me up delivering their goods. It begins to disintegrate after 2:30 p.m., when what produce remains is trundled back into vans by people shouting in Cockney accents, or is bought cheaply, surreptitiously, and illegally by locals like me. I speak of that oldest and most famous flower market—Columbia Road. Every Sunday morning, my studio (thirty seconds' walk from the florabundal epicentre) is garlanded with kangaroo paw, lilies, parrot tulips, tuberose—proof that nature still exists somewhere, even during a London winter.

The market provides many subsidiary attractions. For example, when the English buy bedding plants, they cheer up, and sometimes smile at complete strangers. Once, on a Sunday morning, I was practising my piano with the French doors open. A flower-buying crowd gathered on the street below and started clapping. The delight of Sunday mornings compensates for East End Sunday afternoons.

ROBYN DAVIDSON

Robyn Davidson's books include Desert Places and Tracks, winner of the Thomas Cook Travel Book Award.

The No. 11 Bus
Liverpool Street Station E1

⊖ Liverpool Street

I love travelling upstairs on the front seat of London's double-decker buses to get a bird's-eye view of London. My favourite bus journey is the No. 11 route. Take it from the back of Liverpool Street station. It travels down Threadneedle Street (Bank of England) through the City, past St. Paul's Cathedral, down Fleet Street (one of the most wonderful streets in London) past the law courts to the Aldwych on to the Strand. Past Charing Cross, Nelson's Column, down Whitehall (10 Downing Street), past the Houses of Parliament, and on to Victoria. Then you get to Sloane Square and King's Road (full of great clothes shops). Get off at World's End and walk back down King's Road towards Sloane Square and shop till you drop, ending up at Peter Jones (Sloane Square, www.peterjones.co.uk), my favourite department store.

CORNELIA PARKER

Artist Cornelia Parker has had major solo exhibitions in London, Paris, and New York

9.15 White Cube 2
2000, Rundell Associates
48 Hoxton Square N1
020 7930 5373; www.whitecube.com

⊖ Old Street

LO Shoreditch High Street

RAIL Old Street

The former site of my publishers, Duckworths, 48 Hoxton Square, was bought by Jay Jopling, dealer to the Sensation era, and converted into a conceptual art nexus for this, London's version of New York's Soho. A luminous white cube, indeed, filled with works, depending on Jopling's latest discovery, from Gilbert and George to Damien Hirst to Sarah Morris. Take a walk outside and the full force of an area described by the *Evening Standard* as the art/fashion centre of the universe will appear to be entirely underwhelming. But then you notice the galleries and bars opening up almost before your eyes, and having got your eye in, there'll be no looking back. Soon you'll be wanting one of those half-million-pound loft conversions, and wondering how you ever lived without Tracey Emin. She often thinks the same thing.

PHILIP HOARE

Philip Hoare's books include biographies of Stephen Tennant and Noël Coward; Wilde's Last Stand; and England's Lost Eden

9.16

Geffrye Museum

Old wing: 1714, unknown architect but funded by the Ironmonger's Company; new wing completed 1998, Branson Coates Architecture
136 Kingsland Road E2
020 7739 9893; www.geffrye-museum.org.uk
For directions, check the website or go to www.journeyplanner.org.

9

I based the almshouse in my novel *Fish, Blood and Bone* on the austerely elegant eighteenth-century Geffrye Museum, where each room has been converted to show the art and interior design of different periods in British history—from darkly elaborate Elizabethan through the streamlined late twentieth century of Tom Dixon leather chairs. My favourite local small museum, with an excellent free reading room and regular exhibitions, it's a must for every student or fan of design. There is a peaceful period herb garden surrounding the building, a haven of green in the tarmac, and tombstone grey of Kingsland Road, and a passable café in the Nigel Coates–designed wing (where the staircase resembles something from a Batman movie). For anything more than tea, though, it's better to sample one of the authentic

🍴 Vietnamese eateries on South Kingsland Road, or walk a
few blocks south, where Hoxton offers the latest in trendy
London restaurants and bars.

LESLIE FORBES
Leslie Forbes is a broadcaster and writer whose novels include Fish, Blood and
Bone, a mystery set in London and Tibet.

9.17 V & A Museum of Childhood

Most of the building was originally part of the Victoria & Albert Museum,
then was transported to this site and reconstructed by J. W. Wild in 1860.
Cambridge Heath Road and Old Ford Road E2
020 8980 2415; www.vam.ac.uk

⊖ Bethnal Green
RAIL Cambridge Heath

For a touch of the country house in London, see the doll's
houses or Baby Houses at the Museum of Childhood, a
branch of the Victoria & Albert Museum. The eighteenth-
century Baby Houses were not on the whole made for
children but for young women of aristocratic or gentle
birth, as expensive miniatures in the spirit of a Cabinet of
Curiosities: the best examples are works of art, possibly a
little lost on children. There is much here to delight all ages.

JEREMY MUSSON
Jeremy Musson is an architectural historian.

9.19 Trinity Green

1695, possibly designed by Sir Christopher Wren
Mile End Road E1

⊖ Whitechapel
LO Whitechapel
RAIL Whitechapel

I used to live in Trinity Green, Mile End Road. It is a
collegiate-style square with a chapel and it was built—in
cool, proportioned style—for mariners' widows whose
husbands had not returned. So there are nautical

references everywhere. Half of the Green was bombed in the Blitz, the other half is as it was—but you can't spot the joins. Trinity Green is a jewel, which until recently wasn't even mentioned in the *A–Z*. It was the subject of the very first volume of the *Survey of London*, written by the Arts and Crafts denizen C. R. Ashbee, who called it "an object lesson in national history." A neglected square of London.

CHRISTOPHER FRAYLING

Sir Christopher Frayling, historian, critic, and award-winning broadcaster, has written many books on aspects of cultural history. He was until recently Rector of the Royal College of Art and Chair of Arts Council England.

9.20 Tayyabs

83–89 Fieldgate Street E1
020 7247 6400, www.tayyabs.co.uk
⊖ Whitechapel

🍽 Don't eat the Bangladeshi or Indian food on Brick Lane—head across the Whitechapel Road and join the queue for the real deal. Tayyabs may be glitzier than a Bollywood movie, but the charcoal-grilled lamb cutlets and teeth-grindingly sweet puds don't lie. While you wait, look around. This was one of London's blackest nineteenth-century slums. Today you'll see dark Victorian philanthropic housing, one of London's biggest mosques (cheek-by-jowl with a tiny synagogue; this used to be one of London's main Jewish neighbourhoods), the gigantic flophouse where Karl Marx once stayed, and, behind you, the Royal London Hospital, where Joseph Merrick, the so-called Elephant Man, was treated (after being spotted in freak shows on the Whitechapel Road). His skeleton is still kept in the hospital vaults, alas, only for the eyes of medical students.

TOM DYCKHOFF

Tom Dyckhoff is architecture critic of The Times, architecture and design critic for BBC2's weekly arts magazine programme, The Culture Show, and writes a weekly column for The Guardian's Weekend Magazine.

9.21 Wilton's Music Hall

1877, J. Buckley Wilson
1 Graces Alley, off Cable Street E1
020 7702 9555; www.wiltons.org.uk

⊖ Tower Hill or Aldgate East
DLR Tower Gateway

As the great actress Peggy Ashcroft once said, theatres either have an atmosphere or they don't. This one does, also a secrecy and a mystery, for hardly anyone knows about the place except a few film crews and, in recent years, a caucus of dedicated fringe theatre-goers. Hidden away off Cable Street, Wilton's, London's first and finest surviving Victorian music hall, is an architectural gem used for small-scale operas, commercial purposes, even private functions (the actor and writer Simon Callow threw a black-and-white fiftieth birthday party there), as well as various maverick, unusual theatre productions. It reeks of the spirit of music hall, with its perfect rectangular proportions, barley sugar pillars and pretty balcony running right round the interior, which is narrow and high. Champagne Charlie sang his songs here in the 1860s, John Betjeman heroically saved the place from the bulldozers in the 1960s. In the late 1990s, the Irish actress Fiona Shaw performed T. S. Eliot's poetic lamentation "The Waste Land," the first live performance in more than a hundred years. The theatre came alive again in shudders and echoes of the past. But it does anyway, if you just poke your head through the door. In 2007, a restoration appeal was launched as the World Monuments Fund added the building to its list of one hundred most endangered sites.

MICHAEL COVENEY
Michael Coveney is the chief theatre critic of Whatsonstage.com and author of several biographies, including those of Maggie Smith, Mike Leigh, and Andrew Lloyd Webber.

Jack the Ripper Walking Tour

020 7624 3978; www.jacktheripperwalk.com

⊖   Tower Hill

I know this sounds as corny as the waxworks at Madame Tussauds, but trust me, it ain't. It's my favourite walk offered by the Original London Walks, the group that organizes hourly tours with subjects ranging from Charles Dickens's London to Princess Diana's London, from the Old Jewish Quarter Tour to the Beatles Magical Mystery Tour. Show up at the tube stop, meet your guide, pay your £8, and you're off. In two hours, see and learn more about London than most Londoners will ever know in a lifetime. Jack the Ripper Haunts meets Sunday nights at 7:30 p.m. at the Tower Hill tube and is often led by Donald Rumbelow (the world's leading "Ripper-ologist"). He escorts his group through the East End of London, describing in gory detail the wheres and hows of each murder, finishing at the Ten Bells, the pub where the prostitute-victims drank their final gins. Despite initial protestations from visiting friends, they invariably return to my flat in a Victorian frenzy saying, "That was the best thing we've done in London."

GLEN ROVEN

Glen Roven, four-time Emmy winner, has performed with orchestras around the world.

9

The Green Bridge

2000, Piers Gough

Mile End Park E2 (not on map)

www.towerhamlets.gov.uk

⊖   Mile End

This is a very "unambitious" idea which creates ambitious results—unifying a park and regenerating an urban area.

The delight in the locals is palpable, and hopefully it will have a long-term impact. And most of all it is joyous.

KAREN WRIGHT

Karen Wright is the editor of Modern Painters and co-editor of the Penguin Book of Art Writing.

Forman's Fish Island

Stour Road, Fish Island E3 (not on map)
020 8525 2365; www.formans.co.uk

DLR Hackney Wick
RAIL Hackney Wick

When Lance Forman's century-old salmon smokery was given notice to quit the future Olympic site—along with two hundred and fifty other small-scale businesses—it not only landed probably the best pitch in London, smack bang across the River Lee from the main stadium, but its new address happened to be Fish Island. Honestly. The staff of eighty-five, who salt, smoke, fillet, and pack countless pounds of salmon each week—you can watch through portholes—come to work via Bream, Mornier, and Dace Streets to a pink building designed to look like a dacre (or fillet) of salmon. It's even got a fish-scale roof. The salmon is London Cure; it's utterly different from any smoked salmon I've had before. The smokery has been supplying Fortnum & Mason for over seventy years and claims to have kick-started the luxury smoked salmon industry in Edwardian times. Last year they opened a little restaurant—modern, minimal, with English wines—with a balcony overlooking the Olympic site (dinner Thursday to Sunday, plus breakfast on Saturdays and lunch on Sundays). They plan to moor a narrow boat alongside it in 2012, so you can guzzle salmon and champagne while athlete-spotting.

SOPHIE CAMPBELL

Sophie Campbell is a travel writer and a London tour guide.

9.22 **London Fields Lido**
London Fields Westside E8
www.hackney.gov.uk
⊖ Bethnal Green
LO Hackney Central

For people who've stumbled upon the pleasures of swimming there, the London Fields Lido is nothing short of a temple of worship. Confirmation of this comes in the many pages of glowing adoration inside the comments book at the front door; it tells a story of Londoners from a seemingly endless array of countries who, like me, love this place. Who would have thought that swimming out in the bleak grey British weather would draw so much affection? For those who don't know, a lido is an outdoor public swimming pool, a concept owing its name to the Lido de Venezia and its origins to 1930s, pre-foreign-holiday Britain. In their heyday, upwards of a hundred and seventy were built across the country. Since then, however, almost all have slipped into ruinous and undignified decay. It's taken a twenty-year campaign to get the London Fields Lido back onto its watery feet, and my fellow worshippers and I are eternally grateful to those who made it happen.

Swimming while watching the clouds scoot overhead is a natural pleasure. The lido makes the experience accessible for us sub-superhero types by keeping the water at an invigorating yet non-death-defying twenty-six degrees Celsius all year round, come rain, shine, or even snow, an experience I would fully recommend.

As is often the case in places of worship, I'm always struck by the hushed silence of concentration when I enter. I can leave life's stresses and strains at the door, to be picked up later, having been put into perspective. The fifty-metre Olympic-length pool provides ample space for swimmers to slip into a meditative rhythm accompanied by the steady splashing cadence of others—a feeling that is matched afterwards only by the righteousness that a swim in the elements brings to the rest of the day.

HANNAH STARKEY

Hannah Starkey is a photographer whose work has been exhibited at London's Victoria & Albert Museum, the Tate Modern, and the Centraal Museum in Utrecht.

9.23 Broadway Market

Runs from London Fields Park to Regent's Canal
www.broadwaymarket.co.uk
Open Saturdays from 9 a.m. to 5 p.m.
DLR Hoxton
RAIL Cambridge Heath

Climpson & Sons
67 Broadway Market E8
020 7812 9829; www.webcoffeeshop.co.uk

Fabrications
7 Broadway Market E8
020 7275 8043; www.fabrications1.co.uk

The Cat and Mutton
76 Broadway Market E8
020 7254 5599; www.catandmutton.co.uk

The Dove
24–28 Broadway Market E8
020 7275 7617; www.belgianbars.com

Broadway Market is Borough Market's smaller, hipper cousin. On Saturdays, it is home to a wonderful collection of stalls selling cheese, bread, books, coffee, cupcakes, and vintage clothes. Local craftspeople sell handmade jewellery and accessories, and East London's beautiful, peacocky twenty-somethings gather to allay their hangovers with lunch from one of the array of stalls which sell everything from paella to stew with Ethiopian injera. The shops that line the street are worth a visit in themselves: Climpson & Sons is an independent coffee shop and roastery selling what is quite possibly the best espresso in the east, and Fabrications is another indie devoted to all things knitted, woven, or crocheted. If you find yourself in need of a tipple, the Cat and Mutton serves up sexy pints to the hipsters, and the Dove, with its sprawling interior, board games, and Belgian beers, caters to everyone else.

AMBER DOWELL

Amber Dowell is an editor at Granta Books.

An East London Stroll

Stroll starts at Sheep Lane.

RAIL Cambridge Health

For directions to individual shops, go to www.journeyplanner.org.

9.24 Broadway Bookshop

6 Broadway Market E8

020 7241 1626; www.broadwaybookshophackney.com

9.25 Hackney City Farm

1a Goldsmiths Row E2

020 7729 6381; www.hackneycityfarm.co.uk

(see p. 181)

9.14 Columbia Road Flower Market

Columbia Road E2

www.columbiaroad.info

Sunday mornings only.

(see p. 167)

9.26 Fred Bare

118 Columbia Road E2

020 7729 6962; www.columbiaroad.info

Open Sundays until 2:30 p.m.

9.27 **Far Global**
124 Columbia Road E2
0793 115 1663; www.columbiaroad.info
Open Sundays and by appointment.

9.28 **Jones Dairy**
23 Ezra Street E2
020 7739 5372; www.jonesdairy.co.uk
Open Friday to Sunday.

9.29 **Two Columbia Road**
2 Columbia Road E2
020 7729 9933; www.twocolumbiaroad.co.uk

9.30 **No-One**
1 Kingsland Road E2
020 7613 5314; www.no-one.co.uk

9.31 **Atomica**
125 Shoreditch High Street E1
020 7739 5923; www.atomica.me.uk

9.32 **Caravan**
3 Redchurch Street E2
020 7033 3532; www.caravanstyle.com
Open Tuesday to Friday.

9.33 **Albion**
2–4 Boundary Street E2
020 7729 1051; www.albioncaff.co.uk

On Sundays, I often walk up Sheep Lane towards the
Regents Canal and Broadway Market. The market is truly
a Saturday destination, but I like avoiding the crowds and
having a duck into the Broadway Bookshop, where I've
found many a treasure for both my own reading and gifts
for friends. I then head over the canal bridge towards
Goldsmiths Row and have a look into the Hackney City
Farm, with its amazing slow-cooked roast lamb that is
offered for lunch with root vegetables. The atmosphere is

very relaxed, with chequered tablecloths, numbers given at the counter, and food delivered to the table. After the Sunday roast, it's a further walk across Hackney Road, up into Columbia Road Flower Market. The market is vibrant with colour and all manner of plants, trees, and flowers. I often just want to look at it all, even if I am not buying anything from the many bustling stalls. There are traders calling out to you, "Four bunches for a fiver," and trying to catch your eye. It is very special to see the change of season in what's on offer. I also love the many shops that line the market on either side. In the old days these were few and far between; now they have mushroomed, and there are many to choose from. Most offer some form of garden pots and furnishings, but there is also Fred Bare, which has sold hats and headgear for at least twenty-five years, and Far Global, which sells relics and such, mainly from India, with the sensitivity and care worthy of these items. The shops there are usually open only on the weekend and come into their own on Sundays in particular. One that has stayed the course from the early days is Jones Dairy in Ezra Street, which is good for bread and staples, and features an aged and vintage façade faithfully kept.

Then one heads up to Two Columbia Road to Tommy and Keith Roberts's shop, to have a look at furniture and fittings from the 1940s through to the 1980s. Tommy Roberts used to run Mr. Freedom in Kings Road in the 1960s, and Practical Styling in CentrePoint in the 1980s, and always had a keen sense of style. I then go up Hackney Road past the infamous George and Dragon, and across Kingsland Road to visit No-One, walking through the bar—perfectly situated for a pit stop for coffee or a drink—and far into the back, where this shop features many young and emerging designers of clothes and jewellery. You feel as if you are in Berlin or New York's Lower East Side. Then on up Shoreditch High Street, stopping into Atomica, where all sorts of chandeliers, furniture, lamps, and side tables, all carefully picked, are on offer.

Finally, I continue up Shoreditch High Street to Redchurch Street, where my most favourite shop among many is Caravan. I adore Emily Chalmers and think her wit and spirit make the place read like an elaborate installation, and certainly a labour of love. I have bought numerous things there, and I go often, as her stock always changes and is sourced in a very individual way. Then it's a choice between a coffee and cake at either the Albion or on the roof of Shoreditch House, right in Ebor Street, making a perfect end to the day, looking out over the whole of the East End from up high.

MAUREEN PALEY

Maureen Paley has had a gallery in East London for twenty-six years, dealing in contemporary British, American, and European art.

9.25 Hackney City Farm

1a Goldsmiths Row E2
020 7729 6381; www.hackneycityfarm.co.uk

⊖ Bethnal Green (about a 15–20 minute walk); or Liverpool Street, then the No. 26 or No. 48 bus; or Old Street, then the No. 55 bus

LO Hoxton

RAIL Cambridge Heath

Hackney City Farm gives East Londoners the chance to experience farming right in the heart of the city. For more than twenty years, it has enabled children and adults to get up-close to a range of farmyard animals and to learn about where their food comes from and why that matters. In the heart of London's East End, the farm is surprisingly calm, with animal chatter neatly masking the sound of local traffic.

🍴   The farm is home to the Frizzante (020 7739 2266; www.frizzanteltd.co.uk), which provides Mediterranean cuisine made from fresh seasonal ingredients, as well as a large selection of daily specials, from Italian coffee to delicious cakes.

SOPHIE ROCHESTER
Sophie Rochester is the founder of The Literary Platform, a website dedicated to showcasing projects experimenting with literature and technology.

9.34 Vyner Street

RAIL Cambridge Heath

Things change on Vyner Street. Artists, curators, and galleries come and go, but the street remains a test bed for the art world. Visit it today, and you'll be entering a scene par excellence, perfect for the study of current and future art trends. Patinated cobblestones, low-rise industrial buildings, and the most theatrical of black-cab repair shops furnish this cul-de-sac, which runs over a mere two hundred metres, bracketed by the cycling highway of Regent's Canal and the slightly less bohemian Wadeson Street. This arrangement creates a natural ghetto for emerging art, where artists, dealers, and curators can cut their vocational teeth. At last count, the street was home to more than ten galleries, ranging from the well-established Wilkinson Gallery and Kate MacGarry to aspirational spaces like Nettie Horn and Vegas Gallery, and mayfly projects set up by students or recent graduates hoping to make an impression. The Victory pub (27 Vyner Street) is a constant—a real East End boozer that allots equal floor space to drinkers and pool players and couldn't give a fig about art.

ELLEN MARA DE WACHTER
Ellen Mara De Wachter is a writer and curator based in London.

9

9.35   Victoria Park

Hackney E9

LO   Hackney Wick

RAIL   Cambridge Heath or Hackney Wick

Summer or winter, one of my favourite weekend haunts is Victoria Park—a sprawling green sanctuary dedicated to the people of the East End. A Victorian park through and through, it contains excavated lakes that serve as home to wayward boats and swans, a bowling green, and a Chinese pagoda. A tea house turned café overlooks a large lake to the west and well-stocked pubs turn a healthy trade in fine food and drink at nearly every gate. In the easternmost section, opposite the cricket pitches, are two recesses culled from the old London Bridge where one can sit and watch a long afternoon slowly pass. The area immediately surrounding the park retains a village-like feel and a number of galleries, cafés, and delicatessens have slotted themselves in, adding organic fare and contemporary art to the local bagel or fish and chips. A haven for the urban rambler, Victoria Park can be reached from as far away as Little Venice in Maida Vale by walking or cycling along the tow path of the Grand Union and Regent's Canal.

JOHN SLYCE

John Slyce writes on contemporary art and culture.

9.37   Café Oto

18–22 Ashwin Street E8

020 7923 1231; www.cafeoto.co.uk

LO   Dalston Kingsland

RAIL   Dalson Junction

Dalston's Café Oto has two types of clientele. There are the huddles of East London art students who fringe the former warehouse space, sustaining single cups of coffee across an afternoon of free wi-fi access. Then there is the miscellany of free-jazz veterans, experimental filmmakers, contemporary music composers, and *Wire* magazine subscribers that commingles there in the evening. It is probably the capital's most adventurous music venue, with an events programme of challenging contemporary music that puts the South Bank to shame. Rapidly adopted as the central HQ of the U.K.'s free-improvisation scene, it has put on legendarily obscure 1960s Japanese psych-folk singers, laptop-generated electronica ranging from minimalist to ultra-minimalist, and—just occasionally—the more courageous of indie bands.

Oto's surroundings—old buildings gutted and demolished to facilitate the 2012 Olympic Games—render it not so much an oasis in a cultural desert as a bunker in a war zone. It may be a venue that is regularly name-dropped by the hipper-than-thou, but, mercifully, this isn't reflected in what you'll hear there or who's listening. You won't bump into Damon Albarn or a supermodel. You will, however, bump into earnest young men chewing the sleeves of their charity-shop knitwear whilst discussing the use of silence in the latest Radu Malfatti composition. Chances are they premièred it.

Matthew Milton

Matthew Milton, a folk singer, free-improvisation violinist, music journalist, and editor, has lived in south London all his life.

9

9.38 Ridley Road Market

Ridley Road E8
Closed Sundays.
LO   Dalston Kingsland
RAIL Dalson Junction

🍽🏛 If you savour the multicultural, head for Kingsland High Street in Dalston, Hackney. This bustling stretch of the

Kingsland Road is crowded with nail parlours and barber shops, Turkish restaurants and pool halls, Irish pubs, cosmetic emporiums with a line in voodoo, pound shops, and even a hamam. New clubs open regularly, though the renowned Four Aces around the corner in Dalston Lane has fallen victim to Hackney Council's disastrous modernization of the area.

Here among frail senior citizens, the indigenous Hackneyites, are women swaddled in robes and veils and some of the best-dressed youths in the metropolis.

But the road's greatest attraction is its street market. Brick Lane is more fashionable, while Brixton's covered market is safer from the weather, but for economy and cheerful pandemonium, none compares with Ridley Road. It's served by flotillas of buses, so leave the car on the fringes of Islington or take the London Overground to Dalston Kingsland, just opposite the market entrance. Walking out of the station is like hurling yourself into a twenty-knot current of humanity. Best times to visit are Friday afternoons or Saturday mornings for the real bargains and the exotic fruit and vegetables. You'll find cheap clothing and CDs: reggae, Turkish—traditional and pop—soul, salsa, Malian, and golden oldies. Enormous women's knickers flutter like acetate flags, a wonder to behold.

It wasn't always this way. During the 1940s, when the area was a working-class Jewish neighbourhood, the market was notorious as the scene of spectacular running battles between Oswald Mosley's fascists and the Communist Party, along with Jewish commandos from the 43 Group. Hundreds of local people attended political meetings, and police vans lined the surrounding streets waiting to collect those arrested. Mosley made his last public speech in nearby Hertford Road.

Today the shady aisles behind the barrows are permeated by the spicy-earthy smell of Africa, and Nigerian shops stock arcane vegetables, incense, and the dried body parts of indeterminate species. Some of the merchandise is so mysterious it's difficult to tell whether it's animal, mineral, or vegetable, let alone what its function might be.

Be sure to go right to the market's end, where you'll find the incomparable Turkish Food Centre (89 Ridley Road). Apart from the feta, olives, and watermelon, there is a large bakery where gleaming glass cases display the freshest and most varied selection of baklava in London. Hot flatbread is stacked on high mobile wooden shelves from which you help yourself. Ridley Road raises the spirits and restores the soul. For more conventional urbanites or those who prefer to remain depressed, there's a Sainsbury's next door.

MARY FLANAGAN

Mary Flanagan, an American writer and critic living in London, is the author of three novels: Trust, Rose Reason, and Adèle.

9.39 The Narrow Way
The northern end of Mare Street E5

LO Hackney Central

RAIL Hackney Central

On Saturday mornings in particular you get the great gamut of unofficial London glaring in your eyes and bawling in your ears, all against a backdrop of ancient history: the sixteenth-century St. Augustine's Tower, remnant of a successor to a thirteenth-century church founded by the Knights Templar, lurks behind the former Old Town Hall, which became a bank and is now a betting shop. St. John's Church gardens spread out to the Tower's rear. They bloom with crocuses in February and offers many splendid drunks, some as aged and derelict as the lichen-spotted tombstones. The Narrow Way itself becomes a corridor of potential conversions, ranging from far left proselytisers to pentecostalist believers. In the shops there are Turkish fashions, Asian fashions, the cheap fashions of a teeming Primark. Established High Street chain outlets—McDonald's, Marks and Spencer, building societies, and a rather basic Boots—are outnumbered by phone shops, thrift shops (everything a pound), fancy goods shops, Muslim fruit and veg shops, an outdoor flower stall, and, just around the bottom corner under the railway bridge, a cluster of nail parlours and a pawn shop you could base a sitcom on. There are lots of buses too, sometimes so many that they blockade the entire street. In all its hope and all its sorrow the whole of inner-city London life is here.

DAVE HILL
Dave Hill is the London Guardian's London blogger and commenter.

9.40   Hackney Empire Theatre

1901, Frank Matcham
291 Mare Street E8
020 8510 4500; www.hackneyempire.co.uk

LO   Hackney Central

The greatest of the super-ornate Edwardian theatres. Thanks to an enlightened management it's still putting on real theatrical experiences, from opera to pantomime, not the made-for-radio stuff you get in the West End.

ROWAN MOORE
Rowan Moore is architecture critic of the London Observer.

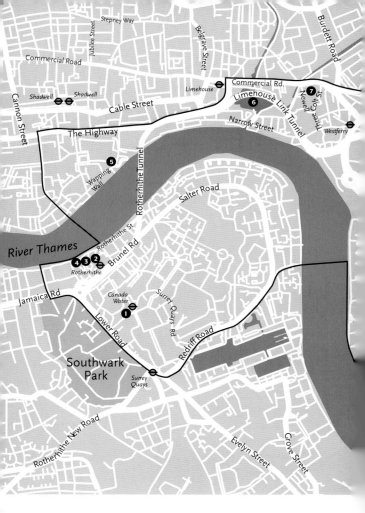

CHAPTER 10
The Docklands

1 Canada Water Station

2 Thames Tunnel

3 St. Mary's Church

4 Mayflower Inn 🍴🍷

5 The Wapping Project 🍴🍷

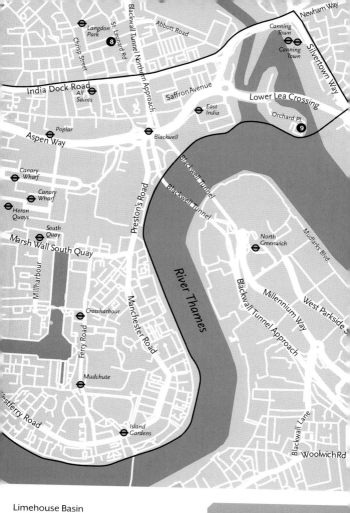

Langdon Park
Chrisp Street
St. Leonard Rd
8
Abbott Road
Blackwall Tunnel Northern Approach
Canning Town
Canning Town
Canning Town
Newham Way
Silvertown Way
India Dock Road
All Saints
Saffron Avenue
Lower Lea Crossing
Poplar
East India
Orchard Pl.
9
Aspen Way
Blackwell
Canary Wharf
Canary Wharf
Blackwell Tunnel
Heron Quays
Blackwall Tunnel
Preston's Road
South Quay
North Greenwich
Mudlarks Blvd
Marsh Wall South Quay
River Thames
Blackwall Tunnel Approach
Millennium Way
West Parkside
Millharbour
Crossharbour
Ferry Road
Manchester Road
Mudchute
Blackwall Lane
Westferry Road
Island Gardens
Woolwich Rd

Limehouse Basin
St. Anne's Limehouse
Balfron Tower
Fatboy's Diner 🍴

The Docklands

A Riverside Stroll

⊖ Tower Bridge

LO Rotherhithe

For most people taking a Sunday stroll along the Thames
Path, Tower Bridge is about as far east as they get. But
accompany the river on its eastern journey past this
exemplary Victorian carbuncle and things begin to get
more interesting.

Beyond the depressing, soulless yuppie warehouse
conversions of Butler's Wharf—ghostly communities
gracing the river like something from a J. G. Ballard
nightmare—lies Bermondsey, where you'll find a stately
home, and beyond that in Rotherhithe, the history of
America. Edward III's Manor House, admittedly a ruin
now, lurks in a rather desultory spot opposite the Angel
pub. Hyperactive kids are about the only people for whom
its ruined walls have any contemporary relevance, but to
think that an ancient seat of the English monarchy lies on
a South London council estate is a wonderful thought, if
for no other reason than to swell the South Bank with a
pride often dented by those north of the river.

Further up is Rotherhithe, a once industrious
shipbuilding community. It's a curious area—in the
seventies it was a menacing National Front enclave, and
now it's just an odd mix of upwardly mobile riverfront
wealth and inland council estates. Derek Jarman used
to have his studio here, and much of his bleak anti-
Thatcherite tirade *The Last of England* was filmed on this
stretch of river. Walk along leafy Rotherhithe Street (the
second longest street in London after Oxford Street), pa
warehouses more Dickensian than Dickens, and you hit
the Mayflower Inn.

It was from here that the Pilgrim Fathers set sail for the New World, and it's in the church opposite the pub that the returning crew of the *Mayflower* are buried.

If it's a sunny day, get yourself a pint and head on out to the deck at the back of the pub, where you can enjoy the open skies. The river affords a respite to London's oppressively claustrophobic architecture. If, as is more likely, the weather is traditionally British, book yourself in for a hearty Sunday roast and gaze at the impressive vista that is London's once thriving riverside.

DAN FOX

Dan Fox is senior editor of Frieze magazine, as well as a writer, filmmaker, and musician.

Canada Water Station to the Mayflower Inn

⊖ Canada Water
LO Canada Water
RAIL Canada Water

10

10.1 Canada Water Station
1999, Eva Jiricna; drum designed and constructed by Buro Happold
Surrey Quays Road SE16

10.2 Thames Tunnel
1825–1843, Sir Marc Brunel
The Brunel Museum
Railway Avenue SE16
020 7231 3840; www.brunel-museum.org.uk

10.3 St. Mary's Church
1716, John James (associate of Sir Christopher Wren)
St. Marychurch Street E16
www.stmaryrotherhithe.org

10.4 Mayflower Inn
117 Rotherhithe Street E16
020 7237 4088

Take the extended Jubilee Underground line to Canada Water. The station is surmounted by a large glass rotunda by Buro Happold (boldly restating in 1990s terms Charles Holden's iconic Arnos Grove Station of 1932–1933) and the adjacent bus station is a powerful and typical work by Eva Jiricna. Then take the East London line one stop to Rotherhithe. Leaving the platform you pass the entrance to Sir Marc Brunel's Thames Tunnel, called the "Great Bore" by *The Times* during its eighteen-year construction from 1825, but actually the great mother of all road and rail passages below water. At St. Mary's Church see the tomb of the Palau Prince Lee Boo, who was brought sightseeing to London from the Pacific in 1783 only to succumb almost immediately to smallpox. The gaunt nineteenth-century warehouses of this once important dockland area are now mostly converted to desirable riverside apartments.

🍴   Finally, stop for lunch in the picturesque Mayflower Inn (the ship began its voyage from Rotherhithe in 1620), where, on a jetty projecting above the Thames, you can enjoy unusually good pub food and fine Suffolk beer.

FRANK SALMON

Frank Salmon is Head of the Department of History of Art at the University of Cambridge.

10.5   The Wapping Project

Wapping Hydraulic Power Station
Wapping Wall E1
020 7680 2080; www.thewappingproject.com

⊖   Wapping
DLR   Shadwell

🍴   Oil. That's what you smell as you walk in. Engineering oil has impregnated the workmanlike green, putty-covered walls of this cavernous space for so many years that it out-guns the fugitive scents of garlic, dough, basil, fish, chocolate, and booze emanating from the kitchen. What chance does the kitchen have? It occupies a fraction of the space; the light, bright half, splashed with poppy-red chairs and white tabletops and the murmur of diners. The other side still houses the hydraulic machinery that once animated the West End—including the safety curtain at the Theatre Royal Drury Lane, the organ that rose through the floor at the Odeon Leicester Square, and the lifts at Claridge's and Selfridges—as well as a labyrinth of galleries and installations. Owner-curator Dr. Jules Wright came here as a location finder and, having found the perfect location, bought it. Here's an East End Sunday: brunch—Brecon lamb and black pudding ballotine—followed by a walk along the dank stones and stairs of Wapping Wall. Judge Jeffreys was arrested here and pirates' bodies hung in the Thames for three tides before justice was considered done. Chin chin.

SOPHIE CAMPBELL
Sophie Campbell is a travel writer and a London tour guide.

10

An East End Canal Walk

10.6 **Limehouse Basin**
Follow the Grand Union Canal north toward Victoria Park.
www.waterscape.com

DLR Limehouse
RAIL Limehouse

London's canals are an underused and undercelebrated amenity. One of the most stimulating walks through the city's past can be found on the banks of the Grand Union Canal. Start early in the morning by taking the Docklands Light Railway to Limehouse and then follow the canal from the Limehouse Basin through the industrial wasteland of Mile End and the formal recreation ground of Victoria Park to the bustling streets of Islington, where a tunnel requires a short detour (and provides a convenient break for lunch). Rejoin the canal for a trip through the urban regeneration of King's Cross and the New Age attractions

of Camden Lock before ending the afternoon in the more
sedate settings of Regent's Park and Little Venice.

Michael Arditti

Michael Arditti is an award-winning novelist, short-story writer, and critic.

10.7 St. Anne's Limehouse

1730, Nicholas Hawksmoor
5 Newell Street E14
020 7987 1502

RAIL Limehouse
DLR Westferry

I used to walk through the churchyard of St. Anne's
Limehouse every morning and evening, and still regard
St. Anne's as Hawksmoor's least-known and most
architecturally satisfying church. It combines great
simplicity in the view of the nave with his characteristic
complexity in the composition of the entrance portico
and tower. I don't live near there now, and I miss it.

Charles Saumarez Smith

*Charles Saumarez Smith is Secretary and Chief Executive of the Royal
Academy of Arts.*

Back-to-front church. Entrance through the apse on the
west side allows the sanctuary to have a wonderfully
imposing façade on the east. The interior is the most
Wren-like of Hawksmoor's churches. However, notice
the scale of the entablature around the circular ceiling.

Robert Livesey

*Robert Livesey is an architect and a professor at the Knowlton School of
Architecture at The Ohio State University.*

10.8 Balfron Tower

1967, Ernö Goldfinger
St. Leonard's Road E14

DLR All Saints

The figure of architect Ernö Goldfinger is by now more o
less recognized—the house he built for himself at 2 Willov

Road in Hampstead in 1938 is open to the public and his thirty-one-storey residential block Trellick Tower of 1967 in the increasingly fashionable North Kensington is often seen in television programmes or in the background of commercials. But Balfron Tower, the slightly earlier and—at twenty-seven storeys—smaller version in the unfashionable East End, is much less known. In combination, however, with Goldfinger's two later and lower blocks alongside, it forms a total composition that is arguably the most potent surviving example of his work and of Modern Movement urban design in London. This is brute concrete used like the noblest stone, but with a ferocity and spatial sophistication fully expressive of the turmoil of the twentieth century.

JAMES DUNNETT
James Dunnett is an architect.

10

10.9 Fatboy's Diner

Trinity Buoy Wharf
64 Orchard Place E14
020 7987 4334; www.fatboysdiner.london.com
DLR East India

In a forgotten corner of the city where the Lee meets the Thames, accessible by the Docklands Light Railway and a walk under a dual carriageway, you will find flats made of container boxes, London's only lighthouse, and a beautiful relic of the American Midwest. Fatboy's Diner is the jewel in Trinity Buoy Wharf's wayward crown. A 1940s Jetstream café transported to Britain in the 1990s, it sells big, greasy burgers and thick, frothy milkshakes. Order a Hot, Fat and Wow and a Vanilla, gaze across the waters at the O2's yellow spikes, and enjoy London's weird loveliness in a silver and red nutshell.

JUDE ROGERS
Jude Rogers writes for The Guardian, The Times, and the New Statesman, and is the co-founder of the quarterly magazine Smoke: A London Peculiar.

A Trip Downriver

Gallions Reach E16 (not on map)

⊖ Canning Town, then **DLR** to Beckton

I knew no one when I first came to London, and I spent
a month or two of Sundays walking about the place,
trying to fill the time when I wasn't at work. My guide
was *Nairn's London*, by the late Ian Nairn, who wrote
daringly about landscape and architecture with an eye
for the unjustly neglected and the obscure. Nairn was
quite capable of estimating some suburban town hall as
more glorious than the Taj Mahal, but his enthusiasm
was infectious, and he sent me (and many more) to places
I would never have otherwise gone.

Gallions Reach was one of them. This muddy stretch of
the lower Thames lies at the eastern end of the old Royal
Docks. When I first visited in 1970, yellow-funnelled
freighters were unloading their cargoes in the Royal
Albert, and the pipes and retorts of the Beckton gasworks
lay smoking and steaming over the way—close (it must be
said) to the exit of the Northern Outfall Sewer. Freighters
and gas works have long since gone (the ruins of the latter
became a fake Vietnam for Kubrick's *Full Metal Jacket*), but
the great architectural oddity of Gallions Reach remains a
listed building: the derelict Gallions Hotel (not open to
the public; Gallions Road, Royal Albert Dock E16). A piece
of 1880s neo-Elizabethan architecture, black and white
with a red-tiled roof, it looks like a Surrey stockbroker's
house, built here by some ridiculous mistake. In fact,
briefly and long ago, it served the travelling rich. Liners
from the distant ports of the British Empire would stop at
Gallions on their way to their final berth upriver so that
their passengers could disembark and reach the city more
quickly. Boat trains met them. Embarking passengers
waiting for outward-bound ships could eat, drink, and

rest at the Gallions Hotel. There's a line in Kipling: "Is it Tilbury and a tender, or Gallions and the Docks?"

The best way to get here is by the Docklands Light Railway to the end of the line at Beckton, or by ferry or pedestrian tunnel—both adventures in themselves—from Woolwich on the river's south bank. Go one way and come back another. North Woolwich has a large sugar refinery on the river, where ships still call. Look west and you can see the Thames Barrier and planes taking off steeply from the City Airport. East lies the estuary and the sea. This is the very edge of London. If it's strangeness you're after, here it is. You might be inspired and think of the Thames as it appears in Kipling, Conrad, and Dickens—the great imperial river—or you might agree with Captain Scott at the South Pole: "Dear God, this is an awful place."

Try to find a copy of Nairn's now out-of-print book. Soon after I read it I met the author and got to know him; we worked for a while for the same newspaper. He was a large man in a shabby blue suit, with an enormous appetite for Guinness and unfiltered Senior Service cigarettes; a person of sincere, powerful, and eccentric enthusiasms. He would often answer the phone by barking "Woof, woof!" rather than the more normal "Hello." His books taught many of us to see London—and Britain—in more interesting ways.

IAN JACK

Ian Jack is a columnist of The Guardian. He edited Granta from 1995 to 2007, and was co-founder of the Independent on Sunday.

CHAPTER 11
From Hyde Park to the River

1 The Victoria & Albert Museum
2 Daquise Restaurant ¶𝖸
3 The Institut Français ¶𝖸
4 Christie's
5 La Bouchée ¶𝖸
6 La Grande Bouchée ¶𝖸
7 The French Bookshop 🏠
8 The Cadogan Hotel
9 Cadogan Square
10 Felt 🏠
11 Royal Hospital Chelsea
12 Chapel
13 Stable Block
14 Oscar Wilde's House
15 Ziani's ¶𝖸
16 Chelsea Physic Garden
17 Thomas Carlyle's House
18 The Albert Bridge
19 Peace Pagoda/Battersea Park
20 Egg 🏠
21 The Grenadier ¶𝖸
22 The Diplomat Hotel
23 Home of Noël Coward
24 Jeroboams 🏠
25 H. R. Stokes 🏠
26 Tomtom Cigars 🏠
27 Fulham News 🏠

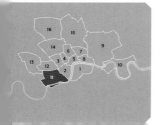

From Hyde Park to the River

SOUTH KENSINGTON & KNIGHTSBRIDG

Sir Henry Cole

11.1 **The Victoria & Albert Museum**
Cromwell Road SW7
020 7942 2000; www.vam.ac.uk
⊖ South Kensington

On a hot summer's day, the Pirelli Garden in the court-yard of the Victoria & Albert Museum is as pleasant a place to be as any in London. Tucked away in a corner o the south side are two small ceramic plaques that record past companions: "In Memory of Jim, Died 1879, Aged 15 Years. Faithful Dog of Sir Henry Cole, of this Museum" and "To TYCHO A faithful dog who died V IAN MDCCCLXXXV."

Cole (1808–1882) was not just "of this museum," he in fact created it, as the South Kensington Museum (its name was changed to the V & A in 1899). Cole was one o those multitalented indefatigable Victorians, a public servant whose achievements included developing the Penny Post, creating the modern Public Record Office, and masterminding the Great Exhibition of 1851. If this makes him sound impossibly worthy, these memorials reveal a more human side, and it is reassuring that creating one of the world's great museums did not mak Cole so self-important that he was unable to commemo rate his dog, who can, indeed, be seen by his side in photographs of the buildings under construction.

In a way, the memorial to Jim works better as a memorial to Cole himself than does the unsatisfactory portrait of Cole to be found on the Ceramic Staircase in the southwest corner of the courtyard, and is in much the same spirit as that archetypal piece of Victorian sentimentality, Sir Edwin Landseer's painting *The Old Shepherd's Chief Mourner*, displayed in the Henry Cole Wing of the V & A.

JAMES BETTLEY
James Bettley is an architectural historian.

11.2 Daquise Restaurant

20 Thurloe Street SW7
020 7589 6117; www.daquiserestaurant.co.uk
☺ South Kensington

🍴 Next to South Kensington tube, just round the corner from Exhibition Road and all the museums, hides this plot of Poland in Central London. Grubby, steamed-up windows obscure a warm, old-fashioned—and wonderfully reasonable—haunt of the Polish émigré community and those in the know. On a cold day, herrings and a shot of vodka, followed by some *golubtsy* (stuffed cabbage) served with all the chaos of family-run kitchens, are the perfect antidote to the pretensions of imperial London outside. In summer, have an Eastern European cream cake and coffee.

If you are lucky, you might still catch a table of military-looking gents on their daily trip from the Polish Club in Hammersmith to the Polish Hearth Club for the evening: some airmen who fought in the Battle of Britain, some victims of unspeakable atrocities in Germany or Russia, others simply émigrés who, history has determined, spend their lives in a foreign land. And London has always, albeit unknowingly, been enriched by wave after wave of immigrants and their children.

ANGUS MACQUEEN
Angus MacQueen's documentary work includes The Death of Yugoslavia, which won a British Academy Award, and Dancing for Dollars, which received an Emmy.

11

Francophile
⊖ South Kensington

11.3 **The Institut Français**
1939, Patrice Bonnet
17 Queensberry Place SW7
020 7073 1350; www.institut-francais.org.uk

11.4 **Christie's**
85 Old Brompton Road SW7
020 7930 6074; www.christies.com

11.5 **La Bouchée**
56 Old Brompton Road SW7
020 7589 1929; www.boudinblanc.co.uk

11.6 **La Grande Bouchée**
31 Bute Street SW7
020 7589 8346

11.7 **The French Bookshop**
28 Bute Street SW7
020 7584 2840; www.frenchbookshop.com

🍴 For the flavour of France in South Kensington visit the
Institut Français. In this marvellously eccentric Art Deco
building you can read *Le Figaro* over an espresso or lunch
in the brasserie, explore the multimedia library, see a film
in the cinema, perhaps one of the great classics by René
Clair or preview one of the newest offerings. There might
even be a wine tasting or a lecture.

The nearby Old Brompton Road is a real cosmopolitan
hub, yet it avoids the crowds and razzmatazz of the King's
Road. Here you can visit Christie's to view the next sale,
which might be pictures, furniture, or pop memorabilia, sit
at a pavement table for coffee, and get a proper French
meal at La Bouchée. Or, go around the corner to Bute Street

for your Camembert and Brie from La Grande Bouchée or
the latest novel from Paris at the French Bookshop.

MICHAEL BARKER

Michael Barker writes and lectures on art, architecture, and decorative arts.
He is co-author of The North of France: A Guide to the Art, Architecture and
Atmosphere of Artois, Picardy and Flanders.

CHELSEA

11.8   The Cadogan Hotel

75 Sloane Street SW1
020 7235 7141; www.cadogan.com
⊖ Knightsbridge or Sloane Square

The Cadogan Hotel, built in 1887, is today a nostalgic
survivor of stately Victorian posh, but in its early years
was a base for fashionable artists and royal assignations.
Its most infamous moment came on April 6, 1895, when
Oscar Wilde, despite the urgent pleas of friends and
authorities alike, remained in Room 118 and waited for
the police to arrest him on charges of "committing acts
of gross indecency with other male persons." He had
been given every opportunity to leave the country, but
Wilde forced his arrest, believing that he would be
cleared in the performance of a trial. Instead, he was
convicted and sentenced to two years hard labour, which
led to his broken health and death shortly thereafter.
The furniture here has been modernized, but Room 118
is still available for bookings and Wilde celebrations.

ROBERT MARX

Robert Marx is an essayist on theatre and opera.

11

11.9 Cadogan Square

Knightsbridge SW1

☏ Knightsbridge or Sloane Square

Cadogan Square and Lennox Gardens in Knightsbridge are lined with late-nineteenth-century buildings (Grade II listed) with exquisite details. They were in part designed by George Devey. Stroll through in the evening to glean glimpses inside of the many beautiful stucco ceilings and grandiose entrance lobbies.

GABRIELE BRAMANTE
Gabriele Bramante is the director of Bramante Architects in London.

11.10 Felt

13 Cale Street SW3
020 7349 8829; www.felt-london.com

☏ South Kensington

Whenever I need a present for a girlfriend or a god-daughter, I head to Felt, on Cale Street in Chelsea. Run by the no-nonsense Eliza, with a soft spot for vintage, this unassuming matchbook-sized jewellery shop always delivers. From £25 hoop earrings and costume clip-ons to a £5,000 Pippa Small cascading gold and aquamarine necklace, Felt is a treasure trove of unusual one-off pieces. On my last visit, I found a 1950s Omega men's watch, some vintage earrings by Kenneth Lane, a ravishing green Dior neck piece, and a crocodile hand-bag, all thanks to Eliza's constant scouring. She celebrates the non-brand and the eclectic, for both the everyday and special treat. "I defy any woman not to find some-thing," she says. Suffice to say, I've never left empty-handed.

ELENA BOWES
Elena Bowes is a culture and travel writer based in London.

Sunday Morning in Chelsea

⊖ Sloane Square

11.11 Royal Hospital Chelsea
1689–1692, Sir Christopher Wren
Royal Hospital Road SW3
020 7730 0161; www.chelsea-pensioners.org.uk

11.12 Chapel
1681–1687, Sir Christopher Wren
Royal Hospital Chelsea SW3
Closed to the public, but you can visit the chapel on Sundays
before 11 a.m. mass.

11.13 Stable Block
1814–1817, Sir John Soane
Royal Hospital Chelsea SW3

(see p. 208)

11.14 Oscar Wilde's House
34 Tite Street SW3
Not open to the public.

11

11.15 Ziani's
45–47 Radnor Walk SW3
020 7351 5297; www.ziani.co.uk

At 10:30 a.m. on a Sunday, walk or drive (park inside) through the front gate of Sir Christopher Wren's Chelsea Royal Hospital, on the Royal Hospital Road. Walk through to the Parade ground and enjoy the banter of the pensioners as they assemble for a parade in their scarlet tunics, black tricorn hats, and white gloves. Watch the sergeant major barking his orders and the governor arriving to inspect the parade.

After the short parade, walk into the Wren chapel for matins; the congregation face one another across a central nave. For the British, the experience is a slice of old Britain; for overseas visitors, it is quite baffling but unforgettable.

After the service, if you know a pensioner, don't miss the chance of a pint in the mess, and if you don't, wander all the same past the mess to the western end for a glimpse of the stables designed by Sir John Soane.

Finish the morning by walking up Tite Street past the house (No. 34) where Oscar Wilde lived, through Tedworth Square into Radnor Walk for a wonderful lunch at Ziani's, one of London's best and friendliest Italian restaurants, tucked away on this side street off the King's Road.

CHARLES MARSDEN-SMEDLEY

Charles Marsden-Smedley's design practice specialises in museum and exhibition design.

11.13   Stable Block

1814–1817, Sir John Soane
Royal Hospital Chelsea SW3
020 7730 0161; www.chelsea-pensioners.org.uk

⊖   Sloane Square

As with jewels, splendour in architecture does not depend on size. On the south side of Royal Hospital Road in Chelsea stands a small but veritable gem created by one of England's greatest architects: Sir John Soane (1753–1837). The surviving Soane public buildings in the capital are familiar landmarks and are all much visited, including Dulwich Picture Gallery (see p. 300), Pitshanger Manor Museum in Ealing, and his former residence, Sir John Soane's Museum (see p. 92), in Lincoln's Inn Fields. The Chelsea Stable Block is widely acknowledged by aficionados as being one of his finest exteriors, yet it remains little known to the general public.

The front (northeast) elevation is an architectural masterpiece in terms of abstract composition. With its concentric brick arches and "layering" of planes of meticulously constructed brickwork, it exemplifies Soane's minimalist primitive style. The underlying geometry of the design is clear for all to see, and detailing and ornament are kept to a minimum. Note the elemental cornice of brick triglyphs and the highly idiosyncratic chimneystacks. For Soane, even horses deserved fine buildings to live in!

BARRY CLAYTON

Barry Clayton is an architect specialising in the conservation of historic buildings.

11.16 Chelsea Physic Garden

66 Royal Hospital Road sw3
Entrance on Swan Walk
020 7352 5646; www.chelseaphysicgarden.co.uk
The garden is open from April to October. Check the website for exact dates.
⊖ Sloane Square

London's most secret garden is the Chelsea Physic Garden, unlocked to the public only on Wednesday and Sunday afternoons between early April and late October. Catch it open if you can for its historical interest and its extraordinary melancholy beauty. Make your way there via Sir Christopher Wren's seventeenth-century Chelsea Royal Hospital (see p. 207), a cosier English equivalent of the Hôtel des Invalides in Paris, inhabited by frail but still roguish scarlet-coated pensioners. Think Byronic thoughts of mutability as you contemplate Wren's Chapel and Hall hung with tattered banners of ancient campaigns.

FIONA MACCARTHY

Fiona MacCarthy is a cultural historian and author of biographies of Eric Gill and William Morris.

11

11.17   ## Thomas Carlyle's House

24 Cheyne Row sw3
020 7352 7087; www.nationaltrust.org.uk
Closed Mondays and Tuesdays.
⊖ Sloane Square or South Kensington

Take a bus or the Circle/District line to Sloane Square on a Wednesday morning. Visit Thomas Carlyle's house, wonderfully preserved and little visited. Climb up to his (semi) soundproofed study and feel glad that you didn't have to cook in the meagre kitchens down below. Lunch at one of the pubs round the corner and go into Chelsea Old Church (64 Cheyne Walk) before spending a leisurely afternoon at the Chelsea Physic Garden (see p. 209), five minutes' walk away.

MIRANDA SEYMOUR
Miranda Seymour is a biographer, novelist, and critic.

Riverside Walk

⊖ Sloane Square

To walk along the Thames Embankment, past Chelsea Old Church, Cheyne Walk, and the Chelsea Royal Hospital (see p. 207), preferably on an autumn evening at the hour favoured by Whistler (a nearby resident), with leaves from the giant plane trees—stirred up by passing traffic—blowing around your legs as you look out over the broad sweep of water, is to experience a moving poetic loneliness within the warmth of the population of a great city.

JAMES DUNNETT
James Dunnett is an architect

11.18   ## The Albert Bridge

1873, Roland Mason Ordish; 1890, modified by Joseph Bazalgette
Between Chelsea and Battersea Park
- South Kensington or Sloane Square

It's an absolutely beautiful nineteenth-century structure,
like a cat's cradle made out of steel. It has a sign on it
telling marching men to break step at the bridge—which
seems to have been news to more recent bridge builders.
MARJORIE M. SCARDINO
*Marjorie M. Scardino is Chief Executive of Pearson PLC, owners of Pearson
Education, the Financial Times Group, and the Penguin Group.*

Chance Encounters

11.19   ### Peace Pagoda

*1985, a gift to the people of London from the Japanese Buddhist Order
Nipponzan Myohoji*
The Peace Pagoda is by the river in the centre of Battersea Park.
www.batterseapark.org
- Sloane Square, then take bus No. 137
RAIL Battersea Park

11

19.5   ### London Russian Orthodox Church

1998
57 Harvard Road W4
020 8742 3493; www.russianchurchlondon.org
- Gunnersbury
LO Gunnersbury
RAIL Gunnersbury

Two small, uplifting, and often repeated pleasures: the
sight of the Golden Buddha in his shrine in Battersea Park
opposite Chelsea Embankment, and of a new arrival—the
gold-starred azure onion dome of the little Russian
church which improbably comes into view on the left as
you come down off the M4 on the Chiswick flyover.
PETER CARSON
*Peter Carson was formerly Editor-in-Chief at Penguin. Now semi-retired, he
works as an editor for Profile Books and translates from Russian.*

Eversleigh Road

Battersea SW11 (not on map)

LO   Clapham Junction

RAIL   Queen's Road Battersea or Clapham Junction

Eversleigh Road is part of the Shaftsbury Estate, south of and parallel to the railway line between Queen's Road Battersea and Clapham Junction stations. A wonderful example of early Victorian town planning for the working class.

PIERS PLOWRIGHT

Piers Plowright retired from BBC Radio in 1997 after thirty years as an award-winning producer.

BELGRAVIA

11.20 ## Egg

36 Kinnerton Street SW1

020 7235 9315; www.eggtrading.com

Closed on Sundays and Mondays.

⊖   Knightsbridge

🕌   A cobblestone's throw from one of my favourite hotels, the Berkeley, is Egg, London's most unique boutique, though the shopkeeper, Maureen Doherty, probably wouldn't like it to be called that. It's just a little white-washed place—a nineteenth-century building, originally a dairy—that sells a cherry-picked collection of items that Maureen (who, before Egg, worked mainly with Issey Miyake) has found on her travels and fallen in love with. I worked here years ago, when I fancied the idea of becoming a fashion stylist; somehow, miraculously, in a world of online everything, it has managed to stay just as under the radar now as then.

The shop—which feels more like it should be in an unexplored corner of Scandinavia than in bankers'

Belgravia—sells diaphanous cotton, linen, and silk separates made in Tibet; lightly quilted blanket-cum-shawls made from unusual, almost Anglo, vintage sari fabric; poetic straw hats made by the German label SCHA; delicate, hand-blown Japanese glassware; and a very small stock of kitten-soft cashmere knitwear that the designer, Sine, can never make enough of.

Egg's customers—perhaps "followers" is more like it—are a mix of dames, divas, gallerists, artists, and style-makers; the late Hardy Amies used to come and perch on a stool, stick in hand, for a gander and a natter, and Donna Karan and Ralph Lauren still make regular pilgrimages.

Maureen has just started stocking some of her wares at the Comme des Garçons Trading Museum, in Tokyo, but, luckily for us, for the time being, she remains, with her two pretty greyhounds, Finn and Lilly, in this little corner of London that time and fashion have yet to erase.

SUMMER LITCHFIELD

Summer Litchfield is a journalist who writes for the Telegraph, the Sunday Times, and other publications.

11

11.21 The Grenadier

18 Wilton Row SW1
020 7235 3074
⊖ Hyde Park Corner

⊪ Near the end of a cobbled mews cul-de-sac in London's most exclusive neighbourhood, Belgravia, is a delightful pub, the Grenadier. A huge Victorian gas lamp, a sentry box, and flower baskets adorn the outside of the pub, where steps lead up to a snug room with a four-hundred-year-old pockmarked chrome bar. Hidden away—even cab drivers have problems finding this one—the pub, some believe, is haunted by the eponymous soldier who is said to have been flogged to death by fellow card players after being found cheating. The pub claims to make London's best Bloody Mary. There's even a cosy restaurant at the back of the pub, serving tasty but quite expensive fare.

NICK WYKE

Nick Wyke is a journalist at The Times and has recently devised a foodies' walking tour of Belgravia in London.

11.22 The Diplomat Hotel

1882, Thomas Cubitt
2 Chesham Street SW1
020 7235 1544; www.thediplomathotel.co.uk
⊖ Sloane Square or Knightsbridge

Nearly everyone who stays here has the dodgy air of someone whom the police are eager to invite over to "help them in their enquiries" (as the British say). In the tiny basement room where a full English breakfast is served—every morning, buffet-style—men in ill-fitting suits, carrying briefcases, speak in strange tongues, very quietly, before slipping out at 8 a.m. Dough-faced matrons serve you your burned toast as if fugitives from some lugubrious German Expressionist movie. The figures at the front desk are nothing if not friendly, though most of them, newly arrived from Poland or points even further east, show only a chance acquaintance with English.

It seems apt that this proud one-star institution, in the middle of Belgravia, is stuffed now only with foreigners; Great Britain has been made visibly greater (or more curious and surprising) in recent years by a flood of non-Britons of every stripe, color, and motivation. And even though plaques on the rooms summon up the great

Victorian names of Knightsbridge all around, the rickety lift looks as if it's about to collapse and the shower stalls are so tiny that instructions on all sides try to prevent sudden drowning. Most of the friends to whom I've introduced the place, even if they come from the developing world, beat a hasty retreat.

But for more than fifteen years now, I've been staying in the Diplomat Hotel on Chesham Street whenever I return to the land of my birth and my upbringing. It sits, incongruous, near the white-columned houses of Eaton Square and Chesham Place. Nearby are any number of much glitzier (and even more overpriced) hotels. A seven-minute walk in one direction brings you to Harrods and the Knightsbridge Tube station (taking you to Heathrow). A seven-minute walk in the other brings you to Sloane Square, and the unorthodox pleasures of the King's Road. Even London's all-knowing taxi drivers often haven't heard of it, and few mortals, after seeing it, wish to return. But I can imagine John le Carré hiding out there, writing one of his stories of false identities and voluntary disappearances. And every year, at Christmas, the manager (originally from Turkey) sends me a classic pocket English calendar, as if to prepare me for any make-believe, but elegantly old-fashioned, self I may want to take on in the year to come. London is full of secrets, and they're not always respectable ones; the Diplomat—as its name suggests— is their shabby and improbable spiritual home.

PICO IYER

Pico Iyer is a longtime essayist for Time magazine and the author of nine books, including Video Night in Kathmandu, The Lady and the Monk, The Global Soul, and The Open Road.

11.23 Home of Noël Coward

1930–1956
17 Gerald Road SW1
Not open to the public.
⊖   Sloane Square

Having moved across the street from grimy Pimlico, Noël Coward, the century's quintessential Englishman—and, by 1931, the highest-earning author in the Western world—had left his mother's boarding house for the whitened sepulchres of Belgravia. No. 17 Gerald Road was hidden away in a mews house and former artists' studio, complete with a gallery and miniature stage on which the Master could perform in private. Sadly, there is now no public access, but you can still look on from the outside and imagine the parties that defined high society: princes of the realm and transatlantic superstars rubbed elbows over cocktails and laughter, whilst Coward himself kept half an ear open for dialogue which would find its way into his latest play.

"It was," commented a contemporary edition of *Vogue* about one such affair, "a party in the enlightened tradition, all very white and witty." Coward would spend the next morning prising tonic bottle caps out of the carpet.

PHILIP HOARE
Philip Hoare's books include biographies of Stephen Tennant and Noël Coward; Wilde's Last Stand; and England's Lost Eden

A Connoisseur's Afternoon
⊖   Sloane Square or Victoria

11.24 Jeroboams

50-52 Elizabeth Street SW1
020 7730 8108; www.jeroboams.co.uk

11.25   H. R. Stokes
58 Elizabeth Street SW1
020 7730 7073; www.henrystokes.co.uk

11.26   Tomtom Cigars
63 Elizabeth Street SW1
020 7730 1790; www.tomtom.co.uk

11.27   Fulham News
200 Fulham Road SW10
020 7351 3435
⊖   South Kensington

11.19   Battersea Park
On the South Bank, across from Chelsea SW11
The Peace Pagoda is by the river in the centre of the park.
www.batterseapark.org

¶¶⊛   There are very few "secrets" in such a busy, gossipy city as
London, but there are some simple, unexploited pleasures.

One of mine would be this. Take a car or a cab to
Elizabeth Street in Belgravia, where you will find a lot of
what you need to nourish body and soul. At Jeroboams,
pick up some good bread and cheese and a bottle of
better-than-average white burgundy; a 1996 Meursault
would do fine. While the cab is waiting, nip into Henry
Stokes's bookshop at No. 58, a small, village-like affair, but
with a well-chosen stock of current titles. Buy something.
In the same street, Tomtom Cigars will sell you a Hoyo de
Monterrey Epicure No. 2. Now divert the cab to Fulham
Road, where you will find the world's best newsagent,
Fulham News. Buy an armful of your favourite papers and
magazines, then have yourself dropped at the Chelsea
Bridge entrance to Battersea Park. I love Battersea Park
because of its oddness: it was built on spoil from the
excavation of the Royal Docks, and asparagus was
cultivated here.

Anyway, select a bench overlooking the river, some-where near the Peace Pagoda (see p. 211). On a weekday you will have the place entirely to yourself so, if you have remembered your running stuff, hide the food, papers, and books and take a turn around the park's perimeter. This is about a mile and a half, so not too demanding, but enough to justify the indulgence of the food, drink, smoke, and reading you are now going to enjoy.

The view from your bench is beautiful and evocative: this is Whistler's and Wilde's Thames. It is wonderful in warm sunshine, even lovelier in autumnal mist. From the bench, as you munch your bread and cheese and slurp the wine, you can enjoy one of the best urban views in Britain: Wren's dignified Royal Hospital and then the gorgeous red brick houses of Chelsea Embankment, these last Britain's most singular contribution to the history of world architecture. If you have brought two bottles, you can sit and wait and watch the sun go down over the eccentric Albert Bridge and the lumpy old Lots Road Power Station. For less than the price of a pretentious meal in a mediocre restaurant, you have had some of the very best London has to offer.

STEPHEN BAYLEY

Stephen Bayley created the Boilerhouse Project at the V & A and was responsible for the Design Museum in London. He is a columnist for The Times.

Newsstands

I really know I'm in London when I catch a glimpse of a newsstand—any newsstand. The fact that there are a dozen newspapers for sale makes me absolutely giddy with delight. As the daughter of two fine newspaper writers (they both would have cringed at the fancy word "journalist"), I feel close to my parents as I pick up an armload of papers every morning, hurry back to my hotel, and emerge, satiated and ink-stained, just in time for lunch. Think of it: there are four national papers alone—*The Daily Telegraph*, *The Guardian*, *The Independent*, and *The Times*. Just a luxurious romp through the obituaries takes a fair amount of time. I know I could look at the London papers online when at home in New York—and I do—but that isn't nearly as wonderful as scattering red-top tabloids and broadsheets all over the bed and floor.

JANE LEAR
Jane Lear is a food and travel writer.

CHAPTER 12
Kensington
Gardens &
Hyde Park

1 Kensington Gardens
2 Kensington Palace
3 The Orangery 🍴
4 Cupola Room
5 Malaysia Hall Canteen 🍴
6 Serpentine Gallery
7 Sunday Softball
8 Hyde Park Corner
9 Edgeware Road

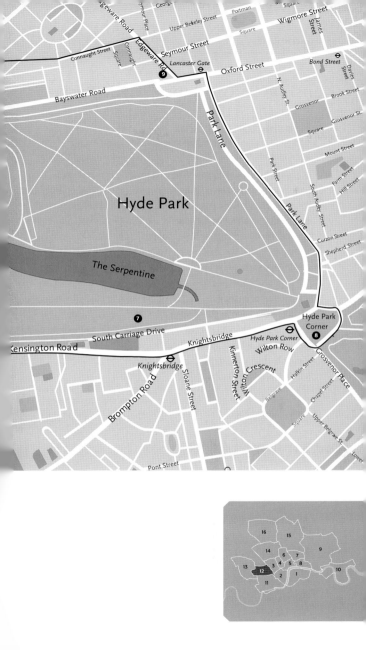

Kensington Gardens & Hyde Park

12.1 Kensington Gardens

020 7298 2141; www.royalparks.org.uk

⊖ Lancaster Gate

Kensington Gardens, with its tremendous avenues, its splendidly bombastic statuary (except the obnoxious Peter Pan), and its two sheets of water, is the most beautiful of the city's famous parks. Walk southward from Lancaster Gate under the majestic plane trees (best in winter—black tracery against London's mother-of-pearl sky). Bear left for a visit to the Serpentine Gallery (see p. 225)—good one-person shows of contemporary art—then meander northwestward through the artfully wooded wilderness (avoid the gooseshit-spattered shores of the Round Pond) to Nicholas Hawksmoor's Orangery, now a restaurant where you can eat lunch for an inordinate price but in unsurpassable grandeur.

LUCY HUGHES-HALLETT

Lucy Hughes-Hallett is an award-winning author and critic. She has received the Catherine Pakenham Award for journalism and the Fawcett Prize for her book on Cleopatra.

12.2 Kensington Palace

1689–1727

Kensington Gardens

0844 482 7777; www.hrp.org.uk

⊖ High Street Kensington or Queensway

An alternative approach: having admired the south front of Kensington Palace from Kensington Road, turn right into Kensington Church Street and second right into York House Place. This leads to Kensington Palace Green, and opposite lies the original eighteenth-century entrance to the palace. A footpath leads past the security gates, used by the various members of the royal family who live in the palace, and through a side gate into the park. Walk around Wren and Hawksmoor's south front of 1689–1695 and the neo-Palladian east elevation of c. 1718, thought to be by Colen Campbell and built between the earlier pavilions of Nottingham House, to the public entrance beyond the Sunken Garden: a charming detour. Once inside, remember to look out from the state apartments, remodelled by William Kent in 1722–1727, from which Charles Bridgemen's garden design of about the same date is still evident in the radiating avenues.

ANNE PURCHAS
Anne Purchas is an architectural historian.

12.3 The Orangery

1705, Nicholas Hawksmoor (under Sir Christopher Wren)
Kensington Gardens W8
0844 482 7777; www.hrp.org.uk

⊖ High St. Kensington or Notting Hill Gate

¶¶ On a rainy London day (or fine day), spring, summer, or fall, take a walk in Hyde Park to Kensington Gardens.

12

Have lunch or tea in the Orangery's high-ceilinged, airy space. Simple stone floor, black iron tables and chairs, crisp white tablecloths (and luscious pastries!). Sit at a table along the back wall to get a long view into the manicured gardens out front. Better yet, stop beforehand at Notting Hill Books (132 Palace Gardens Terrace, 020 7727 5988). Find a book on something one knows nothing about: *Land Tenure of the Ramessides*, or *The History of Notting Hill*, or even a new best seller, all of which will be discounted. Read in the Orangery—no one is rushed. Go around two in the afternoon, when lunch is winding down and tea has not yet started. Afterwards, continue reading by the Round Pond nearby, sitting on a deckchair

provided by the Royal Parks Service. As swans glide and
children play, I have my London.

CECILIA WONG
Cecilia Wong is an interior designer and art historian.

William Kent

12.4 Cupola Room
In Kensington Palace W8
0844 482 7777; www.hrp.org.uk
☉ High Street Kensington or Queensway

2.16 Horse Guards
Whitehall SW1
(see p. 43)
☉ Embankment

In 1722, William Kent, wit, dilettante, and darling of Lord
Burlington's Palladian clique, launched his London career
with the grisaille decoration of the Cupola Room at
Kensington Palace. At the Horse Guards in Whitehall, his
last project in 1755 (where you can view the Changing of
the Guard), he has become "Kentissimo." Remarkably,
you can still walk from one to the other entirely through
the Royal Parks, a distance of some two and a half miles
through central London, and a delightful way to pass a
summer's afternoon.

PETER HOWARD
*Peter Howard, an architect, is co-author of guides to the architecture of Oxford
and Cambridge.*

12.5 Malaysia Hall Canteen
30–34 Queensborough Terrace W2
020 7985 1262
☉ Bayswater or Queensway

🍴 What makes this scarcely signposted basement
room worth a look is a sense of complete cultural

transportation: one moment you are pondering street paintings on the tourist drag next to Hyde Park, the next you are pretty much in Kuala Lumpur. Negeri FM (or some such) blares from the radio; groups of friends chat while solo diners enjoy a plate of Nasi Lemak over copies of the *New Straits Times*. Being directly below the Malaysian High Commission, it's possible that this really is Malaysian soil, legally speaking—and the prices certainly seem that way. As for the breakfast, it involves dried crispy anchovies, so to be honest can never quite be up there with my favourites—but the beef rendang is very good, and I think it'd also make a great lunch or dinner stop if you happened to be in the area and wanted to avoid being fleeced by a dodgy trattoria or the ubiquitous Angus (mis) Steakhouse.

SEB EMINA

Seb Emina, as Malcolm Eggs, edits The London Review of Breakfasts, the world's premier repository of overblown literary breakfast reviews.

12.6 Serpentine Gallery

12

1912, Sir Henry Tanner
Kensington Gardens W8
020 7402 6075; www.serpentinegallery.org
⊖ Lancaster Gate or Knightsbridge

Go to the Serpentine Gallery (free) in Kensington Gardens and then watch the roller-bladers, baseballers, and the rest as you pay respects to Prince Albert, who now boasts the most splendid memorial in town.

GILLIAN DARLEY

Gillian Darley was co-author with Andrew Saint of The Chronicles of London, a historical anthology of London. Her other books include biographies of Sir John Soane, Octavia Hill, and John Evelyn.

12.7 Sunday Softball
Hyde Park SW7

⊖ Knightsbridge

Every Sunday morning, from April to October, a group of expatriate Americans gathers in Hyde Park, opposite the Knightsbridge Barracks, to play softball. This game has been going on since 1962; I've played in it both with my father, in the 1960s, and my sons, in the 1990s. The park is a good place to visit on Sunday mornings, before the museums and galleries open, and if you know how to play, you might even get a game.

On many Sundays red-coated guardsmen parade past the field, accompanied by a band, and play stops briefly, as it does when a child or a dog wanders into left field, which happens a lot. On other occasions, like Remembrance Sunday, immaculate ex-guardsmen file past in bowler hats and pinstriped suits, carrying tightly furled umbrellas, a uniform all but extinct elsewhere in Britain, even in the City.

Then the pubs open (and there are several quiet, attractive ones in the little streets and squares between the park and Harrods). If you spend any time at the game—watching, playing, kibitzing—and feel tourist guilt, walk west a few hundred yards and you're at the Serpentine Gallery or the Albert Memorial, newly gleaming after its interminable restoration.

Zachary Leader
Zachary Leader is a Professor of English Literature at the University of Surrey Roehampton and the author and editor of books on Romantic poetry and twentieth-century British fiction.

12.8 Hyde Park Corner
Intersection of Knightsbridge, Grosvenor Place, Piccadilly, and Park Lane, between Hyde Park and Green Park

⊖ Hyde Park Corner

Constitution Arch
1830, Decimus Burton

Machine Gun Corps Memorial
1925, Francis Derwent Wood

Royal Artillery Memorial
1925, Charles Sargeant Jagger

Hyde Park Corner is a frantic traffic roundabout bordered by Apsley House (Wellington's old home, with the enviable address: No. 1, London); Knightsbridge, the Lanesborough Hotel; the walls to Buckingham Palace Gardens; Green Park; Piccadilly; and Park Lane. Subways from all corners lead to this fascinating oasis.

Here stands Decimus Burton's Constitution Arch, once the entrance to Hyde Park. Now it is marooned and unused, except by royalty; I once witnessed Princess Margaret being driven through it to queue-jump the snarl of traffic. The Arch is topped with a magnificent bronze group: "Peace in Her Quadriga," by Captain Adrian Jones. Captain Jones gave a dinner party for eight friends inside the statue before it was raised to its present position. In the base of the arch there is a tiny police station—the second smallest in London (the smallest is in Trafalgar Square).

Unquestionably the sexiest naked back in London (best viewed in a car coming out of Park Lane) belongs to the bronze David, part of Francis Derwent Wood's Machine Gun Corps Memorial. David leans on Goliath's sword; wreathed machine guns stand either side of him. The statue bears the chilling motto "Saul hath slain his thousands, but David his tens of thousands."

Opposite the Lanesborough is the Royal Artillery Memorial (by Charles Sargeant Jagger). It takes the form of a huge field gun guarded by eloquent bronze gunners,

12

and is inscribed to "a royal fellowship of death." It is positioned so that if a shell were fired from it with sufficient propulsion it would land on the Battlefield of the Somme.

FIDELIS MORGAN
Fidelis Morgan, writer and actor, is the author of a mystery series set in London.

12.9   Edgware Road

Edgware Road, between Bayswater Road and Marylebone Road NW1

⊖   Marble Arch

For me, one of London's strongest features is how it can become somewhere else entirely. Nowhere is this more true than the stretch of the Edgware Road between Marble Arch and the Marylebone flyover, once darkness has fallen. The pavement is suddenly dominated by Arabs, strategically arranged over at least two chairs each, deftly sucking on giant shisha pipes containing apple or strawberry tobacco. Combined with the eerie glow of the lights, it is one of the most interesting nights spent abroad in London.

SHEZ 360
Artist Shezad Dawood has exhibited widely, including at the Tate and the Venice Biennale.

CHAPTER 13
Holland Park & Notting Hill

1   Debenham House
2   Japanese Garden
3   Leighton House
4   Kensington Church Walk
5   St. Mary Abbots Church
6   The Roof Gardens
7   Ezra Pound's House
8   Henry James's House
9   Kensal Green Cemetery
10 St. Francis of Assisi
11 Café Grove 🍽♟
12 Graham & Greene 🎁
13 Olowu Golding 🎁
14 Mr. Christian's Delicatessen 🎁
15 Wild at Heart 🎁
16 Tom's Deli 🍽♟
17 The Westway
18 Westbourne Grove 🍽♟
19 Fresco 🍽♟
20 The Porchester Spa

Holland Park & Notting Hill

HOLLAND PARK

13.1 Debenham House

1906, Halsey Ricardo
8 Addison Road W14
www.debenhamhollandpark.co.uk
No longer open to the public.

⊖ Kensington or Sheperd's Bush

LO Kensington

Holland Park is full of splendid town houses built for nouveau toffs, but none is grander or stranger than 8 Addison Road. It was designed in 1906 by Halsey Ricardo. The exterior elevations are sheathed with semi-vitrified glazing bricks; some blue to reflect the sky, others blue-green to echo the surrounding foliage. Within is a neo-Byzantine dome, dreamed up by a pre-Raphaelite with the unlikely name of Gaetano Meo. But an even greater glory are its tiles (to be found both within and without), all the creation of William de Morgan. These were chosen not only for their intrinsic beauty but because "the finger of time leaves [glazed tiles] obstinate and unaffected." They certainly have lost none of their original vitality. Bathrooms (which all still contain their contemporary fixtures) are populated by creatures extant and extinct, while larger spaces display Orpheus beguiling ferocious beasts with his lute, or the adventures of Jason and the Argonauts. Elsewhere there are quotations from Homer's *Odyssey*.

CLIVE SINCLAIR
Clive Sinclair is the author of novels including Blood Libels and Cosmetic Effects.

13.2   Japanese Garden

Holland Park W8
Entrance on Abbotsbury Road
www.rbkc.gov.uk

⊖   Kensington
DLR   Kensington

The proportions of this replica of a Kyoto garden dismiss
an accusation of "tweeness" or bonsai lookalike. A waterfall,
a low bridge, and a fast-growing collection of flowering
shrubs and *Clematis stellata* make a pleasant enclave raised
from the ground and enclosed by walls of huge stones
brought from Japan. This is a garden worthy of comparison
with the water garden at Lake House, Wiltshire.

EMMA TENNANT
Emma Tennant's novels include Sylvia and Ted *and* The Beautiful Child.

13.3   Leighton House

1866–1879, George Aitchison
12 Holland Park Road W14
020 7602 3316; www.leightonhouse.co.uk

⊖   Kensington
DLR   Kensington

13

The artist Lord Leighton, then at the height of his
fame and prosperity, built this handsome mansion,
one of a number in this area occupied by wealthy
nineteenth-century artists, as both residence and studio,
with the assistance of the architect George Aitchison.
Its chief attraction—wonderfully cool on hot summer
days—is its Arab Hall, decorated with thirteenth- to
seventeenth-century Persian tiles, with a fountain in the
centre and damascene stained glass windows. The home
also contains some splendid pottery by William de
Morgan, also famed in his day as a novelist, and pictures

by Leighton and his contemporaries. Holland Park
is near at hand.

FRANCIS KING

*Francis King is the author of twenty-eight novels, a short-story writer, and a
poet. His books include Act of Darkness, The Domestic Animal, and Cold Snap.*

Until modern times, artists did not paint works with the
intention of having them displayed in public museums;
rather, their destination was usually the private collection
of a patron. Rarely can we experience works of art in the
kind of domestic context they were intended to adorn.
Such an opportunity is provided by Leighton House, the
home and studio of Frederick, Lord Leighton (1830–1896).
The classical exterior was very unusual for the time
(contrast it with Webb's Gothic studio for Val Prinsep next
door) and emulated an Italianate villa, reflecting the
theme and style of Leighton's own paintings. With
Alma-Tadema and Edward Poynter, Leighton set himself
to oppose Pre-Raphaelite Romantic realism. Many of his
paintings, some in his earlier style reminiscent of the
Florentine quattrocento, others in his later refined
pseudo-Hellenistic classicism, are displayed in the house
along with his sculpture.

There are numerous inventive details throughout. For
example, the window positioned above the fireplace (the
flue ingeniously concealed by an S-bend) features a
sliding, mirrored shutter affording a view to the garden
on the ground floor. More evident, however, are the
richly colored interiors; the red walls and black woodwork, for example, imitate a Venetian palazzo. The house
established Aitchison as a master of decoration. In 1877 he
added the celebrated Arab Hall, based on the chamber of
the twelfth-century Islamic Palace of La Zisa at Palermo,
to display Leighton's collection of Saracenic tiles. William
de Morgan designed new tilework, Boehm carved the

capitals, and Walter Crane contributed the mosaic frieze. The back door for the models, the generous promenades for the clients, and the luxurious studios are reminders of the successful artist's social position in mid-Victorian era. The exuberant ornamentation evokes Oscar Wilde's description of the house and studio of the fashionable artist Basil Hallward in *The Picture of Dorian Gray*.

PETER J. HOLLIDAY

Peter J. Holliday is Professor of Art and Classical Archaeology at California State University in Long Beach.

13.4 Kensington Church Walk

Just east of Kensington Church Street, off Holland Street w8

✪ High Street Kensington

Take a turn up this small alley, whose entrance is by the side of the Chelsea Old Town Hall. Quite suddenly you are in a quiet York stone walkway and churchyard which continues further to a small row of single-storey shops with a pretty forecourt. There are benches to sit on, birdsong, antiques, and antiquarian books. Perfect for a quiet respite.

RALPH STEADMAN

Ralph Steadman is a cartoonist, illustrator, printmaker, and writer.

13

13.5 St. Mary Abbots Church

1868–1872, Sir George Gilbert Scott
Kensington Church Street w8
020 7937 5136; www.stmaryabbotschurch.org

✪ High Street Kensington

A lunchtime concert at St. Mary Abbots Church on the corner of Kensington High Street and Kensington Church Street, with its peaceful cloister, is an uplifting experience. Here students from the Royal College of Music will transport one into another world.

ANNE PURCHAS

Anne Purchas is an architectural historian.

13.6 The Roof Gardens

1938, Ralph Hancock
99 Kensington High Street W8
020 7937 7994 or 020 7368 3993; www.roofgardens.virgin.com
Call ahead for hours as the gardens are often closed for private functions.

⊖   High Street Kensington

If you're tiring of the summer crowds in Kensington, turn down shaded Derry Street and look for a large, imposing doorway marked 99 Kensington High Street. It appears to lead to the offices of some well-heeled company, but go inside, sign in at reception, take a lift up to the roof, and then step out into one of London's strangest secret gardens. Floating an improbable thirty metres above the traffic of Kensington High Street, and sprawling out over one and a half acres, the Roof Gardens boast fully grown oak and fruit trees, a stream stocked with fish, and four resident flamingos, named Bill, Ben, Splosh, and Pecks. There are fine views over the crowded cityscape of Kensington and Chelsea. Opened in 1938 atop what was then the Derry and Toms department store (part of the Barkers group), the gardens were created at the behest of Barkers' vice president, and designed by Ralph Hancock (architect of the Gardens of the Nations at Rockefeller Center, New York). Today the Roof Gardens are owned by the Virgin Hotels group and open for public viewing on select days only: phone in advance of your visit to check access, and then wander through a 1930s department-store president's dream of a gracious shopping experience.

HELEN GORDON
Helen Gordon is a journalist, editor, and the author of Landfall.

Literary Neighbours
⊖ High Street Kensington

13.7 **Ezra Pound's House**
10 Kensington Church Walk w8
Not open to the public.

13.8 **Henry James's House**
34 De Vere Gardens w8
Not open to the public.

Not long after arriving in London, Ezra Pound moved into 10 Church Walk, Kensington, where he lived from 1909 to 1914. You are likely to be regarded with suspicion by the residents as you stand in the tiny square gazing upwards at the second-floor window where Pound worked on the translation of *Cathay*, and brushed up *Lustra* for publication.

One day not long ago I went to make an imaginative claim on Henry James's house at 34 De Vere Gardens (where, unlike Pound's house, there is a blue plaque), where he lived between 1886 and 1902, overseeing, among much else, the publication of his great London novel, *The Princess Casamassima*. I was tickled to discover that it was just a short hop away from Pound's place. But surely there was no connection between these two expatriate Americans, one grounded in the nineteenth century, the other an architect of the twentieth? Then, flicking through a biography of Pound in the library a few days later, I came across the information that when he arrived in London and moved into Church Walk, he had a dislike of fiction, "of which, anyway, he was ignorant, apart from the novels of Henry James."

JAMES CAMPBELL
James Campbell's books include Talking at the Gates, A Life of James Baldwin, and This Is the Beat Generation.

NOTTING HILL

13.9 Kensal Green Cemetery

1833
Harrow Road W10
www.kensalgreencemetery.com

⊖ Kensal Green

LO Kensal Green

RAIL Kensal Green

Kensal Green was the smartest as well as the earliest of London's great public cemeteries. Normally next to empty—but never creepy—it contains around two hundred and fifty thousand bodies, from Isambard Kingdom Brunel (1859) to Thackeray (1863) and downwards. It is the quintessence of late Romanticism: heart-piercing epitaphs, crumbling statuary, a sea of grasses and shaggy trees. All the pomp and vibrancy of Victorian London has ebbed away, leaving this a charnel house of jumbled monuments. To see the tomb of William Mulready the painter, in a November dusk, under its pall of chestnut trees is to come close to a rare sort of bliss—and just off the Harrow Road, too.

ROGER BOWDLER

Roger Bowdler works at English Heritage as head of designation in the Heritage Protection Department. He is the chairman of the Mausolea and Monuments Trust.

13.10 St. Francis of Assisi

1859–1860, Henry Clutton; 1861–1863, John Francis Bentley, additions
Pottery Lane W11
020 7227 7968; www.stfrancisnottinghill.org.uk

⊖ Holland Park

This is the first public building (neo-Gothic Arts and Crafts movement) built by Sir John Francis Bentley, the first Catholic architect in the Post-Reformation England. Small in size and tucked between the parish school, the rectory and an access yard. The whole ensemble is enclosed by a reddish brick wall that completes the charm of a village parsonage in the heart of the old Holland Park area. Sir Francis Bentley later built Westminster Cathedral.

AL ORENSANZ

Al Orensanz is a sociologist and semiologist, and the director of the Angel Orensanz Foundation in New York.

Portobello Morning

Θ Ladbroke Grove

13.11 **Café Grove**
253a Portobello Road W11
020 7243 1094

13.12 **Graham & Green**
4 Elgin Crescent W11
020 7243 8908; www.grahamandgreen.co.uk

13.13 **Olowu Golding**
367 Portobello Road W10
020 8960 7570

13.14 **Mr. Christian's Delicatessen**
11 Elgin Crescent W11
020 7229 0501; www.mrchristians.co.uk

13.15 **Wild at Heart**
222 Westbourne Grove W11
020 7727 3095; www.wildatheart.com

13.16 **Tom's Deli**
226 Westbourne Grove W11
020 7221 8818; www.tomsdelilondon.co.uk

13

I bought my flat smack in the middle of Notting Hill at the beginning of the Bosnian War. I needed a peaceful place to return to, to connect with human beings after living in a war zone. A walk down Portobello Road at 9 a.m. on a weekday brings me back to earth. I buy flowers and fresh-ground coffee; then I sit outside at the Café Grove, eating an omelette and reading *The Times*. Then shop— Graham & Greene and a stop at the amazing clothes designer Olowu Golding. I visit Mr. Christian's on Elgin Crescent for fresh bread, brownies, cookies, olives, and soup. Then a walk down Westbourne Grove: I buy flowers at Wild at Heart before meeting friends for the best cappuccino outside Rome at Tom's Deli. Everyone knows one another. The market vendors call out, "Hello Darling!" It feels very much like a world within a world.

JANINE DI GIOVANNI

Janine di Giovanni has written four books, including Madness Visible: A Memoir of War, and has won numerous prizes for her reporting from war zones.

13.17   Driving Along the Westway

Between Edgware Road and Ladbroke Grove

London is a city that rarely entered the twentieth century, and to find this stretch of motorway little more than a stone's throw from Marble Arch is a poignant reminder of what might have been. Join it by travelling west along the Marylebone Road, not far from 221b Baker Street, Sherlock Holmes's notional address. The Westway is a continuous overpass some three miles in length, running towards White City, home to BBC Television, and then to Shepherd's Bush, where Pissarro's house is still standing.

By international standards the Westway is unremark- able, and affords a view of some of the most dismal housing in London. But that is not its point. Rising above the crowded nineteenth-century squares and grim stucco terraces, this massive concrete motion-sculpture is a heroically isolated fragment of the modern city London might once have become. There are few surveillance cameras and you can make your own arrangements with the speed limits. Corbusier remarked that a city built for speed is a city built for success, but the Westway, like Angkor Wat, is a stone dream that will never awake. As you hurtle along this concrete deck you briefly join the twentieth century and become a citizen of a virtual city-state borne on a rush of radial tyres.

J. G. BALLARD

The late J. G. Ballard was the author of eighteen novels, including Crash, Cocaine Nights, and Empire of the Sun, which was based on his childhood in a Japanese internment camp and later made into a film by Steven Spielberg.

On the map it looks bizarre: a broad blue flyover bang in the middle of the city speeding from nowhere to nowhere. But if you get the chance to go on it when no one else is about—heading west—there is a rare moment of freedom to be had as you soar up into the sky leaving the long reach of Marylebone behind you, lifting above the steel drums of the Carnival; the road curves, offering possibilities unimaginable before falling back inexorably to the small comedies of Shepherd's Bush, Ealing, and Notting Hill.

ROMESH GUNESEKERA

Romesh Gunesekera's novels include Reef, Heaven's Edge, and The Match.

13

13.18 Westbourne Grove Restaurant Row

Between Queensway and Kensington Park Road w2

⊖ Bayswater or Royal Oak

🍴 No one in their right mind reveals their secret, favourite restaurant, because then it is no longer a secret and every Tom, Dick, and Sally turn up and squeeze you out. But here's a compromise. I reveal Westbourne Grove as the real heart of London restaurant land. In its half mile between Queensway and Kensington Park Road, the Grove and its side streets have restaurants representing twenty-one national cuisines, all good and all eminently affordable. I know. I live in the middle of them and have tried them all.

Phillip Knightley

Phillip Knightley is an author and a journalist whose books include Australia: A Biography of a Nation.

13.19 Fresco

25 Westbourne Grove w2
020 7221 2355; www.frescojuices.co.uk

⊖ Bayswater or Royal Oak

🍴 This is not a trendy, state-of-the-art Notting Hill café. This is a small, family-run Middle Eastern restaurant open day and night. They serve fresh carrot and ginger juice, Mediterranean mezze, hot pita bread—and they have the best shwarma outside Beirut. Close your eyes and you're in Jerusalem, Damascus, Cairo.

Janine di Giovanni

Janine di Giovanni has written four books, including Madness Visible: A Memoir of War, *and has won numerous prizes for her reporting from war zones.*

A Day at the Spa

13.20 The Porchester Spa

Queensway w2
020 7792 3980; www.nuffieldhealth.com

⊖ Bayswater or Royal Oak

9.18 Spa London

York Hall Leisure Centre
Old Ford Road E2
020 8709 5845; www.spa-london.org

⊖ Bethnal Green

The proliferation of small private health clubs has seen the demise of most of the grand Turkish baths built by local authorities at the beginning of the twentieth century. But the little wooden boxes of the sauna cannot rival the pleasures of steaming halls. The Turkish bath at the Porchester Centre is the most magnificent survival. It even uses the old Latin names for the various areas. The East End used to have several such places, but the Poplar Vapour Baths disappeared a long time ago and the cavernous Russian Baths at York Hall in Bethnal Green have now been transformed by private enterprise into a lavish modern spa—where nonetheless some of the old Cockney camaraderie still endures.

Duncan Fallowell

Duncan Fallowell is an author and cultural commentator. His books include Going As Far As I Can: The Ultimate Travel Book.

CHAPTER 14
Regent's Park

1. Gardens of St. John's Lodge
2. Queen Mary's Garden
3. Open Air Theater
4. London Zoo
5. St. Mark's Gate
6. Primrose Hill
7. Cachao
8. Lemonia
9. Primrose Hill Books
10. R. J. Walsh
11. Cecil Sharp House
12. Lodging House
13. Abbey Road Studios
14. Lord's Cricket Ground

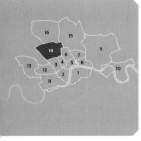

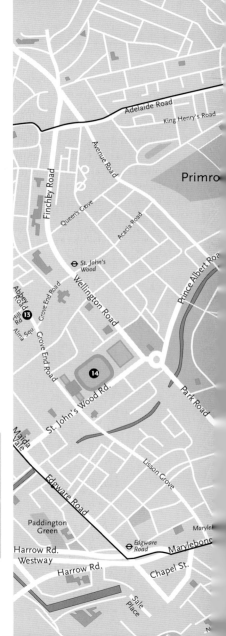

Erskine Rd
Ainger Rd
Peck
Berk
Chalcot Rd
Gloucester Avenue
Chalcot
Cres
Rothwell
St.
Fitzroy Rd
Princess Rd
Regent's Park Rd
Gloucester Ave

8
10
7
9
6
5
11

fill Rd

St. Pancras Way
Chalk Farm Road
Kentish Town Rd.
Camden Road
Royal College Street
St. Pancras

Camden Town ⊖

12

St. Mark's Gate
Parkway
Delancey St.
Camden High Street
Camden Street
Bayham Street
Plender St.
College Place

Outer Circle
Broad Walk

4

Regent's Park

Crowndale Road
Oakley Square
Eversholt Street
Mornington Crescent ⊖
Hampstead Road

Albany Street

Boating Lake
Inner Circle

1
3
2

Chester Road

Euston
Cardington St.
Euston ⊖
Euston Square ⊖
Gower Street
Drummond Street

Allsop Place

Baker Street

Euston Road

Warren Street ⊖
Great Portland Street ⊖
Regent's Park ⊖
Fitzroy Square
Tottenham Court Road
Whitfield Street

Marylebone High Street
Portland Place
Great Portland Street
Hallam Street

Cleveland Street

Goodge Street

Paddington Street

New Cavendish Street
Duchess Street

Newman Street

George Street
Manchester Square

Regent's Park

High Summer in Regent's Park

The Inner Circle, Regent's Park NW1

020 7486 7905; www.royalparks.org.uk

⊖ Baker Street or Regent's Park

14.1 Gardens of St. John's Lodge

1994, Colvin & Moggridge Landscape Architects

14.2 Queen Mary's Gardens

14.3 Open Air Theatre

0844 826 4242; www.openairtheatre.org

Go to the Regent's Park when you want to be outside but it's too hot to walk. Take a picnic to the formal garden adjoining the east side of St. John's Lodge. It's a supremely civilised composition of topiary and rosy arbours, stone fountains and velvet lawns, and mercifully few people even know it's there. Afterwards make your way across Queen Mary's rose garden, feeding your scraps to the ducks, to take in a performance at the park's much acclaimed Open Air Theatre.

Lucy Hughes-Hallett

Lucy Hughes-Hallett is an award-winning author and critic.

Go to the Open Air Theatre, then to the lake; hire a boat and row aimlessly around the island for an hour. After that, catch newlyweds being photographed in the flashiest part of the gardens, or just sit and sniff roses in Queen Mary's gardens.

Gillian Darley

Gillian Darley was co-author with Andrew Saint of The Chronicles of London, a historical anthology of London. Her other books include biographies of Sir John Soane, Octavia Hill, and John Evelyn.

14.4 Penguin Pool

1933, Berthold Lubetkin
London Zoo
Regent's Park NW14
020 7722 3333; www.zsl.org
⊖ Camden Town

An icon of modern architecture, the space is at once a constructivist sculpture, minimalist building, and structural delight.

ROBERT LIVESEY
Robert Livesey is an architect and a professor at the Knowlton School of Architecture at The Ohio State University.

14.5 A Stroll in Regent's Park

Enter Regent's Park from St. Mark's Gate
www.royalparks.org.uk
⊖ Camden Town

🍴 Start with lunch in Regent's Park Road—at Odette's for French treats in a room of mirrors (130 Regent's Park Road), or Lemonia for Greek delights in a noisy bustle (89 Regent's Park Road). Then limber up by crossing nearby Primrose Hill and enter the park by St. Mark's Gate, bowling along the Broad Walk with the Zoo to the right. All of this area in London's most beautiful park has been renovated and improved, climaxing in the sensational Italian Gardens abutting the Euston Road—a formal oasis of bushes, flower beds, small trees, fountains, and hedges—restored in the original Victorian design. Regent's Park is an ever-changing landscape of treasures and pleasures. One nook I particularly like is near the Open Air Theatre, an idyllic, enclosed corner with the magnificent Triton Fountain, the muscular merman blowing away on his conch with naked bronze ladies revelling in the spume at his fin.

MICHAEL COVENEY
Michael Coveney is the chief theatre critic of Whatsonstage.com and author of several biographies, including those of Maggie Smith, Mike Leigh, and Andrew Lloyd Webber.

14

14.6 Primrose Hill
⊖ Swiss Cottage or Chalk Farm

14.7 **Cachao**
140 Regent's Park Road NW1
020 7483 4422; www.cachaotoycafe.com

14.8 **Lemonia**
89 Regent's Park Road NW1
020 7586 7454

14.9 **Primrose Hill Books**
134 Regent's Park Road NW1
020 7586 2022; www.primrosehillbooks.com

14.10 **R. J. Welsh**
156 Regent's Park Road NW1
020 7722 5113

Primrose Hill is a good place for a refreshing walk, and
provides a splendid view of London. It is just to the north of
the Zoo, separated from Regent's Park by the Regent's Park
Canal, and is less than ten minutes' walk from the Swiss
Cottage underground station on the one hand and Chalk
Farm underground on the other. There was once a sort of
altar on its summit (nothing to do with the Druids who
congregate there to celebrate the summer solstice),
engraved with a diagram of the view identifying its main
features, chief among them the dome of St. Paul's. But the
view has become so complicated (the dome is still visible but
dwarfed by many tall buildings) that the "altar" has been
removed. Many of the park's great trees have gone, too,
swept away by a storm in 1978; but their successors are
growing on well, and there is plenty of green shade in which
to have green thoughts. Pre-AIDS, this little park led a double
life: by day a haven for children's picnics, gentle groups of
baseball players, and dog walkers; after dark, a well-known

romantic trysting place for gay men. But now owls and the occasional fox have the nights more or less to themselves.

🍴🍷🍲   At the foot of the hill, to the left if you are facing the Zoo, is short, pretty Regent's Park Road. It is well supplied with shops both useful and elegant, and boasts more than its fair share of excellent cafés—for the shameless sweet tooth I must recommend the American-style pancakes at Cachao. It also has a lovely Greek restaurant, Lemonia; a famous old-fashioned hardware shop, R. J. Welsh; and arguably the best small bookshop in London (both new and secondhand books), Primrose Hill Books. Locals have been heard to claim that you could manage perfectly well without ever setting foot outside this, their friendly and civilized village.

DIANA ATHILL
Diana Athill's books include Stet, Don't Look at Me Like That, and Somewhere Towards the End. She was awarded an OBE in 2009.

Climb the 206 feet to the top of Primrose Hill and see London lying at your feet. Where people now fly kites, duels were once fought. Almost two centuries ago, in 1821, the editor of *Blackwood's Magazine* inflicted a mortal wound on the editor of *The London Magazine* for accusing him of being so ungentlemanly as to make money out of his writing. Nearer our own times, Pongo in *101 Dalmations* started the twilight barking from the top of the hill. Zigzag down between the trees Frank Auerbach paints with such vibrancy (one or two of those paintings are in the Tate Modern) towards the elegant sweep of the Snowdon aviary in London Zoo. Cross the road into Regent's Park, taking an almost hidden path to the right down to Regent's Canal. As you stroll along the tow path you get a free glimpse of various beasts behind bars to your left as well as an occasional elephant taking the air. If you look carefully along the wall on the right you can still see the rope marks

14

left by the horses pulling barges—you may even see Britain's
oldest narrowboat being drawn by Queenie and Bonny.

EVA TUCKER
Eva Tucker's novels include Berlin Mosaic and Becoming English.

Belsize Park to Primrose Hill
⊖ Chalk Farm or Belize Park

I am by temperament a South Londoner, having been
born there. But I seem to have settled (for nearly thirty
years now) in northwest London. Not fashionable and
expensive Hampstead, but Belsize Park, which shares the
NW3 postal district number with Hampstead but lacks
some of its pretentiousness. My nearest open space is
Primrose Hill, and I like it partly because it's one of the
most inaccessible open spaces in London. I suggest
approaching Primrose Hill on foot through the long
Victorian and Edwardian streets in the area, permanently
in a condition of decay cut short just in time by refurbishment. Look out for blue plaques, depending on your
route—Frederick Delius (44 Belsize Park Gardens NW3),
Sylvia Plath (3 Chalcot Square NW1), and the socialist
historian H. N. Brailsford (37 Belsize Park Gardens NW3)
are among those I pass regularly.

By any route, walk to the top of Primrose Hill, a bare
unadorned area of short but not aggressively trim grass
fringed by trees—on a clear day, this is the best vantage
point in North London for seeing how the city has grown
and developed, and dignified itself with fine buildings
and spoilt itself with deplorable ones.

ALAN BROWNJOHN
*Alan Brownjohn is a poet. His most recent collection of poetry is Ludbrooke and
Others. He has also published four novels including The Way You Tell Them.*

14.11   Cecil Sharp House

2 Regents Park Road NW1
020 7485 2206; www.efdss.org
Check the website for schedule of events.
⊖   Camden Town

It may be a grand, 1930s-built, listed building in Camden, but Cecil Sharp House is in several ways a big village hall. Every one of its many rooms appears to have a piano in it. The musty air downstairs always seems to smell ever so slightly of gas. The bar stocks ales—ales, not beers—that have rustic but respectable names, and they are served by a big man with an unruly large beard. If there's food on offer, it will probably be egg sandwiches. Named in honour of Cecil Sharp, England's most important folk-song collector, the mansion is home to the English Folk Dance and Song Society. On the second floor resides the Vaughan Williams Memorial Library, a storehouse of ancient broadside ballads, dances, and orally transcribed traditional songs. Needless to say, you have to be a member to use it, but that somehow suits the pungently arcane atmosphere of the place. Besides, there are plenty of other decidedly home-woven activities going on: clog dances, ceilidhs, folk-song workshops, accordion lessons, Serbian choristry and, of course, morris dancing, on a weekly basis. Enterprising young promoters of the "nu-folk" contingent are also indulged from time to time. But even when hosting a gig that chimes with some accidental Zeitgeist, the fustiness of Cecil Sharp House remains admirably non-recuperable.

MATTHEW MILTON
Matthew Milton, a folk singer, free-improvisation violinist, music journalist, and editor, has lived in south London all his life.

14

14.12 Lodging House

8 Royal College Street NW1
Not open to the public.
⊖ Camden Town
LO Camden Road

The house at 8 Royal College Street (formerly Great College Street), where Rimbaud and Verlaine stayed in 1873, is best viewed from adjoining Plender Street, which runs west from Royal College. Here you can view the façade, now painted white, as the two delinquent poets would have seen it on their way home from Soho or Hampstead Heath. The pair lived here for only a few weeks, between May and July, but it occupies a significant place in Rimbaud's work in particular, and in the pair's alarming love story.

It is believed that the "Foolish Virgin" section of *A Season in Hell* represents their domestic life at the time. In this portion, Verlaine is the dramatic speaker:

"On several nights, his demon seized me, we rolled around together, I wrestled with him!—At nights, often, drunk, he lies in wait in the streets or in the houses, to frighten me half to death.—They will cut my throat, truly; it will be disgusting."

From Great College Street, Verlaine fled to Brussels. Rimbaud followed a few days later, and Verlaine shot him in the wrist, an act for which he was imprisoned. A few years ago, the house was sold, but the new owner remains sympathetic to its literary heritage. An oblong white plaque commemorates the poets' stay.

JAMES CAMPBELL
James Campbell's books include Talking at the Gates, A Life of James Baldwin, *and* This Is the Beat Generation.

14.13   Abbey Road Studios

3 Abbey Road NW8
020 7266 7000; www.abbeyroad.co.uk
Not open to the public.
⊖ St. John's Wood or Maida Vale

There are certain religious pilgrimages that all music fans (teenage and grown) must undertake. Fans of Jim Morrison visit Père-Lachaise in Paris; fans of Elvis trek to Graceland. And in London, Beatles fans go to Abbey Road to see the legendary studio where the Beatles spent seven years recording.

Take the tube to St. John's Wood, where a five-minute walk leads down Grove End Road to the corner of Abbey Road. You know you are there when you start to see graffiti on the wooden benches lining the road: "Niels Tiebosch loves Beatles"; "Julie + James, 9/11/00, Love is all you need." Then you hit that famous sign: Abbey Road 8. The zebra crossing, instantly recognizable, is just past the street sign. Close your eyes and picture John, Ringo, Paul, and George parading across. Don't, though, try to pose for a photo: it's actually a very busy intersection full of motorists annoyed by camera-happy tourists.

Abbey Road Studios, at No. 3 Abbey Road, is a part of EMI. Skyrocketed into fame because of the Beatles, it has actually been in existence since 1927, when Captain Osmund "Ozzy" Williams decided to build a recording studio in North London. In the 1930s, Sir Edward Elgar conducted the London Symphony in "Land of Hope and Glory," and in the 1940s, Glenn Miller recorded there. It wasn't until June 6, 1962, that the Beatles made their first visit to the studio (with Pete Best, not Ringo). The first song that the Beatles (as we know them) recorded there the next year was "Love Me Do," in Studio 2. The Abbey Road LP, the Beatles' tenth and final album to be recorded,

14

was released on September 26, 1969. The photo of Paul on the crossing, shoeless, led to rumours that he was dead.

Today the outside wall of the studios is covered in graffitied writings in English, Spanish, Japanese, Hebrew, French, and German. They range from the mundane ("Tom Walker wuz here") to the profane (pictures of John in an act that shall remain unnamed) and from the average fan ("The Beatles rule—my fave band, from Jackie") to the diehards ("Yesterday is so much better thanks to you, from Peter").

Be warned: Abbey Road Studios has no visitors' facilities. While the staff smile rather symphathetically at the earnest and eager fans who try to enter, they politely suggest a visit to the tiny Beatles Coffee Shop (attached to the St. John's Wood tube on Finchley Road, 020 7586 5404). The co-owner, Richard Porter, has been a London Beatles tour guide since 1988 (www.beatlesinlondon.com).

LEXY BLOOM
Lexy Bloom is a senior editor at Vintage and Anchor Books.

14.14 Lord's Cricket Ground

St. John's Wood Road NW8
020 7616 8500; www.lords.org

⊖ St. John's Wood

Note the general architecture, especially the stand built by Michael Hopkins (1985–1987). Delicious Indian flavour reminiscent of New Delhi. I played there many times as a schoolboy and from Oxford and having been brought up in Calcutta, always felt a pang of recognition.

Alas, the media centre, looking as if it had just landed from outer space, is out of keeping (built by Future Systems, 1995–1998).

ALAN ROSS
The late Alan Ross was Editor of the London Magazine and author of memoirs, poems, travel books, and biographies.

Cruise from Little Venice to Camden Market

Little Venice to Camden Town by barge, along the Grand Union Canal (seasonal)
Jason's Canal Trips: 020 7286 3428; www.jasons.co.uk.
Waterscape: 084 5671 5530; www.waterscape.com; London Waterbus Company: 020 7482 2550; www.londonwaterbus.com
⊖ Warwick Avenue

To journey by the canal is to see a place from an entirely different perspective, and this short trip, about twenty minutes, is no exception. It starts in Little Venice, with its respectable, fashionable villas and houseboats; dives into a tunnel; comes up briefly for air in an estate of low-cost housing; then goes back under a bridge, and immediately you are among millionaires' mansions on the edge of Regent's Park. Beyond them is the tranquillity of the park in a deep cutting with overhanging trees. The canal bisects the London Zoo; we saw gazelles and heard the squawk of tropical birds. Just after the Zoo, the barge takes a sharp left turn by a floating Chinese restaurant before arriving in Camden.

The barge drops you right at the centre of the Camden market. The day we went, there was a cloudless sky with bright sharp sunlight, so that the arrival at the crowded market, with is bright colours and exotic smells, owed more to a Conrad arrival at some riverside town on the Congo than to a North London market.

CHARLES MARSDEN-SMEDLEY
Charles Marsden-Smedley's design practice specialises in museum and exhibition design.

CHAPTER 15
Islington

1 Chapel Market 🎁
2 Camden Passage Antiques
   Market 🎁
3 Colebrooke Cottage
4 The Old Queen's Head 🍴🍷
5 Steve Hatt Fishmongers 🍴🍷
6 George Orwell's Flat
7 Estorick Collection of
   Modern Italian Art

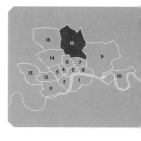

Islington

15.1   Chapel Market

Chapel Market, off Liverpool Road and Upper Street N1
Closed Mondays.

✚   Angel

🏛   Tucked away behind busy Upper Street—a couple of
minutes' walk from the Angel tube station—this is one of
London's oldest street markets. The word is that the stall
holdings are hereditary, held in the family for generations. Certainly over the years that I've known the market
the faces have aged but seldom changed. Wheeled wooden
stalls flank the long narrow street, offering everything
from CDs and track shoes to glitzy earrings and secondhand books. But the central feature is fruit and vegetables—
great glowing piles of oranges, lemons, grapefruit,
mangoes, pineapples, peaches . . . elegant displays of
impeccable cabbages, carrots, lettuces, avocados,
fennel . . . Everything you've ever heard of and some
that you haven't. The flower stalls are Aladdin's caves,
brilliant with great shocks of chrysanthemums, foaming
gypsophila, cornucopias of tulips. And the balloon
man wanders through the crowds tethered to a cloud of
silver helium hearts and globes like Mary Poppins.
PENELOPE LIVELY
Penelope Lively is a novelist and short-story writer.

15.2   Camden Passage Antiques Market

Off Upper Street N1
www.camdenpassageislington.co.uk
Check website for hours.

✚   Angel

🏛   Go to Portobello Road Market, if you must, but the real
antiques market is at Camden Passage. It is confined to an

area known as The Angel. Everything—low end to high end, finger jewellery to oak armoires—is on display and for sale.
JAY ANTHONY GACH
Jay Anthony Gach is a composer. His concert music has been performed, recorded, and broadcast internationally.

Islington Stroll
⊖ Angel

15.3 ### Colebrooke Cottage
64 Colebrooke Row N1
Not open to the public.

15.4 ### The Old Queen's Head
44 Essex Road N1
020 7354 9993, www.theoldqueenshead.com

A short walk from City Road, through the park that separates Duncan Terrace from Colebrooke Row, takes the dispirited or merely hungry to Regent's Canal in Islington, where it emerges from a 970-yard tunnel. This unexpected oasis from the clattering of local traffic is the perfect sheltered spot for lunch. After a few steps down a bank, convenient benches are placed along the path, overlooked on the far side of the canal, by the backs of the great houses of Noel Road. Sickert, who had a studio there, named his engraving of this view *The Hanging Gardens of Islington*.

15

Leaving the Canal and walking along Colebrooke Row towards St. Peter's Street, it is easy to imagine the rural scene it was until 1861, where the New River ran before the present road was constructed. In less than a quarter of a mile the river could be crossed by three bridges, from which schoolboys fished. The last house on the left, at 64 Colebrooke Row, is Colebrooke Cottage, once detached and since altered, where Charles Lamb and his sister

Mary lived from 1823 to 1827. "Elia," that most amiable of all the Romantics, described this cottage with delight:

> ". . . a white house; with six good rooms in it; the New River . . . runs . . . close to the foot of the house, and behind is a spacious garden, with vines I assure you. . . . You enter without passage into a cheerful dining room . . . and above is a lightsome drawing room, three windows . . . I feel like a great lord, never having had a house before . . ."

A glance across the road and on the upper storey of 55 Colebrooke Row just reveals on brickwork the faded painted lettering of a nineteenth-century hostel, stating the terms: "Women only 9d and 1/- per night. 4/6 and 6/- per week" (7p and 5p, 21p and 20p approximately).

A short turn up St. Peter's Street leads left to Essex Road, possibly the dullest street in London, and the location of The Old Queen's Head. A minute's walk from Upper Street, this pub was rebuilt on the site of the original Elizabethan inn, unhappily demolished in 1829. Considered one of the finest examples of domestic period architecture, the original pub had a magnificent wooden carved fireplace and ceiling, which were transplanted into its replacement. Quite a feat to try to work out the details of the woodwork, but the subject is Diana and Actaeon, with appropriate decorations, of Venus, Bacchus, and Plenty.

GEOFFREY ELBORN

Geoffrey Elborn, a biographer and critic, has written about lives of Edith Sitwell and Francis Stuart.

15.5 **Steve Hatt Fishmongers**

88–90 Essex Road N1
020 7226 3963
⊖ Angel
RAIL Essex Road

Steve Hatt's is surely the best fish shop in London, not only because of the variety and quality of the fish on sale but because Steve is impressively knowledgeable about all things to do with cooking and eating fish. The mussels are particularly worth a try: excellent value and always juicy.
FELICITY LUNN
Felicity Lunn is a curator and critic.

15.6 **George Orwell's Flat**

27b Canonbury Square N1
Not open to the public.
⊖ Highbury & Islington
LO Highbury & Islington
RAIL Highbury & Islington

For nine months, I lived at 27b Canonbury Square, the two-bed flat where George Orwell wrote and published *Animal Farm* and lots of journalism, and thought up much of *1984*. Canonbury was down-at-heel when Orwell was there in the 1940s with his first wife and their son, but not now. Yet while the Square's garden, opposite a plaque in Orwell's honour, is lovingly manicured, and Orwell's flat has been completely renovated (though a photo of Orwell at his typewriter guards the study from any change), an air of the past remains. Whenever I climbed to the top of the stairs at 27b, holding the black-painted rail, I could imagine bumping into Winston Smith, moving slowly because of his varicose ulcer, "resting several times on the way." And though the bare cold stairwell didn't smell of "boiled cabbage and old rag mats," it was easy to imagine how it could. It was a sad place for Orwell: his first wife

15

died suddenly, leaving him with a new baby, and he contracted the tuberculosis that would kill him. But the peaceful, almost secret garden at the back brings to mind the happier times: the appearance of *Animal Farm*, the arrival of baby Richard, and the moments when *1984* began coming together in his mind.

JOANNA BIGGS
Joanna Biggs is an editor at the London Review of Books.

15.7 Estorick Collection of Modern Italian Art

39a Canonbury Square N1
020 7704 9522; www.estorickcollection.com
⊖ Highbury & Islington
RAIL Highbury & Islington

This unique, interesting, and little-known gallery, housed in Northampton Lodge, a beautiful early-nineteenth-century house in Islington, contains the only collection of Futurist Italian painting in Britain. The work on show is exclusively by Italian artists, and it includes paintings by Modigliani, Di Chirico, Balla, and Severini. The collection was formed by Eric Estorick (1913–1993), an American political scientist and art dealer.

LUCRETIA STEWART
Lucretia Stewart is the author of, among other books, Tiger Bam: Travels in Laos, Vietnam and Cambodia.

Holloway Road

Holloway Road, between Highbury Corner and Highgate Hill (not on map)
⊖ Holloway
LO Upper Holloway

Indian Ocean Tandoori

359 Holloway Road N7

Cash X Change
352 Holloway Road N7

Holloway Express Shop
304 Holloway Road N7

Archway Tavern
Archway Close N19
⊖ Highgate

I suspect that few visitors to London would actively seek out the Holloway Road. Unlike Oxford Street, Leicester Square, Portobello Road, or Brick Lane, it is not what guidebooks are fond of calling a "destination."

As a tributary of the A1 in and out of London, it is more commonly a bit of the city hurried through to get to other destinations. After all, even football fans scurrying along it to and from Arsenal's newish Drayton Park ground have the stadium, not the street, on their minds.

A veil is possibly best drawn over the thoughts of anyone beating a path to the Fettered Pleasures or Showgirls fetish-wear shops that sit at its Highbury end. And, I'll admit, as a "city secret" its charms will probably remain stubbornly enigmatic to most. And I am hardly selling it here and now by also suggesting that perhaps the best way to experience it is from the top deck of a bus. But as the home turf of that fictional Victorian commuter Mr. Charles Pooter, it seems fitting enough to me. Placed above shop fronts, level and in motion, not only does the Holloway of Pooter's own day become a little more visible but so equally do many other fragments of London's past. Barrelling along from Highbury Corner to the foot of Highgate Hill, you'll encounter a bewildering array of building styles, not all of them especially pretty, and virtually every shop and café fascia and sign font ever to grace a London street over the past century or more. The

15

now increasingly rare Taj Mahal frontage of the Indian
Ocean restaurant alone deserves listing as a prime
example of period seventies catering design.

But above some of the gaudier new additions, you can
also spy weathervanes and minaret domes from the late
Victorian and Edwardian eras. Not quite obscured by the
plastic signage of the Cash X Change at No. 352, you can
still find traces of the once elegant wooden doors,
windows, and turrets of the entrance to the old Jones
Brothers department store.

A small black plaque above the cider-and-ciggie-
vending Holloway Express Shop confirms that the
"Telstar" record producer Joe Meek once worked
his magic here at number 304. And as Holloway Road
peters out, you'll find yourself before the former
Archway Tavern (now Dusk Til Dawn), a pub that graced
the record sleeve of the Kinks' "Muswell Hillbillies,"
chosen, apparently, because it had the worst country-
and-western band Ray Davies had ever heard.

TRAVIS ELBOROUGH

*Travis Elborough is the author of The Bus We Loved: London's Affair with the
Routemaster and Wish You Were Here: England on Sea.*

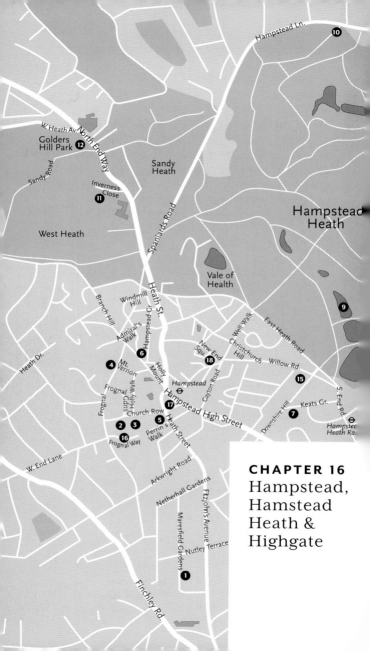

Hampstead Ln.

10

W. Heath Av. North End Way

Golders
Hill Park **12**

Sandy Road

Inverness
Close

11

West Heath

Sandy
Heath

Spaniards Road

Hampstead
Heath

Vale of
Health

Heath St.

9

Windmill
Hill

Branch Hill

Well Walk

East Heath Road

Admiral's
Walk

D Hampstead

New End
Squ.

Christchurch
Hill

6

Heath Dr.

Mt.
Vernon

4

Holly Walk

Holly
Mount

Willow Rd.

15

Clayton Road

Hampstead

7

Keats Gr.

S. End Rd.

Frognal Gdns.

Frognal

Church Row

Hampstead High Street

17

18

Downshire Hill

Hampstead
Heath Rd.

2 **3**

Perrin's
Walk

5

Heath Street

Frognal Way

16

W. End Lane

Arkwright Road

Netherhall Gardens

Fitzjohn's Avenue

Maresfield Gardens

Nutley Terrace

1

Finchley Rd.

CHAPTER 16
Hampstead,
Hamstead
Heath &
Highgate

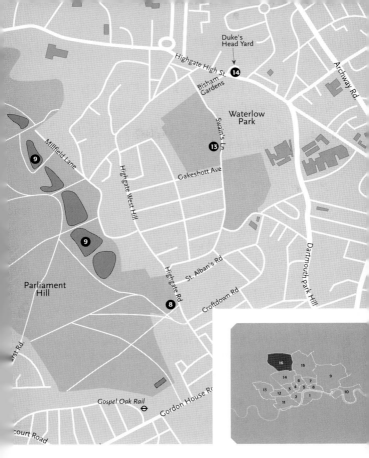

1   Freud Museum
2   St. John-at-Hampstead Graveyard
3   St. John-at-Hampstead
4   Former home of Charles de
    Gaulle
5   Abernethy House
6   Fenton House
7   Keats's House
8   Parliament Hill Café 🍴🍷
9   Highgate Ponds
    A. Women's Pond
    B. Men's Pond
    C. Mixed Pond

10 Kenwood House
10 Brew House 🍴🍷
11 Hill Garden
12 Golders Hill Park 🍴🍷
13 Highgate Cemetery
14 Studio House
15 House designed by Ernö
    Goldfinger
16 Sun House
17 Louis Patisserie 🍴🍷

18 Livingstone Studio (see p. 77) 🎁

Hampstead, Hampstead Heath & Highgate

16.1 Freud Museum

20 Maresfield Gardens NW3
020 7435 2002; www.freud.org.uk
⊖ Finchley Road
LO Finchley Road & Frognal

In a perilous last-ditch flight from the Nazis, Sigmund
Freud arrived in London with his family in 1938, moving
into the substantial red brick house in Hampstead which
he predicted would be "his last address on this planet."
The following year he died of cancer of the throat. This,
the most atmospheric of all London museums, is
strangely little known. At its heart is Freud's own study
and consulting room, drawing its peculiar aura of
enchantment from his famous collection of antiquities in
bronze, stone, and terracotta, sent on from Vienna, and
enriched by the colour and texture of the carpets and
hangings. Most magnificent of these is the five-sided
deep-red-and-blue rug, woven by one of the tribal groups
of the Qashqai confederacy of Western Iran, draped over
the couch employed by Freud for his analyses. Dream on.
FIONA MACCARTHY
*Fiona MacCarthy is a cultural historian and author of biographies of Eric Gill
and William Morris.*

16.2 St. John-at-Hampstead Graveyard

Church Row NW3
020 7794 5808; www.hampsteadparishchurch.org.uk
⊖ Hampstead

Hampstead's parish register, which was started in 1560,
contains the entry "Noe burialls in 1566." The present
parish church, St. John's, wasn't built until 1747, which

means that the graveyard is a better place for making contact with earlier centuries. The first parish church, St. Mary's, existed in the thirteenth century, and in 1837, when Constable was buried at the bottom of the slope, there were several layers of older bones beneath his coffin.

Inside the wrought-iron gates, you have to duck under an overgrown holly bush and make your way down an uneven path between tombstones that have been tilted by subsidence to eccentric angles, while many have been damaged by the ice of successive winters.

Only a minority of the inscriptions is still legible. Erosion, moss, ice, and stains on the stone have damned some of the dead to anonymity, while other headstones have been overpowered by shrubs, ivy, weeds, brambles, and pine needles aspiring to the condition of compost. Some tombstones, once proudly vertical, are horizontal and fragmented, while others, flat and horizontal from the outset, are modestly pursuing the coffins into the earth.

Once I was told off here by a man in a raincoat. Why was I letting my daughter dance on his grandfather's grave? What were my religious beliefs? But, far from being vertically in line with the stone, the old man's remains would have been shifted by subterranean movements. Other bones were below the small feet.

RONALD HAYMAN

Ronald Hayman's books include biographies of Nietzsche, Kafka, Sartre, Proust, Thomas Mann, Jung, and the Marquis de Sade.

16

Church Row

⊖ Hampstead

Lord Alfred Douglas's House

Church Row NW3

16.3 St. John-at-Hampstead

Church Row NW3
020 7794 5808; www.hampsteadparishchurch.org.uk

16.4 General Charles de Gaulle's House

99 Frognal NW3
Not open to the public.

The best walk in London is down Church Row in NW3.
After his exile and disgrace as the boyfriend of Oscar
Wilde, Lord Alfred Douglas lived here, though I don't
know at which number. You could ring all the bells and
ask. At the end of the road there is a ravishing little
graveyard to the right which contains the remains of
Hugh Gaitskell, Kay Kendall, Anton Walbrook (the
ringmaster from La Ronde), and Joan Collins's mother.
Our Lady guards Beerbohm Tree. To the left, in the
grounds of the church itself, you will find the grave of
John Harrison—immortalised by Michael Gambon in the
television film of *Longitude*. You will also get an extraordinary view south towards the river. Then you should head
on to Frognal, turn right, and at No. 99 you will find the
house where General de Gaulle lived as leader of the Free
French throughout the Second World War. I find it
heartstopping to think of him here, directing the French
war effort from a house in Hampstead. Of course if you
want to follow the theme of the Resistance, you then have
to go to the French House in Soho (49 Dean Street W1,
020 7287 9109; www.frenchhousesoho.com) to see where
de Gaulle's juniors all ate and drank. But, for me, the
pub will never be as evocative as the big, leafy house in
North London.

DAVID HARE

David Hare is a playwright and screenwriter. His twenty-seven plays include
Plenty, Skylight, Via Dolorosa, and Stuff Happens.

16.5 Abernethy House

1819
7 Heath Street NW3
Not open to the public.
⊖ Hampstead
LO Hampstead Heath
RAIL Hampstead Heath

"Robert Louis Stevenson slept here" is among the world's most common graffiti. In the summer of 1874, he stayed in Hampstead, in Abernethy House, Mount Vernon. At the time, Hampstead was considered the healthier part of London, and Stevenson's lungs needed any kindness they could get. One day, looking from the side window giving on to Holly Place, Stevenson spied some little girls playing with skipping ropes, which moved him to write the lovely essay "Notes on the Movements of Young Children." It is still a pleasant spot today, with no cars and few pedestrians.

JAMES CAMPBELL
James Campbell's books include Talking at the Gates, A Life of James Baldwin, and This Is the Beat Generation.

16.6 Fenton House

1686
Hampstead Grove NW3
020 7435 3471, www.nationaltrust.org.uk
Check website for hours and tour schedule.
Open March to November.
⊖ Hampstead
LO Hampstead Heath, Finchley Road & Frognal (1 mile)

16

Fenton House has a secret garden, high-walled in warm, worn red brick, where roses and clematis climb, and flowering terraces lead to a quiet, ancient, gnarled orchard. The house, a perfect example of London Queen Anne, as copied in Victorian doll's houses, stands back from the street on Windmill Hill, Hampstead. The museum shows musical instruments—especially seventeenth- and eighteenth-century harpsichords—and in the summer there are concerts. It's such a hidden place of enchantment, I'm loath to give away its presence.

MARINA WARNER
Marina Warner is a writer of fiction and cultural history, a curator, and an art critic.

16.7 Keats's House

1816
Wentworth Place, Keats Grove NW3
020 7332 3868, www.keatshouse.cityoflondon.gov.uk
Check website for hours and tour schedule.

⊖ Hampstead (1/2 mile)
LO Hampstead Heath
RAIL Hampstead Heath

He was only twenty-five when he died, but by then he'd written some of the greatest poems in the English language. Tuberculosis overtook him before he could marry the girl he loved, but they had one summer of intense happiness, living in semi-detached houses with a shared garden and a thin party wall.

At the end of 1818, the twenty-three-year-old John Keats moved from lodgings in Well Walk, Hampstead, to share a nearby house with a friend, Charles Brown. Keats paid him £5 a month for the room and the meals. The bigger house on the other side of the thin wall belonged to a friend of theirs, Charles Wentworth Dilke. Then only two years old, the houses were jointly known as Wentworth Place, and they'd been designed to look like a single house. One front door was in the middle, with the other tucked inconspicuously around the corner of the building.

Nobody now thinks of Hampstead as being outside London, but two years later, when the painter Constable settled his ailing wife and their children into Well Walk, he wrote: "I'm glad to get them out of London for every reason." Hampstead was still a secluded village, surrounded by fields. There were encampments of Gypsies on the Heath, and cattle grazed there.

The eighteen-year-old Fanny Brawne was living with her widowed mother, a younger brother, and a younger sister in a cottage at the corner of Downshire Hill and the road which was called Red Lion Hill until it became Keats Grove. After meeting Fanny at the end of 1818, he described her as "beautiful and elegant, graceful, silly, fashionable and strange." A few days later he wrote: "she is ignorant—monstrous in her behaviour—flying out in all directions." But soon they were unofficially engaged.

In the spring of 1819, when Dilke moved out of his house, the Brawnes moved in. Keats and Fanny saw each other almost every day, and went for walks on the Heath. She inspired some of his best poems, and by May he'd completed five odes, including the one to the nightingale, which took him only a few hours. He wrote it under a plum tree in the garden.

Brown always let his house in the summer, and Keats, who went with him to the Isle of Wight and Winchester, suffered such pangs of jealousy that he wanted to break off the engagement. He told Fanny he was trying "to force you from my mind . . . I love you too much to venture to Hampstead. I feel it is not paying a visit but venturing into a fire." He decided to live in Westminster and work as a journalist. But seeing her when he went to collect his things from the house, he had to give up the idea of leaving her. "You dazzled me. There's nothing in the world so bright and delicate."

Told by his doctors to spend the next winter in Italy, Keats left Wentworth Place in September. Fanny prepared

16

his clothes for the journey, and lined his travelling cap with silk. His last words to her were written from Naples in a letter to her mother dated October 24, 1820, but he'd written his last full letter to Fanny in August. "I wish I was either in your arms full of faith or that a Thunder bolt would strike me."

Unlike the lovers, the semi-detached houses were soon married. They were bought at the end of the 1830s by a retired actress, Eliza Chester, who'd been known as "Prinny's Last Fling," Prinny being the Prince Regent. Making the two houses into one, she had the staircase removed from the smaller house, and in the bigger she made the two parlours into one, adding a wing to contain another large drawing-room. But you can still see most of the original furniture, and three locks of Keats's brown hair.

RONALD HAYMAN

Ronald Hayman's books include biographies of Nietzsche, Kafka, Sartre, Proust, Thomas Mann, Jung, and the Marquis de Sade.

16.8 Parliament Hill Café

Parliament Hill, off Highgate Road, between the tennis courts and the bandstand NW3
020 7485 6606; www.cityoflondon.gov.uk

⊖ Tufnell Park

LO Gospel Oak

🍴 Don't miss the café at the bottom of Parliament Hill Fields. Go on a winter morning and you'll have it all to yourself. You can get an okay cappuccino and leaf through back copies of *Ham and High*. Then walk along, past the Lido and the strength-through-joy running track, and all of London is spread out on your left. If it's clear you'll see from Canary Wharf right across to Hammersmith. The London Eye presents a graceful ellipse bang in the middle of the frame, just between the Post Office Tower and Big Ben, and if it's really clear you'll see the south downs, and get a sense of the scale of the city sprawl, and its green boundaries. Walk past the empty benches with their maudlin dedications, where dozens of over-fed crows congregate listlessly in the cold weather. Then turn right up the hill, past grand Hampstead houses. Twenty minutes' brisk walk will bring you to Kenwood House (see p. 278).

ROGER MICHELL

Roger Michell is a film and theatre director of, among others, Persuasion and Notting Hill.

16.9   Highgate Ponds

Hampstead Heath, near East Heath NW3
020 7332 3773; www.cityoflondon.gov.uk
Open from May to mid-September.
For directions go to www.journeyplanner.org.

A personal favourite with visitors in the summer are the ponds at Highgate. It surprises out-of-towners who have suffered a hot day of London tubes and stress that you can swim in fresh water in the open air—with a view over the City. There are three ponds: men's and women's and mixed (the water flows through the women's first!), and in late summer the temperature is delightful. The atmosphere is very relaxed; it is not at all "naturist." Indeed, the mix is indicative of London's cultural diversity: Orthodox Jews with their ringlets pinned up; old, young, fit, and unfit. The women's pond, I'm told, is rather more sociable.

I recommend the stiff walk back up the hill to the Flask Tavern (77 West Highgate Hill N6, 020 8348 7346), a Georgian pub at Highgate Village; if it is getting cold by then, they have braziers outside.

IAN KELLY

Ian Kelly is an actor and writer. His publications include Shakespeare Cinema.

16

16.10 Kenwood House

Hampstead Lane NW3
020 8348 1286; www.english-heritage.org.uk
☻ Archway, Golders Green, then No. 210 bus
LO Gospel Oak or Hampstead Heath
RAIL Gospel Oak or Hampstead Heath

Go to Kenwood for one of the great picture collections in the capital. Then make for the Heath, just beyond the Kenwood fence, where there are fantastic trees for the small and the agile to climb and places to picnic where you won't be disturbed all afternoon.

GILLIAN DARLEY

Gillian Darley was co-author with Andrew Saint of The Chronicles of London, a historical anthology of London. Her other books include biographies of Sir John Soane, Octavia Hill, and John Evelyn

The best way to explore the grounds is on a twenty-minute circular lakeside walk. Go through the trellis tunnel at the side of the house, cross the terrace, take the steps down the grassy bank, and cross the fenced pasture to the right of the lake, looking back at the house to take in the fall of light on its façade. Cross the bridge to the right of the lake, follow the path through the woods, bearing left, and you'll end up back at the Brew House (see p. 279), situated behind the house in the old stable block. Inside can be quite crowded, but there is a spacious and sheltered walled garden.

Locals visit Kenwood all year round to walk, to jog, and to picnic, but seasonal highlights include the banks of daffodils in early spring, the massive flowering rhodo-dendrons in May, and the lakeside classical concerts programmed for many evenings throughout the summer. One tip: if you drive to Kenwood, avoid the cramped car park. Leave your car on Hampstead Lane, just opposite Compton Avenue, and enter by the East Lodge. The secluded right-hand path takes you in style right to the front door.

CHRISTOPHER GEELAN AND SARAH GORDON

Christopher Geelan and Sarah Gordon are the Artistic Directors of the Young Shakespeare Company.

Self-Portrait

c. 1663, Rembrandt

The Rembrandt self-portrait, tucked away in the leafy setting of Kenwood House on Hampstead Heath, has haunted me since I was a teenager, a hundred years ago. Yes, there is a sunny Franz Hals there and yes, there is an exquisite Vermeer there. But the Rembrandt just hypnotises me, as it always has. The eyes of the master are tragic and yet the face and the whole pose are full of dignity and inner strength. I never can take my eyes off the picture and if my eyes can stray for a short while onto the marvellously sumptuous painting of the fur on his garment, they soon lock back onto his eyes, sad and defiant. Possibly the greatest painter who ever lived and certainly one of his greatest paintings. And so close to my doorstep when I grew up in Hampstead. I was lucky. It was just luck the painting was there and I was so nearby. And it will always be there!

BERNARD JACOBSON

Bernard Jacobson has had a gallery in London for more than forty years, dealing in modern and contemporary British, American, and European art.

16

16.10   ## The Brew House

In the Kenwood House
Hampstead Lane NW3
020 8341 5384; www.companyofcooks.com
Archway or Golders Green, then the No. 210 bus

On a sunny morning in spring or summer or on a crisp day in autumn, go and eat breakfast in the Brew House at

Kenwood. Load your tray with eggs, bacon, sausage, grilled tomato, and mahogany-brown tea and carry it out to one of the tables in the garden. You can look at the fig trees and argue about whether a fig has ever ripened in England, you can fend off the sparrows and robins, and when you have finished your breakfast you can stroll round the corner for a look at the best small art collection in the world.

NICCI GERRARD AND SEAN FRENCH
Nicci Gerrard and Sean French, both journalists, write thrillers together, including Killing Me Softly, The Safe House, and Complicit.

16.11 Hill Garden

1905–1911; 1925, Summer House and extension of Pergola by Thomas Mawson
Inverforth Close, off North End Way NW3
⊖ Hampstead

If you like surprises, this is a must—London's most secret garden. Secluded and beautiful, this is quintessential landscape architecture. The rolling hillside is defined by the colonnaded walkway, with its painted Tuscan Doric columns, quasi-temples, and pagodas, its rhythm reflected in its stone paving. Formal lawns and pools have been inserted into the hillside, and wonderful trees and borders are all around. It is all immaculately kept, the colonnade has been recently restored, and on most days you have this haven of peaceful contemplation all to yourself.

EDWARD BURD
Edward Burd, an architect, was for thirty years a partner at Hunt Thompson Associates, where he worked primarily on conservation and social housing projects.

16.12 Golders Hill Park

Hampstead Heath, next to the West Heath NW3
020 7332 3511; www.camden.gov.uk
⊖ Golders Green or Hampstead

Less known than the main Hampstead Heath, Golders
Hill Park (at the far west corner of the Heath) makes
for a perfect afternoon out. The formal Flower Garden
and Pergola provide respite from the centre of London,
while the play structures entertain young children
for hours. Inflatables and a variety of clowns and
magicians visit Golders Hill Park in the summer holidays,
and the Italian ice cream parlour has some of the best
homemade ice cream in London.
FELICITY LUNN
Felicity Lunn is a curator and critic.

Bird Chorus and Bat-Watching

Check website for walks in Hampstead Heath and Waterlow Park;
www.cityoflondon.gov.uk/hampstead
Walks run during the summer months, peaking in July and August.

If you can get to Hampstead Heath by 4 a.m. on an April or
May morning you can set off in the company of other
people you can't yet see and be led into the woods. At first
there's nothing to hear, then a few peep peeps, then all
within a few minutes a good racket sets up as you greyly
begin to make out your feathered companions. When
I've been, the guide's style has been an appealing mixture
of the laid-back and the knowledgeable: able to chat and
smoke, yet simultaneously single out all sorts of different
bird voices. Some are familiar enough, even in London,
but others, like those of migrants, such as blackcaps and
chiffchaffs, can be heard only for those few weeks of spring.

The bat walks start on summer evenings and attract
all sorts of people, some keenly carrying little black

16

electronic boxes called Bat Detectors. Even if the bats don't show up it's a lovely walk. But they generally do, and then the Bat Detector owners get very excited, sorting out which bat is which according to the frequency of its squeaks. What I like are the names of the bats: Pipistrelle, Daubenton's, Noctule, Natterer (this last, being rarer here, the cause of great jubilation when it appears).

There are also bat walks in Waterlow Park, Highgate, from which you get a wonderful view of London—so good that Sir Sydney Waterlow, Lord Mayor of London, 1872–1873, donor of the park, has been standing on his plinth, pipe in one hand, hat and umbrella in the other, admiring it ever since he was placed there, almost a century ago.

RUTH PAVEY

Ruth Pavey writes for national publications on contemporary fiction, crafts, and horticulture.

16.13 Highgate Cemetery

Swains Lane N6

020 8340 1834; www.highgate-cemetery.org

The cemetery is divided into East and West sections. The East, home to Karl Marx's grave, is open from 10 a.m. to 4 p.m. every day. Visiting the West requires a guided tour. For directions check the website or go to www.journeyplanner.org.

When I was working as a writer in Hampstead I needed somewhere peaceful but stimulating to walk to in the afternoons. It was a long journey across the Heath to Highgate Cemetery, but when I got there I entered a mysterious world like a walled-in but nevertheless apparently boundless jungle—thick undergrowth and huge trees encroaching on elaborate tombs like the half-hidden temples of Cambodia. There were domes, porticos, spires; a sunken mausoleum like an ancient Egyptian excavation; a colossal monument to a horse. At the centre, like the presiding deity of a sacred grove, there was on its plinth the massive bust of Karl Marx, his formidable head jammed down onto his shoulders, in an area kept reverentially clear around him with perhaps a faded wreath or two. There was a strange potency in the great apostle of materialism being commemorated in such a wild and almost mystical place. The cemetery had long since been closed to new burials, and in the 1970s it was open to the public only on certain days of the week or year—so this added to the sense of secrecy and taboo.

NICHOLAS MOSLEY

Nicholas Mosley, novelist and biographer, won the Whitbread Book of the Year Award in 1990 for Hopeful Monsters.

Architectural Stroll

⊖   Highgate

Highpoint I and II

1933–1935 (I) and 1938 (II), Lubetkin, Bertold & Tecton
Highgate North Hill N6 (not on map)
www.housingprototypes.org

16.14   Studio House

1939, Tayler & Green
Duke's Head Yard N6

16.13   Highgate Cemetery

Swain's Lane N6
020 8340 1834; www.highgate-cemetery.org
The cemetery is divided into East and West sections. The East is open from 10 a.m. to 4 p.m. every day. Visiting the West requires a guided tour. For directions check the website or go to www.journeyplanner.org.

16

16.15   House designed by Ernö Goldfinger

1939
2 Willow Road NW3
020 7435 6166; www.nationaltrust.org.uk
Check website for hours and tour schedule.

16.16 **Sun House**
1935, Maxwell Fry
9 Frognal Way NW3

16.17 **Louis Patisserie**
32 Heath Street NW3
020 7435 9908

English insularity kept modern architecture at bay in the early twentieth century, and only in the 1930s was there a scattered, rather timorous acceptance of it. There is no better way to see this belated embrace of Modernism than to spend an afternoon walking between Highgate and Hampstead. Take the underground to Highgate and head for North Hill, where you will find two blocks of flats by the Russian émigré Berthold Lubetkin: Highpoint I and Highpoint II. Both are indebted to Le Corbusier, but the latter upset the purists with two Erechtheum caryatids at its entrance—a definite hint of the surreal.

Continue into Highgate village and, off High Street, enter inconspicuous Duke's Head Yard for Tayler & Green's 1939 Studio House, with more Corbusian echoes. Cemetery lovers might then detour down Swain's Lane to visit London's most atmospheric example. Otherwise take the narrow, continually interesting Fitzroy Park to the edge of Hampstead Heath. Choose from a variety of routes and enjoy expansive views towards the city as you make for 2 Willow Road on the far side of the Heath. This was designed by the Hungarian émigré Ernö Goldfinger and, owned by the National Trust, is now open to the public. A walk up Willow Road brings you to Hampstead and your final destination—Maxwell Fry's white-walled Sun House, in Frognal Way, which, well maintained, still radiates the excitement of the new. There's an excellent patisserie in nearby Heath Street, opposite the end of eighteenth-century Church Row.

ANDREW MEAD

Andrew Mead is a journalist, writing on architecture, art, and landscape.

Highpoint I and II

1933–1935 (I) and 1938 (II), Lubetkin, Bertold & Tecton
Highgate North Hill N6 (not on map)
www.housingprototypes.org

Highgate

Conventional plans are transformed by simple modernist devices. The caryatids on II are either announcing the decline of Modernism or indicating Lubetkin's breadth of sources.

ROBERT LIVESEY

Robert Livesey is an architect and a professor at the Knowlton School of Architecture at The Ohio State University.

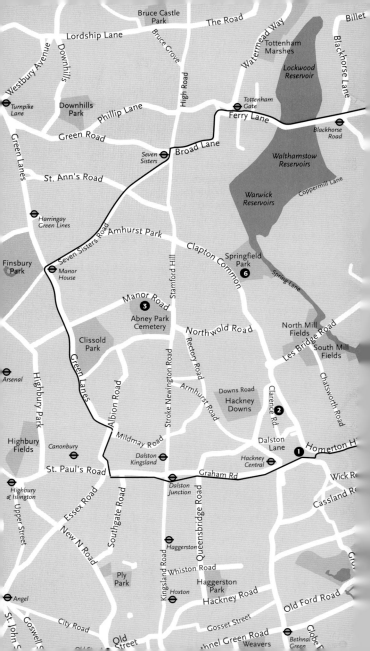

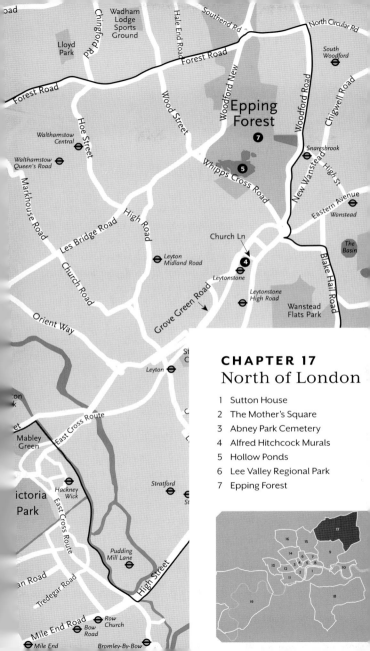

CHAPTER 17
North of London

1 Sutton House
2 The Mother's Square
3 Abney Park Cemetery
4 Alfred Hitchcock Murals
5 Hollow Ponds
6 Lee Valley Regional Park
7 Epping Forest

North of London

17.1 **Sutton House**

1535
Homerton High Street E9
020 8986 2264; www.nationaltrust.org.uk
LO Hackney Central
RAIL Hackney Downs

Extraordinary survival. Built for one of Henry VIII's strong-arm men, Sir Ralph Sadleir, who lived to sit in judgement on Mary, Queen of Scots; now National Trust. Exhibitions, concerts, excellent restaurant, rooms to hire and a strong educational programme. Splendid panelling—worth the effort to get there.

ANN SAUNDERS
Ann Saunders's books include Regent's Park, Art and Architecture of London, and St. Paul's Cathedral. She is Honorary Editor to the London Topographical Society and Editor Emeritus to the Costume Society.

9.36 **Arcola Theatre**

24 Ashwin Street
020 7503 1646; www.arcolatheatre.com
At press time, the Arcola Theatre had moved to Ashwin Street in Hackney. See map 9 on p. 156 for location.
LO Dalston Kingsland
RAIL Dalston Junction

The Arcola Theatre lacks many things that other theatres have: a proscenium arch, elaborate scenery, mezzanine seats, fancy dressing rooms, a curtain. But it has something much more important—a fierce commitment to taking risks and producing new plays. Begun in a Hackney warehouse where, legend has it, J. M. W. Turner once mixed his paints, the Arcola is one of my favourite places in London.

ERIC SCHLOSSER
Eric Schlosser is an investigative reporter, the author of Fast Food Nation, and a playwright whose work has been performed at the Arcola Theatre and Shakespeare's Globe.

17.2 The Mother's Square

1987–1990, HTA Architects Ltd.
Behind Mother's Hospital
Lower Clapton Road E5
LO Hackney Central or Clapton

Here, the powerful sense of place transcends the graffiti, derelict cars, and rubbish, to prove that low cost architecture does not mean low quality—of ambition, concept, design, or construction. In an impoverished neighbourhood, this housing development, primarily for people on low incomes, shines like a jewel. The design is rigorous, with a nod toward Palladio, and flats, houses, and old people's accommodation are all incorporated within it. If all social housing was like this, all social classes would be queuing up for the opportunity to live in it.

EDWARD BURD
Edward Burd, an architect, was for thirty years a partner at Hunt Thompson Associates, where he worked primarily on conservation and social housing projects.

17.3 Abney Park Cemetery

Opened 1840, buildings and landscapings by William Hosking
Stoke Newington Church Street N16
020 7275 7557; www.abney-park.org.uk
RAIL Stoke Newington

Abney Park is a romantic wilderness off Stoke Newington High Street and Church Street, every bit as interesting as Highgate Cemetery. There is a monument to Isaac Watts (hymn writer), who is actually buried in Bunhill Fields, and General William Booth (founder of the Salvation Army) was buried here in 1912. But there are splendid urns, inscriptions, lions, angels, beasts, and a policeman's helmet, dogs, and cruisers too. All part of life's rich pageant.

PIERS PLOWRIGHT
Piers Plowright retired from BBC Radio in 1997 after thirty years as an award-winning producer.

17

William Booth of the Salvation Army found his final resting place here. His tomb is quite a head-turner. And there are many others, equally appealing, some—my special favourites—with tiny, ancient photographic ceramics glued to the front of them (the dead staring blankly into the camera lens, and then beyond it, into eternity), others, with poignant poems—sometimes whole families, killed in influenza epidemics—many in terrible disrepair; fallen angels, lop-sided plinths, toppling urns.

Just outside, after your walk, you can order a pristine cappuccino at a tight-arsed but relentlessly bohemian local brasserie.

Nicola Barker
Nicola Barker's novels include Wide Open, Darkmans, and Burley Cross Post Box Theft.

Leytonstone

⊖ Leytonstone

17.4 Alfred Hitchcock Murals
1999, City Arts & Greenwich Mural Workshop
In Leytonstone Station E11
www.greenwichmuralworkshop.com

17.5 Hollow Ponds
Whipps Cross Road E11
020 8532 1010; www.waterscape.com

The seventeen mosaics that greet commuters at Leytonstone tube station are a surprising burst of colour in an otherwise grimly lit and faintly depressing under-pass. Each one depicts a key scene from the life or the films of Alfred Hitchcock—a local lad who, I presume, escaped at the earliest available opportunity—and are expressive, unusual pieces of public and popular art. Yet in all the years I've lived in Leytonstone, I've never seen one person stop and look at them, nor touch the exposed shards of vitreous glass tesserae. I did once, but a pair of schoolkids laughed at me.

These odd, tucked-away, luminescent gems are typical of the slightly strange character of Leytonstone. Until the late sixties it wasn't considered a part of London at all; it was Essex suburbia. And if you turn right out of the underground station and walk along Fairlop Road, you can see why: the neat lines of terraced housing, their pebble-dashed or stone-clad exteriors often protected by motorised gates and customised hatchbacks, spread out over the course of about a square mile. The quiet is stunning, punctuated only by the howls of ambulances from the nearby hospital. Turn left at the Tube, however, and you're in the heart of a small and ebullient town centre.

While far from the bohemian stylings of Walthamstow Village—a quick bus ride away—Leytonstone has a better-than-expected smattering of restaurants and a couple of decent pubs. It's loud and noisy, the traffic is horrendous, and the McDonald's and the Tesco are open twenty-four hours a day. But as you walk up the high street towards the Green Man Roundabout, you begin to notice trees in the middle distance. The A10 that cleaves the town in two, and the complicated ramps and crossings it provokes, cannot alter the fact that just a few yards away is the beginnings of the Epping Forest.

If I were to lay a line as to where London stops and suburbia truly begins, it would be at Hollow Ponds, a short walk from the Green Man Roundabout, where boats can be hired and ice creams eaten. The fuss and noise of the traffic melts away here; the sweat and temper of the city dissipates. Over the road, the Alfred Hitchcock Hotel reminds you where you are, but otherwise the feeling is of being utterly lost. Walking around those ponds is a perfect reminder of the small joys—like the Hitchcock

17

murals—that are dotted around this part of East London: tucked away, ignored, and wonderfully unexplored.

STUART EVERS

Stuart Evers writes about books for The Guardian and The Independent, among other publications.

17.6 Lee Valley Regional Park

Springfield Park E5

08456 770 600; www.leevalleypark.org.uk

For directions, go to www.journeyplanner.org.

Lee Valley Regional Park stretches twenty-six miles along the river Lee from Ware in Hertfordshire to East India Dock basin. My bit goes from Springfield Park on the fringes of Stoke Newington down to Hackney Marshes, which now abuts the new Olympic development. From the Park ridge, you sweep down into the valley and onto a track through a wild, glamorous, urban park landscape. There is more sky than you usually see in cities. Under the pylons and elevated rail track carrying graffitied trains across this expanse, there are highland cattle grazing in fields. In summer, wild burdock and cow parsley grow five feet high along the banks of the river where bulrushes rustle. There is a wonderfully lonely bird sanctuary where through special hatches you can watch tufted ducks, pochards, goosanders, swans. Hawks circle. Herons lurk. The river is as you might expect—a brackish London backwater. There are intriguing houseboats moored along the banks. Rowers slice past, avoiding the bobbing detritus, the occasional upended shopping trolleys, and swans. You don't see many people, but those you do see reflect London's population: strolling Hasidic families, flash girls with piercings, weirdos, and trampers, and every kind of dog and owner.

MELANIE MCFADYEAN

Melanie McFadyean is a journalist. She writes for numerous publications, including The Guardian, The Independent, Granta, and the London Review of Books.

17.7   ## A Day Trip to Epping Forest
In Loughton, between northeast London and Essex
www.cityoflondon.gov.uk
For directions, go to www.journeyplanner.org.

Epping Forest, London's finest woodland, stretches north for almost six miles, a good day's outing, and absorbs thousands of recreationists into its glades of oak, beech, hornbeam, and birch. Stop for tea amid throngs of bikers by the Robin Hood roundabout. Walk around two ancient hill forts, buried in woodland. Watch a cricket match on a clearing which is the lid of the sunken orbital M25 motorway. End the day by the log fire of the Forest Gate Inn (111 Bell Common, Epping, 01992 572 312), a down-to-earth hostelry, everything a country pub should be (and generally isn't).

MICHAEL HEBBERT
Michael Hebbert is Professor of Town Planning at the University of Manchester and author of London: More by Fortune Than Design and Dismantlers.

Queen's Wood
Muswell Hill Road N10 (not on map)
www.fqw.org.uk
Highgate

A true gem of untouched woodland next to Highgate tube station. No views, no children's playgrounds, no picnickers, just a valley of ancient trees with an empty, rundown pond in the middle. The wood is perfect for that half hour of silent commune with the wood sprites, an antidote to the peopled greenery that makes up most other London parks.

Each tree and overgrown pathway stands in silent tribute to one of those grand preservation campaigns that explode magnificently into the public consciousness and then disappear into the mists. In the 1890s, the battle for

17

Churchyard Bottom, as the wood was less elegantly known, occupied the columns of local and national newspapers as well as a good chunk of parliamentary time.

An Appeal Committee included such forgotten heroes as the Rt. Hon. G. J. Shaw-Lefevre and Thomas Skinner, Esq. (What fun to be able to rescue, even momentarily, two of their names.) It was set up to pay off the rapacious Ecclesiastical Commissioners, who considered that making money for the propagation of religion served a higher purpose than preserving the environment. The huge sum of £30,000 was eventually raised to protect the trees from the urban spread that ate up the countryside of North London in the twentieth century.

A hundred years ago the renamed Queen's Wood was well looked after, boasting a fence, a lodge, and a tearoom, as well as four full-time keepers. The woods were in constant use as a place of escape for the masses on their way to Alexandra Palace, that Victorian folly, first broadcast home to the BBC and now an ice rink with a view. Today a penurious local council leaves the place to run wild. Nature flourishes gloriously in this lack of attention—an oasis for foxes, birds, and the occasional strange human souls doing their own things, the ¶ tearoom, the Queens Wood Lodge Cafe off Muswell Hill Road, serves a delicious and suitably organic mix of hot food and cakes.

So if you are ever wavering over a contribution to a campaign to save something for posterity and think, "What's the point," catch the Northern Line to Highgate and meditate under one of the great beeches in Queen's Wood.
ANGUS MACQUEEN

Angus MacQueen's documentary work includes The Death of Yugoslavia, which won a British Academy Award, and Dancing for Dollars, which received an Emmy.

Alexandra Palace

Originally completed in 1873 by Alfred Meeson and John Johnson;
rebuilt in 1875
Alexandra Palace Way, Wood Green N22 (not on map)
020 8365 2121; www.alexandrapalace.com

⊖ Wood Green, then the W3 bus to the Main Court entrance

RAIL Alexandra Palace Station is located right at the Wood Green
entrance to the park.

Every world city has its white elephants; what would we
do without them? London has a fine example on its
northern rim: Ally Pally, opened in May 1873 and
destroyed by fire within two weeks. Rebuilt in two years,
it has had a chequered history and was the site of the
BBC's first public television broadcast. I like it most on the
closest Saturday night to the 5th of November, when the
skies light up with the Ally Pally fireworks, commemorating
itself as much as Guy Fawkes, and all across the city
bonfires burn.

ROMESH GUNESEKERA
Romesh Gunesekera's novels include Reef, Heaven's Edge, and The Match.

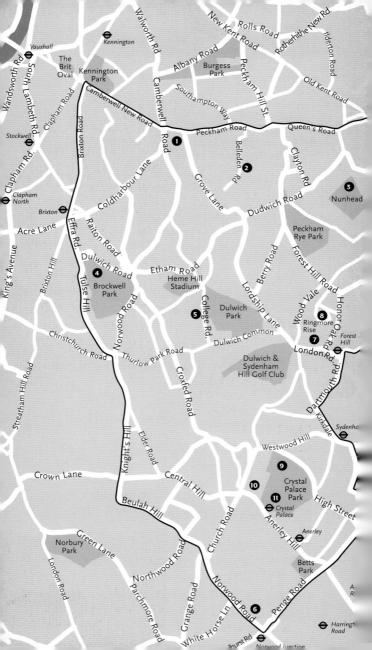

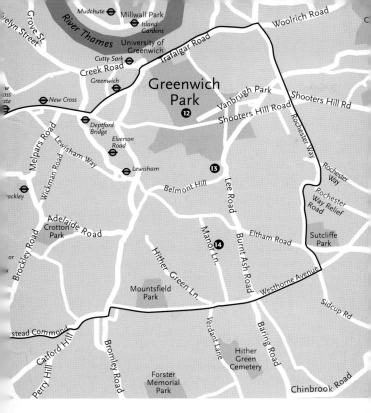

CHAPTER 18
South & Southeast of London

1 Johanssons 🍽🍷
2 Review Bookshop 🎁
3 Nunhead Cemetery
4 Brockwell Lido
5 Dulwich Picture Gallery
6 Stanley Halls
7 Horniman Museum
8 Ringmore Rise
9 Crystal Palace Park
10 Crystal Palace Museum
11 Crystal Palace Park Farm

12 Greenwich Park
13 Blackheath
14 The Ice House

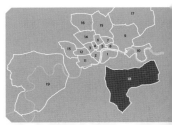

South & Southeast of London

18.1 Johanssons

2 Grove Lane SE5
020 7701 4944
RAIL Denmark Hill

I write often in Johanssons. It's a really cosy place, but it's big enough that you don't feel like you're taking the piss by sitting on one coffee for a couple of hours. The people working there are friendly and the food is good. Have a black coffee and a cinnamon toasted ciabatta. In the winter there's an open fire; in the summer there's a vine-sheltered garden to sit in. Lovely.
EVIE WYLD
Evie Wyld's first novel is After the Fire, a Still Small Voice.

18.2 Review Bookshop

131 Bellenden Road SE15
020 7639 7400; www.reviewbookshop.co.uk
RAIL Peckham Rye

Review is a small independent bookshop on the road I grew up on in Peckham. It has everything I want in a bookshop—titles chosen for the quality of their writing, not their sales figures; an atmosphere of quiet community; and a nice long dog called Gus. It's the best bookshop in London.
EVIE WYLD
Evie Wyld's first novel is After the Fire, a Still Small Voice.

18.3 Nunhead Cemetery

1840
Linden Grove SE15
020 7732 9535; www.fonc.org.uk
RAIL Nunhead

As the population of London grew in the early nineteenth century, parish churchyards couldn't cope with the increase of bodies requiring burial; so began a major programme of cemetery building. Parliament authorised the construction of private cemeteries, and between 1832 and 1841 seven magnificent burial grounds were built. Nunhead (one of the two south of the Thames) was consecrated in 1840, and although it is perhaps the least known, it is arguably the most beautiful.

It does not contain as many celebrated inhabitants as northern counterparts such as Highgate (although its collection of music-hall artists, cricketers, and trade unionists makes for fascinating discoveries); it is the overall effect of this semi-wild landscape that gives the cemetery its unique charm. Although it is gradually being restored, its potent mix of overgrown nature and miniature histories remains, along with a wonderful array of butterflies, woodpeckers, foxes, bats, and remarkable flora—just a fifteen-minute train from Victoria.

There are fabulous chapels and catacombs, as well as beautiful vistas (one view in particular, of St. Paul's through the trees, has been created to dramatic effect), but most compelling are the commemorations of forgotten moments of history: the monument to the Scottish Political Martyrs, which reflects Southwark's radical roots, and the Sea Scout monument, commemorating the nine Walworth Scouts drowned in an accident on the Thames, are poignant memorials in amongst all the domestic stories.

The tireless work of the Friends of Nunhead Cemetery has restored the Gothic beauty and preserved the unique atmosphere of this Victorian gem.

PAUL BAGGALEY
Paul Baggaley is the Publisher of Picador.

18

18.4 Brockwell Park Lido

Brockwell Park
Dulwich Road SE24
020 7274 3088; www.brockwelllido.com; www.fusion-lifestyle.com
⊖ Brixton (20-minute walk)
RAIL Herne Hill

The Friday evening summer barbecues at Brockwell Park Lido, an outdoor swimming pool, are a South London institution. Located between rarefied, rich, white Dulwich and predominantly black Brixton, it's the place to come to see multicultural London at its most vibrant and enjoyable. Swim, lounge, read, chat, eat, or just people-watch—this is quintessential London: inclusive, frantic, and fun.

JONATHAN COX
Jonathan Cox is a primary-school teacher and a former editor and writer for Time Out City Guides.

18.5 Dulwich Picture Gallery

1811–1815, Sir John Soane
College Road SE21
020 8693 5254; www.dulwichpicturegallery.org.uk
RAIL West Dulwich (15-minute walk); or North Dulwich (15-minute walk)

Hidden away in the leafy suburbs of South London, within less than an hour's travel from the centre, is the world's seminal building in gallery design. In the early nineteenth century, Dulwich College School (founded by the Elizabethan actor Edward Alleyn) acquired the nucleus of an art collection, originally intended for the King of Poland, which included major works by Canaletto, Claude, Gainsborough, Poussin, Rembrandt, Rubens, and Watteau, among others. The Regency architect Sir John Soane, presented with a limited budget, constructed between 1811 and 1815 one of the first custom-built public art galleries ever. He devised a masterpiece of abstract classicism in brick, dressed with Portland stone detailing, in which he pioneered a system of top-lighting. Recently restored, with a sensitively placed visitors' centre nearby, the gallery provides an afternoon's feast of architecture and painting in the arcadian setting of Dulwich village.

JOHN WILTON-ELY

John Wilton-Ely, an art historian, is a Fellow of the Society of Antiquaries and the Royal Society of Arts. He is the author of Piranesi as Architect and Designer.

A Drive Through Norwood

www.croydon.gov.uk

LO Forest Hill

RAIL Crystal Palace or Forest Hill

18.6 Stanley Halls

1903, W. F. Stanley
12 South Norwood Hill, South Norwood SE25 (not on map)
020 8253 1038

18.7 Horniman Museum

1901, C. Harrison Townsend
100 London Road, Forest Hill SE23
020 8699 1872; www.horniman.ac.uk

18.8 Ringmore Rise

Lewisham SE23

London is not a city in the European sense. It is, rather, an agglomeration of ever-eliding suburbs with a tiny urban core. It is a precursor of Los Angeles, a horse-drawn, Victorian L.A. And, thus, its essence is to be found in those suburbs, which are captivating places to walk in and to drive around, even if the notion of actually living in them is less appealing. Upper Norwood is an anthology of High Victorian Gothic domestic architecture—Church Road, Auckland Road, and Belvedere Road are splendid sites of this style in its psychotic decadence. The curious

18

may divert to South Norwood, where the cutler W. F. Stanley (inventor of the vandal's weapon of choice, the Stanley Knife) designed and built the wonderfully bizarre Stanley Halls in an idiom that has no precedent.

North of Norwood, at Forest Hill, the Horniman Museum is one of the very rare instances of a fine public building by an Arts and Crafts architect, C. Harrison Townsend. Behind it, from Ringmore Rise, a road of undistinguished houses of the early 1930s, are the best views of central London: one doesn't look across the city, one looks down on it.

JONATHAN MEADES

Jonathan Meades has written and performed in some fifty polemical essays for BBC TV, including the series Off Kilter. He is the author of seven books, among them Pompey and The Fowler Family Business.

Crystal Palace

LO   Crystal Palace
RAIL   Crystal Palace

18.9   **Crystal Palace Park**

1851–1854, Joseph Paxton
Thicket Road SE20
The dinosaurs are in the southwestern corner of the park.

18.10   **Crystal Palace Museum**

Anerley Hill SE19
Southwest corner of the park
020 8676 0700; www.crystalpalacemuseum.org.uk

18.11   **Crystal Palace Park Farm**

The Croft, Ledrington Road SE20
0208 778 5572; www.crystalpalaceparkfarm.co.uk
For directions, go to www.journeyplanner.org.

There have been dinosaurs at Crystal Palace since 1854, when Joseph Paxton created the park as a permanent home for the glass and iron building that housed the Great

Exhibition. The prehistoric beasts survived the fire of 1936, which destroyed the Palace, and today one of the joys of encountering them is watching as children suddenly spot the enormous antlers of a megaceros—Irish elk—through the branches of trees, a massive iguanadon or a cluster of marine reptiles in a lagoon. The lakes, islands, and thickets where these and others live form a geological time trail, constructed by distinguished experts of the day. If some of the models, sculpted by Waterhouse Hawkins to the instructions of Sir Richard Owen, Director of the Natural History Museum, are anatomically incorrect, they represent an important stage in our understanding of prehistoric life. They were created just ten years after the first discovery of dinosaur remains in Britain.

The vast fountains, the Atmospheric Railway, the aviators and balloonists, the Cup Finals, and the visiting crowned heads are long gone, but mementoes of the Crystal Palace's former glories, and of the fire, can be viewed in the charming and informative small museum on Anerley Hill, run by the Crystal Palace Foundation, an independent trust.

Other attractions in the park include the maze, a boating lake, a small zoo for children too young to appreciate its intrinsic sadness, a mini-railway, play-ground, visiting funfairs and fireworks displays, the Concert Bowl, and the National Sports Centre. If, however, you'd prefer a sweet and surreal celebration of the park on video, *The Pleasure Garden*, a short film directed in 1952 by James Broughton, photographed by Walter Lassally, stars Hattie Jacques as the magical genius loci, John Le Mesurier, Lindsay Anderson, and Kermit Sheets. It won the Prix du Film de Fantaisie Poétique in Cannes in 1954.

SHENA MACKAY

Shena Mackay's books include Dunedin, The Orchard on Fire, and The Atmospheric Railway: New and Collected Stories.

18

It stood for a mere six months in Hyde Park, but the astonishing Crystal Palace remained atop Sydenham Hill for eighty-two years before burning down in 1936. All that remains of the Palace are the long ballustraded promenades that formerly fronted it and the rather battered sphinxes that once proudly stood sentinel over the world's most impressive greenhouse. The small Crystal Palace Museum nearby tells the story of the Palace in Sydenham. It's housed in the old engineering school where John Logie Baird established his television company. And the television associations continue to this day—the towering Crystal Palace TV mast can be seen from as far afield as Hampstead Heath.

The location, one of the loftiest in London, still affords exhilarating views over the capital, and down through the charmingly semi-dilapidated park. Yet, all is set to change as the London Development Agency's "Masterplan" swings into action over the next few years. The famous Grade I–listed dinosaurs in the Tidal Lakes have been spruced up, and the children's Crystal Palace Park Farm has reopened. A host of major renovations are to follow, including tree planting following the footprint of the Palace, a new café and playground, and removal of the mess of roads and car parks that currently scar the centre of the park.

A new, partially sunken sports centre will be built and the not universally loved 1960s National Sports Centre tarted up. Sport is the other great association with Crystal Palace. Motor races were held in the park from the 1930s to the 1970s, and, from 1895 to 1914, twenty FA Cup Finals were played here, attracting crowds of up to one hundred thousand. WG Grace once led the London County Cricket Club on the cricket ground (and captained the national lawn-bowling team here). In 1866, aged just eighteen,

Grace won a national 440-yard hurdle race at Crystal Palace, just one day (some sources say two) after he scored 224 not out for All-England against Surrey at the Oval, establishing his reputation as the most versatile sporting star of his time.

JONATHAN COX
Jonathan Cox is a primary-school teacher and a former editor and writer for Time Out City Guides.

8.12 Greenwich Park

www.royalparks.org.uk and www.friendsofgreenwichpark.org.uk
For directions check the website, or go to to www.journeyplanner.org.

Statue of General Wolfe

At the end of Blackheath Avenue, in the centre of the park

Queen's House

1635, Inigo Jones
Romney Road, just north of the park
www.nmm.ac.uk

The Royal Hospital (Old Royal Naval College)

1685-1692, Christopher Wren, Nicholas Hawksmoor, and John Vanbrugh
Northern end of the park
020 8269 4799; www.oldroyalnavalcollege.org

The Royal Observatory

1675, Sir Christopher Wren
At the end of Blackheath Avenue, in the centre of the park
020 8858 4422; www.nmm.ac.uk

The Fan Museum

12 Crooms Hill, northwest corner of the park
0208-305 1441; www.fan-museum.org

National Maritime Museum

Romney Road, north end of the park
www.nmm.ac.uk

18

Ranger's House

The Wernher Collection
Chesterfield Walk, west side of the park
020 8853 0035; www.english-heritage.org.uk

Vanbrugh Castle

1719, John Vanbrugh
On Maze Hill, northeast side of the park
Not open to the public.

Easily the most beautiful park in London; where else has a deer park, a sausage café (next to the Royal Observatory, www.honestsausage.com), undulating valleys, massive ancient trees, and the most splendid yet forgotten view of Central London? Stand at the statue of General Wolfe, of Quebec fame, and all London is laid out before you—as well as, alas, the skyscrapers of the Docklands. But this is just for starters, as below stands the greatest agglomeration of architecture in Britain. The early-seventeenth-century Queen's House by Inigo Jones was the first real classical building in Britain, a cool, pale, minimalist bolt of the European Renaissance in a still medieval land. In front is the Royal Hospital, designed by a *Who's Who* of British architecture: Christopher Wren, Nicholas Hawksmoor, and John Vanbrugh (who built a castle-like brick home, Vanbrugh Castle, on the east side of the park—still there—to watch progress). You want more? How about the home of time itself? In the Royal Observatory you can see—for free—where, from this very spot, Enlightenment scientists mapped the globe and the heavens, and carved up the planet into east and west. There is an actual line embedded in the ground so you can straddle both hemispheres. From Christopher Wren's main building, Halley spotted his comet. There's a great museum, too, including John Harrison's marine time-keeper. And there's more! The Fan Museum; the National

Maritime Museum; and Ranger's House, with its incredible collection of porcelain! I could go on, but I'll leave it for you to discover Greenwich Park's many pleasures.

TOM DYCKHOFF

Tom Dyckhoff is architecture critic of The Times, architecture and design critic for BBC2's weekly arts magazine programme, The Culture Show, and writes a weekly column for The Guardian's Weekend Magazine.

18.13 Blackheath

RAIL Blackheath

Few tourists come to Blackheath, thinking it's too far away, although it's in fact just twelve minutes from London Bridge, or twenty-two minutes from Charing Cross. It's a shame that any visitor to London would miss out on the city's hidden village. So many people think of London as a collection of villages, the Great Wen gobbling up the countryside in the eighteenth, nineteenth, and twentieth centuries. Most villages had their stint as artistic escapes, but Blackheath is one of the few to really retain its village-like atmosphere—weirdly so, considering the urban soup of Lewisham right around the corner. Exit the train station and enter a Miss Marple drama. Two churches, cricket green, duck pond, eighteenth-century houses, and at the top of the hill, turning left out of the station, the vast, treeless, hilltop expanse of the heath ⅊ (stopping for coffee and cake at Hand Made Food, 40 Tranquil Vale, www.handmadefood.com). It's not quite remembered why Blackheath is called the black heath: some think it refers to its black soil, others to its bleakness, still more to the story that plague victims were buried here. Either way it has the most compelling atmosphere of any of London's commons: something to do with the huge sky, high on the hill. This used to be the haunt of highwaymen. Shooter's Hill still passes through.

18

On the heath you'll find kite-flyers on gusty days, travelling circuses and funfairs on holidays (they've come here since the sixteenth century), and sad-looking donkeys giving rides to children. Blackheath also has the highest concentration of classic modernist private houses after the more famous Hampstead, the wealthier creative classes experimenting with new-fangled design from the late 1940s onwards. Blackheath Park is the best place to start. It's located right out of the station, top of the hill, first left. Along its length you'll spy houses by camp modernist Patrick Gwynne (the graphite grey one that looks like a Bond villain's lair) and Peter Moro (lead designer on the Royal Festival Hall), plus, peeling off its lanes, countless Span estates, the now forgotten success story of post-war housing: not bleak tower blocks but beautifully landscaped, Scandinavian-style houses and flats, now mostly lived in by architects and artists.

TOM DYCKHOFF

Tom Dyckhoff is architecture critic of The Times, architecture and design critic for BBC2's weekly arts magazine programme, The Culture Show, and writes a weekly column for The Guardian's Weekend Magazine.

18.14 The Ice House

c. 1830
Manor House Gardens, Lee SE12
Brightfield Road
020 8318 1358; www.lewisham.gov.uk
The Ice House is open to the public upon request.

LO   Hither Green or Lee

On a very hot Sunday—the first or third Sunday between July and September—take an overland train to Lee or Hither Green. Walk through Manor House Gardens and find the set of metal steps which lead down to a brick-built ice house and tunnel. Ice from the pond was packed into the well and kept for up to two years. Fruit and vegetables from the Manor House orchards and kitchen gardens were kept fresh in the adjoining chambers. Imagine the chilled flowers which were used as table decorations. A block of ice made a fountain as it slowly melted and spilled from the top of a tower of plates which displayed the flowers. Then climb back above ground and buy an ice cream from the kiosk.

CHRISSIE GITTINS

Chrissie Gittins is a poet, playwright, and short-story writer.

CHAPTER 19
Southwest & West of London

1 Fulham Palace Garden
2 Bedford Park
3 Chiswick House
4 Gunnersbury Park Museum
5 London Russian Orthodox Church (see p. 211)
6 Osterley Park
7 Kew Gardens
8 Richmond Park
9 King Henry's Mound
10 Richmond Lock
11 Garrick's Temple
12 Strawberry Hill House

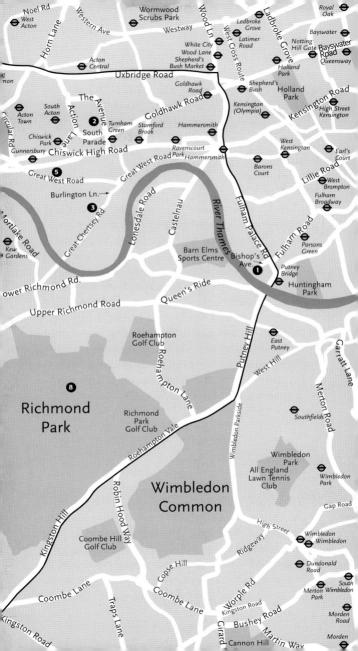

Southwest & West of London

19.1 Fulham Palace Garden

c. 1750
Bishop's Avenue SW6
020 7736 8140; www.fulhampalace.org
⊖ Putney Bridge
RAIL Putney Station

One day, when I was checking the view from the site of
Mary Shelley's Putney home for a biography I had
recently completed, I found myself gazing at the walls
which enclosed the bishop's palace at Fulham. Crossing
the river by what would have been the old timber bridge
in her day, I circled the garden wall and wandered
through the West Gate to find myself in a gloriously
landscaped private garden, shaded by cedars and leading
down to what is currently (before restoration) one of
London's most enchanting walled gardens, complete with
box hedges, delicately collapsing greenhouses in which
peaches still smother the walls, and a cloud of yellow
butterflies nestling against the red brick.
MIRANDA SEYMOUR
Miranda Seymour is a biographer, novelist, and critic.

19.2 Bedford Park

1875–1886, Richard Norman Shaw, among others
www.bedfordpark.org
⊖ Turnham Green

Bedford Park, begun in 1875, was the first planned garden
suburb. Its significance was first noted by Herman
Muthesius in his book *Das Englische Haus*. John Betjeman
suggested it was England's greatest contribution to
international architecture. Designed largely by Norman

Shaw, it also has buildings by E. W. Godwin, E. J. May, and Maurice Adams.

PETER MURRAY

Peter Murray, Hon. FRIBA. is chairman of Wordsearch, chairman of the New London Architecture centre, and director of the London Festival of Architecture.

19.3 Chiswick House

1729, William Kent
Burlington Lane, Chiswick W4
020 8995 0508, www.chgt.org.uk
The house is open from April to October. The gardens are open year-round. Check the website for hours as the house is often closed for private functions.
⊖ Turnham Green (3/4 mile)
RAIL Chiswick (1/2 mile)

Andrea Palladio (1505–1580) was Europe's most influential architect: the style of every colonial building in the U.S. and Canada can be traced back to his buildings in Vicenza and other towns in northern Italy, or to his villas in the Veneto. The third Earl Burlington, no mere dilettante but a consummate architect, visited some of Palladio's buildings and, from his sketches and Palladio's *Quattro Libri*, created Chiswick House in 1729, with some help from fellow architect William Kent.

Exquisite inside and out, the house is small: only seventy feet square. Said the wit Lord Hervey, it "is too small to inhabit, and too large to hang on one's watch." With enfilades of rooms and even bedchambers in the grand French style, it is arranged on two floors, plus wine cellars, and is the best imaginable place for holding the grandest of parties; indeed, that was and remains its purpose.

The best people partied there: after the Burlingtons came the promiscuous Duchess of Devonshire, Georgiana (she liked Chiswick House so much she bought the place).

19

In 1844, her son Bertie, the future King Edward VII, greeted the Tsar of Russia with a twenty-one gun salute and asked Queen Victoria and Prince Albert along too; Bertie also put on one hell of a show for the Shah of Persia in 1873. Today, Chiswick House can be rented for private parties for up to ninety-six guests.

In the summer of 2010, the estate was reopened after a mammoth restoration. Now, as before, it offers statuary vistas, temples, streams, ponds, and grottos in the new natural "English" style. Most of the grand garden land-scapes of the following century, including New York's Central Park, were inspired in part by Chiswick.

IAIN MACKINTOSH

Iain Mackintosh is a producer, designer of theatre spaces such as Glynde-bourne and the Cottesloe, and curator of fine-arts exhibitions of theatre painting and theatre architecture.

I love Chiswick House as a piece of Palladian Italy marooned in suburban Chiswick. Amid a wasteland of mock Tudor terraced houses stands a fragment of the warm south: a perfect Renaissance design, complete with obelisks, classical statues, formal gardens, and a pagan temple. Even in the depths of an English winter it never appears to succumb to the gloom of its surroundings.

WILLIAM DALRYMPLE

William Dalrymple is an award-winning travel writer and historian. His books include From the Holy Mountain, White Mughals, and Nine Lives: In Search of the Sacred in Modern India.

19.4 Gunnersbury Park Museum

Popes Lane, Acton w3
020 8992 1612; www.visithounslow.com
www.gunnersburyfriends.org

Gunnersbury House

Late 1700s, John Webb

⊖ Acton Town

Bounded to the east by the North Circular and to the south by the M4 and the Martini Tower, Gunnersbury Park is a hundred-and-eighty-five-acre open green space on the borders of Ealing and Acton. An estate since the Middle Ages, it is now dominated by the two stucco halls—Gunnersbury Park and Gunnersbury House—which, last owned by the Rothschilds, now form a museum devoted to the heritage of Ealing and Hounslow. But it's the grounds that make it extraordinary: a surprising secret garden in one of those parts of London dominated by the incessant buzz of modern transportation systems—the roads, the Tube, the permanent throttle back of jets on their Heathrow landing pattern.

The best way to experience Gunnersbury is to turn immediately to the right once you get through the front gates: through a small garden protected from the road by a high brick wall, past the Temple and the boating pond—which in summer is full of delighted childish squeals—and westwards to the large open space which rises northwards from the lights of the M4—partially obscured by huge poplars—to the detached thirties houses that front on Popes Lane. In the far southwest corner, there is the Folly and the Potomac Lake: a small pond constructed out of a clay pit that plays host to meditative night-time fishermen.

Space in London is highly concentrated, and one of the things that has always amazed me about Gunnersbury

19

Park is that you can be so close to major roads and yet still feel so secluded. The walk along the south side is completely covered by an umbrella of horse chestnuts—a deep boskiness that protects you until you walk back up north for the first proper view of the great house that you approach up a sharp incline to the long terrace. Walking to the west, you get a full view of the Orangery before returning, via the café, to the Temple and the exit— a forty-five-minute or so pause from the stomach-churning exigencies of metropolitan life.

Before my parents moved to W8 in 1967, Gunnersbury was my local park: we lived a quarter of a mile away in Baronsmede, while my grandparents built their detached thirties property, Manor House, right opposite Gunnersbury's front gates. This suburban corner is central to who I am, and now that I no longer live in London I revisit it as a touchstone of the way things were, are, and still might be. My favourite time is at dusk, when there's no one around except the owls and, in summer, the bats: the familiar views (which to some might seem banal) remind me of my good fortune in having this free, imaginative space on my childhood doorstep.

JON SAVAGE

Jon Savage is a historian of popular culture. His books include England's Dreaming: Sex Pistols and Punk Rock and Teenage: The Creation of Youth, 1875–1945.

19.6 Osterley Park

1576, original house; remodelled 1761–1780 by Robert and James Adam
Jersey Road, Isleworth TW7
020 8232 5050; www.nationaltrust.org.uk
Check website for hours and directions. Closed November to March.
⊖ Osterley (1 mile)
RAIL Isleworth (1½ miles)

Less than forty-five minutes' journey by underground from central London and a fifteen-minute walk will bring you to the most perfectly preserved masterpiece of the Adam brothers, set in an idyllic park within sound (alas) of Heathrow. Osterley Park, originally built as a country seat for the Elizabethan tycoon Sir Thomas Gresham in 1576 (the Queen actually slept here that year), was remodelled with supreme elegance by the Adam brothers for the Georgian bankers Francis and Robert Child, in the latest fashionable taste. Given to the National Trust in 1949, the house retains in unique completeness the original Adam furnished interiors, devised with a flair and panache that caused a sensation in the 1770s. The novel Etruscan Dressing Room, in part inspired by Wedgwood and Herculaneum, remains one of the first conscious attempts to create a modern style of interior design. The house also has the dubious distinction of having turned away as visitors Thomas Jefferson and John Adams in 1786 because they had failed to acquire tickets in advance and Mrs. Child was at the Newmarket races! Be sure, therefore, to check the opening arrangements.

JOHN WILTON-ELY

John Wilton-Ely, an art historian, is a Fellow of the Society of Antiquaries and the Royal Society of Arts. He is the author of Piranesi as Architect and Designer.

19

19.7 Kew Gardens

Royal Botanic Gardens, Kew TW9
020 8332 5000; www.kew.org
Θ Kew Gardens
LO Kew Gardens

Waterlily House
1852, Richard Turner

Palm House
1844–1848, Decimus Burton

I find the Waterlily House, built in 1852, a small, strange oasis of warmth, and the Palm House, opposite, a place of serendipity. The underground aquarium, with its wonderful epigram—"without algae there can be no life on earth"—is a real surprise.

ROMESH GUNESEKERA
Romesh Gunesekera's novels include Reef, Heaven's Edge, and The Match.

Stroll Along the Grand Union Canal

Stroll starts at Windmill Lane, just north of Osterley Park.
Follow the Grand Union Canal south toward Kew Gardens, and then on to Brentford where it joins the Thames.
www.waterscape.com

During weekdays the canals are little frequented, except by occasional, unusually solitary fishermen. Except when a boat chugs by, there is total silence. My favourite of these walks is from Windmill Lane (with a remarkable road, rail, and canal crossing) to Kew Gardens to view Hanwell Locks (six in all) to the vast canopied warehouse of Brentford Dock.

FRANCIS KING
Francis King is the author of twenty-eight novels, a short-story writer, and a poet. His books include Act of Darkness, The Domestic Animal, and Cold Snap.

19.8 # Richmond Park

Kingston Vale SW15
020 8948 3209; www.royalparks.org.uk
⊖ Richmond, then bus No. 65 or No. 71
LO Richmond

Richmond Park seems locked in *A Man for All Seasons* world of English oaks and huge antlered stags. Part formal plantation, part wild heath, it's the best walking territory in London—especially in spring when the rhododendrons are in flower.

WILLIAM DALRYMPLE
William Dalrymple is an award-winning travel writer and historian. His books include From the Holy Mountain *and* Nine Lives: In Search of the Sacred in Modern India.

19.9 # King Henry's Mound

Pembroke Lodge, Richmond Park TW10
020 8948 3209; www.royalparks.org.uk
⊖ Richmond
LO Richmond

This is London's most secret yet most dramatic view. Walk beneath the ancient oak trees and through the gardens of Pembroke Lodge to the top of the Mound. From there, on a clear day, you will see St. Paul's Cathedral, ten miles away, framed by trees as if through a keyhole.

DAME JENNIFER JENKINS
Dame Jennifer Jenkins is President of the Ancient Monuments and formerly Chair of the National Trust, the Consumers Association and the Historic Buildings Council for England.

19

19.10 Richmond Lock and Footbridge

1894
Harbour Services: 020 8940 0634; www.waterscape.com

⊖ Richmond

RAIL St. Margaret's

Every London guidebook recommends Richmond riverside, its magnificent eighteenth-century bridge, and the glorious curve of the Thames under Richmond Hill and through Petersham Meadows. Richmond is also famous for high spring tides which submerge the cars of unsuspecting visitors. Less well-known is the device that preserves this riverscape when the tide ebbs. Walk a few hundred yards downstream from Richmond riverside, under Twickenham Bridge, and you come to a fine late Victorian hydraulic contraption (painted in cream and *eau-de-nil*) which combines four elements: a barge lock, a pedestrian footbridge, a set of rollers for punts and skiffs, and three massive gantries holding sixty-six-foot-wide sluices. On the ebb tide these gates are lowered into place with a splash. They impound a five-foot depth of water. As the tide rises they're hoisted back into their gantry. A fine spectacle, twice daily.

Michael Hebbert
Michael Hebbert is Professor of Town Planning at the University of Manchester and author of London: More by Fortune Than Design *and* Dismantlers.

19.11 Garrick's Temple

1756, architect unknown; 1758, Louis-François Roubiliac, marble statue of William Shakespeare
Situated opposite Garrick's Villa on Hampton Court Road (near its intersection with Thames and Church Streets)
020 8831 6000; www.garrickstemple.org.uk
Garrick's Temple is open on Sundays (2 p.m. to 5 p.m.) from April to

September. The garden is open daily throughout the year.

⊖ Richmond, then R68 bus

TRAIN Hampton Court Station, then R68 bus; or Hampton Station, then 111 or 216 bus

Garrick's Temple to Shakespeare was the first building in the world to have been built in honour of Shakespeare. In the middle of the eighteenth century, actors, authors, and connoisseurs built their villas alongside the Thames, a four or five hours' carriage ride from town. In 1755, David Garrick, Britain's then-greatest actor, built his villa upstream from Hampton Court Palace. In front of the villa, right on the bank of the Thames, Garrick erected this well-preserved but tiny octagonal temple with an Ionic columned portico. It is said to be modelled on an earlier decorative temple in Lord Burlington's gardens at Chiswick. The villa still stands today, now broken up into private flats, yet it and the temple still evoke the coupling of Shakespeare and Garrick, who in the mid-eighteenth century successfully strived to become Shakespeare's representative on earth.

In 1758, Garrick dedicated a life-size portrait of Shakespeare by the sculptor François Roubiliac, one of the artists who at Garrick's behest helped to reinvent Shakespeare as a national hero. The statue here is a facsimile, but it looks much better than the original, which stands on a shelf, shorn of its plinth, in the lobby of the British Library. The temple sits in a carefully re-created eighteenth-century garden, and its interior walls are covered with facsimiles of paintings celebrating Garrick and the Temple, by Zoffany and other artists.

IAIN MACKINTOSH

Iain Mackintosh is a producer, designer of theatre spaces such as Glynde-bourne and the Cottesloe, and curator of fine-arts exhibitions of theatre painting and theatre architecture.

19

19.12 Strawberry Hill House

1747–1792, Horace Walpole
268 Waldegrave Road, Twickenham TW1
Check website for tours, www.friendsofstrawberryhill.org.

⊖ Richmond, then travel either by South West Trains to Strawberry Hill or by No. 33 or R68 bus

RAIL Strawberry Hill Station from Waterloo. Turn left out of the station onto Tower Road, then right onto Waldegrave Gardens. At the end of the road, turn left onto Waldegrave Road.

Strawberry Hill House at Twickenham, a little to the west of London, was the creation of the eccentric antiquarian and man of fashion Horace Walpole (1717–1797). He built it as a rustic Thames-side retreat from his busy Mayfair life, and it took the form of a sham castle with theatrical Gothic interiors. He thereby initiated the movement in architecture known as the Gothic Revival. To go with it he invented the genre of the Gothic novel, by publishing *The Castle of Otranto* in 1764. Yet Walpole was quintessentially a figure of the eighteenth century (his wide-ranging correspondence is considered without contemporary equal), and therefore as medieval fantasies go, Strawberry Hill is deliciously lighthearted. Horace was childless, and over the centuries his pleasure dome fell into dilapidation and was placed on the English Heritage at Risk Register. But in 2002 the Strawberry Hill Trust was established to oversee its restoration.

The house is very near Eel Pie Island, whose hotel had a famous ballroom where the Rolling Stones began their performing career in the early 1960s. The hotel burned down in 1971. Eel Pie Island is privately owned.

DUNCAN FALLOWELL
Duncan Fallowell is an author and cultural commentator. His books include Going As Far As I Can: The Ultimate Travel Book.

INDEXES

INDEX OF CONTRIBUTORS

TIM ADAMS is a staff writer at *The Observer*, where he was formerly Literary Editor. He lives in Highgate, North London, with his wife and two daughters. pp. 71, 96

DAVID ALEXANDER is an author of fiction and nonfiction. He has written and published in virtually every literary category, including novels, novelettes, short stories, poetry, essays, and film scripts, and a miscellany of other forms, some of them unclassifiable. His most recent book is *The Building: A Biography of the Pentagon*. p. 44

BRIAN ALLEN is Director of Studies at the Paul Mellon Centre for Studies in British Art in London and adjunct professor of History of Art at Yale University. He is also a Fellow of the Society of Antiquaries of London. p. 151

MICHAEL ARDITTI is an award-winning novelist, short-story writer, and critic. His novels include *Easter*, *A Sea Change*, and *The Enemy of the Good*. pp. 19, 193

JOHN M. ASHWORTH has been the chairman of the British Library Board, the director of the London School of Economics, and the British government's chief scientist. In 2008 he received a knighthood for public service. pp. 109, 153

DIANA ATHILL was, for almost fifty years, a director for the publishing house Andre Deutsch Ltd., and worked with some of the most important writers of the twentieth century. Her nonfiction books include *Stet*, *Instead of a Letter*, *Yesterday Morning*, and a novel, *Don't Look at Me Like That*. In 2009 Athill's memoir *Somewhere Towards the End* was the winner of the Costa Biography Prize, and she was awarded an OBE. p. 248

P. W. ATKINS was Professor of Chemistry at Oxford University until his retirement in 2007. He is the author of many widely used textbooks, and books on science for the general public. p. 57

PAUL BAGGALEY was a bookseller in London for many years, a director at the Harvill Press where he produced a list of classic London novels, and an editor at Random House and Harper Collins. He is now the publisher of Picador. p. 298

ANDREW BALLANTYNE studied and practised architecture before moving into an academic career. He has written about a wide range of topics in architectural history and theory, and his books include *Architecture: A Very Short Introduction*; *Deleuze and Guattari* for Architects; *Paliochora on Kythera*; and *Tudoresque: Histories of a Popular Architecture*. He is Professor of Architecture at Newcastle University. p. 58

The late J. G. BALLARD was the author of eighteen novels, including *Crash*, *Cocaine Nights*, and *Empire of the Sun*, which was based on his childhood in a Japanese internment camp and later made into a film by Steven Spielberg. p. 240

MICHAEL BARKER writes and lectures on art, architecture, and decorative arts. He is co-author of *The North of France: A Guide to the Art, Architecture and Atmosphere of Artois, Picardy and Flanders*. p. 204

NICOLA BARKER's novels include *Wide Open* (winner of the International IMPAC Dublin Literary Award), *Darkmans* (short-listed for the Man Booker Prize and winner of the Hawthornden Prize), and *Burley Cross Post Box Theft*. In 2005 she was named as one of *Granta* magazine's Best of Young British Novelists, and her work has been translated into over a dozen languages. p. 289

PAUL BARKER writes widely on social, cultural, and architectural issues and is the former editor of the opinion weekly *New Society*. He is a senior research Fellow at the Young Foundation. His latest book is *The Freedoms of Suburbia*. p. 159

ALAN BAXTER is the engineering designer of many new landmark buildings and is involved in the conservation of historic structures in London. p. 136

STEPHEN BAYLEY was responsible for the Design Museum and created the Boilerhouse Project at the V & A. His books include *Woman as Design*, and he is a columnist on *The Times*. He currently runs a small design business in Soho. pp. 12, 216

ANDY BECKETT is a feature writer for *The Guardian* and the author of *When the Lights Went Out: Britain in the Seventies*. He has lived in London since 1994, and has never escaped from the page of the *London A–Z*, which covers Islington and Stoke Newington. pp. 24, 69

JAMES BETTLEY is a freelance architectural historian whose projects include a revised edition of the *Pevsner Architectural Guide to Essex*. He was Head of Collection Development at the National Art Library, Victoria and Albert Museum, 1997–2000, having previously worked at the British Architectural Library of the Royal Institute of British Architects at the Design Museum. p. 202

JOANNA BIGGS is an editor at the *London Review of Books*. p. 263

LEXY BLOOM is a senior editor at Vintage and Anchor Books, imprints of the Knopf Doubleday Publishing Group at Random House, Inc., in New York. pp. 32, 253

ROGER BOWDLER works at English Heritage as head of designation in the Heritage Protection Department. He is the chairman of the Mausolea and Monuments Trust. p. 238

ELENA BOWES is a culture and travel writer based in London. She writes for the Indagare travel website, *Travel & Leisure*, *Town & Country*, and *Budget Travel*, among other publications. p. 206

ELLIOT BOYD, a member of the Royal Institute of British Architects, is an architect practicing in London. p. 20

GABRIELE BRAMANTE is the director of Bramante Architects in London. p. 206

ALAN BROWNJOHN is a poet. He has also published four novels, *The Way You Tell Them*, *The Long Shadows*, *A Funny Old Year*, and *Windows on the Moon*. p. 250

EDWARD BURD, an architect, was for thirty years a partner at Hunt Thompson Associates, where he worked primarily on conservation and social housing projects. He lectured at the Bartlett School of Architecture and was for many years an assessor for the Civic Trust Awards. pp. 39, 280, 289

JAMES CAMPBELL'S books include *Talking at the Gates*, *A Life of James Baldwin*, and *This Is the Beat Generation*. pp. 237, 252, 273

SOPHIE CAMPBELL lectures on travel writing and is a London tour guide. She writes for the *London Daily Telegraph*, *The London Financial Times*, and *Condé Nast Traveller*, among other publications. pp. 192, 174

PETER CARSON was formerly editor-in-chief at Penguin. Now semi-retired, he works as an editor for Profile Books and also translates from the *Russian*. His translations include Chekhov's Plays and *Turgenev's Fathers and Sons*. pp. 61, 146, 211

ADAM CHODZKO is a multimedia artist. p. 109

SUSANNAH CLAPP is theatre critic of *The Observer* and the author of *With Chatwin*, a memoir of Bruce Chatwin. p. 137

BARRY CLAYTON is an architect specialising in the conservation of historic buildings. His expertise in the works of Sir John Soane has led to his involvement in the restoration of the House and Entrance Gateway at Tyringham in Buckinghamshire, and the ongoing major reconstruction of Soane's last major country house, Pell Wall in Shropshire. p. 208

MICHAEL COVENEY is the chief theatre critic of Whatsonstage.com and author of several biographies, including those of Maggie Smith, Mike Leigh, and Andrew Lloyd Webber. pp. 172, 247

JONATHAN COX is a primary school teacher and a former editor and writer for *Time Out City Guides*. pp. 300, 304

WILLIAM DALRYMPLE is an award-winning travel writer and historian. His books include *From the Holy Mountain*, *White Mughals*, and *Nine Lives: In Search of the Sacred in Modern India*. pp. 314, 319

GILLIAN DARLEY is co-author, with Andrew Saint, of *The Chronicles of London*, a historical anthology of London. Her other books include biographies of Sir John Soane, Octavia Hill, and John Evelyn, and *Villages of Vision: A Study of Strange Utopias*. Her most recent book is *My Vesuvius*. pp. 25, 99, 120, 225, 246, 278

ROBYN DAVIDSON has had homes in Sydney, London, and the Indian Himalayas. Her books include *Tracks*, winner of the Thomas Cook Travel Book Award, and *Desert Places*, shortlisted for the same prize. p. 167

Artist SHEZAD DAWOOD has exhibited widely in the UK and internationally, including at the Tate and the Venice Biennale. pp. 162, 228

GILES DE LA MARE was director of Faber & Faber from 1969 to 1998, and is now the chairman of Giles de la Mare Publishers, founded in 1995. p. 100

ELLEN MARA DE WACHTER is a writer and curator based in London. Since 2007, she has been the exhibitions curator at 176 Zabludowicz Collection, the project space for a major international collection of contemporary and emerging art. She edits and contributes to exhibition catalogs and to various international art publications. p. 182

AMBER DOWELL is an editor at Granta Books. p. 177

LESLEY DOWNER's most recent books are works of fiction: *The Courtesan and the Samurai* and *The Last Concubine*. Her nonfiction books include *Geisha: The Secret History of a Vanishing World*. She writes on occasion for *The Sunday Times Magazine* and *The Financial Times*. p. 151

BRUCE DUCKER is the author of nine books, including the novels *Lead Us Not into Penn Station*, *Dizzying Heights*, which was short-listed for the James Thurber Award, and God's Heel Basin. p. 27

JAMES DUNNETT, an architect and lecturer, translated Le Corbusier's *The Decorative Art of Today* in 1987. pp. 196, 210

JOE DUNTHORNE was born in Swansea in 1982. He is the author of a poetry pamphlet, *Faber New Poets 5*, and a novel, *Submarine*, which won the Curtis Brown Prize and is being made into a film by Warp Films. He currently lives in London and is a striker for the England Writers' Football Team. p. 166

TOM DYCKHOFF is architecture critic of *The Times*, architecture and design critic for BBC2's weekly arts magazine programme, *The Culture Show* and writes a weekly column for *The Guardian's Weekend Magazine*. His recent seven-part BBC2 series, *Saving Britain's Past*, examined Britain's obsession with heritage. pp. 171, 305, 307

ROBERT DYE RIBA is an architect who has worked with Sir James Stirling and Fred Koetter. p. 145

GEOFFREY ELBORN, a biographer and critic, has written about the lives of Edith Sitwell and Francis Stuart. He is currently writing about Patricia Highsmith. pp. 78, 261, 264

TRAVIS ELBOROUGH is the author of *The Bus We Loved: London's Affair with the Routemaster*; *The Vinyl Countdown: The Album from LP to iPod and Back Again*; and *Wish You Were Here: England on Sea*. pp. 69, 131

PAUL ELLIMAN is an artist and designer based in London and Detroit. He is a visiting critic at Yale University School of Art, and has exhibited at the Tate Modern in London and the New Museum in New York, among other places. pp. 143, 144

A native of London, ROBERT ELMS is a broadcaster whose daily show on the BBC is a passionate song of praise for the city he loves. He is also the *GQ* travel editor, a journalist who has written for many major newspapers and magazines, and the author of three books. p. 158

SEB EMINA, as Malcolm Eggs, edits *The London Review of Breakfasts*, the world's premier repository of overblown literary breakfast reviews. p. 224

STUART EVERS, a former bookseller, writes about books for *The Guardian* and *The Independent*, among other publications. His first book of fiction is *Ten Stories About Smoking*. p. 290

DUNCAN FALLOWELL, born in London in 1948, is an author and cultural commentator. His books include *Going As Far As I Can: The Ultimate Travel Book*. He is currently making a series of short art films. pp. 35, 40, 96, 242, 322

MICHELE FIELD is a writer on food issues and on the materials environment. pp. 75, 76

OPHELIA FIELD is a biographer, a journalist, and a policy analyst in the field of refugees and human rights. She is the author of *The Favourite: Sarah, Duchess of Marlborough* and *The Kit-Cat Club*. p. 76

MARY FLANAGAN, an American writer and critic living in London, is the author of three novels (*Trust*, *Rose Reason*, and *Adèle*) and two collections of short stories (*Bad Girls* and *The Blue Woman*). p. 185

LESLIE FORBES is a broadcaster and writer whose novels include *Fish, Blood & Bone*, a mystery set in London and Tibet, and *Waking Raphael*, set in Urbino, Italy. p. 169

DAN FOX is senior editor of *Frieze* magazine, and is based in New York. He is also a writer, filmmaker, and musician. pp. 66, 165, 190

SIR CHRISTOPHER FRAYLING was until recently Rector of the Royal College of Art and Chair of Arts Council England. An historian, critic, and award-winning broadcaster, he has written seventeen books on aspects of cultural history—the latest being *Horace Walpole's Cat* and *Ken Adam: The Art of Production Design*. p. 170

PHILIP FRENCH is *The Observer*'s film critic, author of Westerns, and co-editor of *The Faber Book of Movie Verse*. He was named Critic of the Year in the 2009 National Press Awards. p. 74

SEAN FRENCH and NICCI GERRARD, both journalists, write thrillers together, including *Killing Me Softly*, *The Safe House*, and *Complicit*. p. 279

JAY ANTHONY GACH is a composer of concert music and music for the media. He is a recipient of the Rome prize in Music from the American Academy in Rome and a Fellow of the London College of Music. p. 260

JEREMY GARFIELD-DAVIES is an architectural and art historian. A former director of Mallett in London and New York, he advises privately on the research, restoration, and acquisition of works of art for some of the most important private and public collections worldwide. He is also currently co-writing the seminal book on the history of English gilt wood furniture. pp. 34, 38

CHRISTOPHER GEELAN is an artistic director of the Young Shakespeare Company. p. 278

NICCI GERRARD and SEAN FRENCH, both journalists, write thrillers together, including *Killing Me Softly*, *The Safe House*, and *Complicit*. p. 279

KENNETH SEEMAN GINIGER is a book publisher, editor, and anthologist living in New York City. p. 59

JANINE DI GIOVANNI has written four books, including *Madness Visible: A Memoir of War*, and has won numerous prizes for her reporting from war zones, including two Amnesty International awards, the National Magazine Award, and Foreign Correspondent of the Year. She acts as a consultant for the United Nations and currently lives in Paris, where she is working on a book about war reporting and motherhood. pp. 239, 242

CHRISSIE GITTINS is a poet, playwright, and short-story writer. p. 308

VICTORIA GLENDINNING is a prize-winning biographer and journalist. Her books include lives of Vita Sackville-West, Trollope, and Jonathan Swift, the novel *Electricity*, and *Love's Civil War*, a collection of diary entries and letters between Elizabeth Bowen and Charles Ritchie. pp. 73, 98

CAROLINE GOODSON is an archaeologist and historian. pp. 93, 149

HELEN GORDON is a journalist, editor, and the author of *Landfall*. She was formerly an associate editor at *Granta* magazine. She lives in East London. pp. 118, 236

SARAH GORDON is an artistic director of the Young Shakespeare Company. p. 278

Sculptor ANTONY GORMLEY'S work has been exhibited worldwide. He was awarded the Turner Prize in 1994 and made Officer of the British Empire in 1997. His large-scale installations include *Angel of the North* (Gateshead) and *Another Place* (Liverpool). p. 115

ROMESH GUNESEKERA was born in Sri Lanka and now lives in London. His first novel, *Reef*, was shortlisted for the Booker Prize and was awarded a Premio Mondello Prize in Italy. His other books include *Heaven's Edge* and *The Match*. He is a Fellow of the Royal Society of Literature. pp. 241, 295, 318

DAVID HARE is a playwright and screenwriter. His twenty-seven plays include *Plenty*, *Skylight*, *Via Dolorosa*, and *Stuff Happens*. p. 271

RONALD HAYMAN'S books include biographies of Nietzsche, Kafka, Sartre, Proust, Thomas

Mann, Jung, and the Marquis de Sade. pp. 271, 274

EDWIN HEATHCOTE is an architect, writer, and designer living and working in London. He is the architecture and design critic of *The Financial Times*, co-founder of the door-handle manufacturer Izé, and the author of over a dozen books. pp. 71, 141

MICHAEL HEBBERT is Professor of Town Planning at the University of Manchester and author of *London: More by Fortune than Design and Dismantlers*. pp. 293, 320

ANGELA HEDERMAN is editor and publisher at The Little Bookroom in New York. p. 84

DAVE HILL is the London *Guardian*'s London blogger and commenter. He was named the *UK Press Gazette*'s Digital Journalist of the Year in 2009. p. 186

PHILIP HOARE lives in London and Southampton. His books include biographies of Stephen Tennant and Noël Coward; *Wilde's Last Stand*; *Spike Island*; and *England's Lost Eden*. In 2009 his book *Leviathan, or The Whale* won the BBC Samuel Johnson prize for nonfiction. pp. 128, 168, 216

PHIL HOGAN is a novelist and a staff writer at *The Observer*. p. 17

PETER J. HOLLIDAY is Professor of Art and Classical Archaeology at California State University in Long Beach. He lived in London when he was a graduate student and is now a frequent visitor. pp. 121, 233

PETER HORROCKS, a barrister, is a freeman of the City of London. He is a former chairman of the Sherlock Holmes Society of London, runs the Covent Garden Minuet Company, an eighteenth century dance group, is a Fellow of the Royal Asiatic Society, and is a player of real tennis. pp. 37, 38, 41, 58, 90

PETER HOWARD, an architect, is co-author of guides to the architecture of Oxford and Cambridge. p. 83, 224

The late DAVID HUGHES was an award-wining crime writer. He published eleven novels, among them *The Pork Butcher* and *The Little Book* as well as the author of many books of nonfiction. He was a Fellow of the Royal Society of Literature. p. 98

LUCY HUGHES-HALLETT the award–winning author and critic. She has written widely on literature, art and theatre, winning the Catherine Pakenham Award for journalism and the Fawcett Prize for her book on Cleopatra. She is the author of *Heroes: Saviours, Traitors and Supermen,* and *Cleopatra*. pp. 16, 222, 246

JOHANNA HURWITZ is the award-winning author of seventy popular children's books. She lectures to students, teachers, parents, and librarians from Mississippi to Mozambique. p. 87

SIR NICHOLAS HYTNER is a film and theater producer and director. He has been the artistic director of London's National Theatre since 2003. p. 44

PICO IYER is a longtime essayist for *Time* magazine and the author of nine books, including *Video Night in Kathmandu*, *The Lady and the Monk*, *The Global Soul* and *The Open Road*. p. 214

IAN JACK edited *Granta* from 1995 to 2007. Previously, he helped to found and later edited *The Independent* on Sunday. He writes regularly for *The Guardian*, and lives with his family in Highbury, North London. p. 197

BERNARD JACOBSON has had a gallery in London for more than forty years, initially publishing prints and subsequently dealing in modern and contemporary British, American, and European art. p. 279

DAME JENNIFER JENKINS is president of the Ancient Monuments and formerly Chair of the National Trust, the Consumers Association, and the Historic Buildings Council for England. pp. 62, 319

ROBERT KAHN, the creator and series editor of City Secrets, is an architect in private practice in New York. p. 56

IAN KELLY is an actor and writer. His publications include *Shakespeare Cinema*. pp. 150, 277

FRANCIS KING is the author of twenty-eight novels, a short-story writer, and a poet. A President Emeritus of International PEN and a Fellow of the Royal Society of Literature, he is a recipient of the honour Commander of the British Empire. His books include *Act of Darkness*, *The Domestic Animal*, and *Cold Snap*, and *The Dividing Stream*, winner of the Somerset Maugham Prize. pp. 233, 318

PHILLIP KNIGHTLEY is an author and a journalist whose books include *Australia: A Biography of a Nation*. He has lived in Notting Hill for forty-five years. p. 241

ZACHARY LEADER is a Professor of English Literature at the University of Surrey Roehampton and the author and editor of books on Romantic poetry and twentieth-century British fiction, including *The Life of Kingsley Amis*. Though an American, he has lived in London for more than forty years. p. 226

JANE LEAR, a food and travel writer based in New York City, is the former senior articles editor at *Gourmet* magazine. A contributor to *The Gourmet Cookbook: More than 1000 Recipes* and *Gourmet Today: More than 1000 All-New Recipes for the Contemporary Kitchen*, she also co-wrote (with chef Floyd Cardoz) *One Spice, Two Spice: American Food, Indian Flavors*. pp. 26, 135, 218

London-born SUMMER LITCHFIELD, formerly arts editor of *UK Esquire*, is a freelance journalist writing for the *Telegraph*, the *Sunday Times*, and other publications. She writes extensively about restaurant culture and is working on her first novel. p. 212

PENELOPE LIVELY is a novelist and short-story writer. She was born and grew up in Egypt and now lives in London. p. 260

ROBERT LIVESEY is an architect and a professor at the Knowlton School of Architecture at Ohio State University. pp. 43, 123, 159, 195, 247, 285

MARIO VARGAS LLOSA, the Peruvian writer and politician, is author of *The Time of the Hero*, *The Green House*, *Conversation in the Cathedral*, *The War of the End of the World*, and *The Bad Girl*, among other novels. He is also the author of noteworthy criticism. In 1990 Vargas Llosa ran for the Peruvian presidency. In 2010, he received the Nobel Prize in literature. p. 110

FELICITY LUNN is a curator and critic. She was curator at the Whitechapel Art Gallery from 1990 to 1998, and director of Germany's Kunstverein Freiburg from 2005 to 2008. She has taught at numerous art schools and universities, has written regularly for *Artforum International* and *Frieze*, and has curated exhibitions in the U.K., Switzerland, the Netherlands, France, and Austria. pp. 263, 281

FIONA MACCARTHY is a cultural historian and author of biographies of Eric Gill and William Morris. pp. 20, 48, 209, 270

SHENA MACKAY is a Fellow of the Royal Society of Literature. Her books include *Dunedin*, the Booker-shortlisted *The Orchard on Fire*, and *The Atmospheric Railway: New and Collected Stories*, the title story of which is about the railway that existed briefly in Crystal Palace Park. p. 302

IAIN MACKINTOSH's lifetime in the theatre has encompassed work as a producer, as the designer of theatre spaces such as Glyndebourne and the Cottesloe, and as the curator of fine-arts exhibitions of theatre painting and theatre architecture at venues including the Royal Academy and the Hayward Gallery London. He is the author of *Architecture, Actor and Audience*, and has written articles and given lectures at conferences and universities around the world. pp. 313, 320

ANGUS MACQUEEN's documentary work includes *The Death of Yugoslavia*, which won a British Acadamy Award, and *Dancing for Dollars*, which received an Emmy. pp. 203, 293

IMOGEN MAGNUS has worked as a theatre designer and costume designer for films and television. She now writes on historic gardens and teaches. p. 128

PATRICK MARBER is a writer. His plays and screenplays include *Dealer's Choice*, *Closer*, *Notes on a Scandal*, and *Don Juan in Soho*. p. 148

CHARLES MARSDEN-SMEDLEY's design practice specialises in museum and exhibition design. pp. 207, 255

ROBERT MARX has served as the director of the theater program at the National Endowment for the Arts and the New York State Council on the Arts, and was executive director of the New York Public Library for the Performing Arts at Lincoln Center. He is an essayist on theater and opera, has produced Off-Broadway plays, and is the voice frequently heard on the intermission features of the

Metropolitan Opera's radio broadcasts. pp. 21, 60, 91, 134, 205

BRIAN MASTERS writes about crime and art. His books include *Killing for Company*, which won the Gold Dagger Prize for nonfiction in 1985, and an autobiography, *Getting Personal*. He is also an authority on gorillas and dukes. pp. 40, 100

CAROL MCDAID is an editor and journalist for *The Observer*. p. 52

As a freelance journalist, MELANIE MCFADYEAN writes for numerous publications, including *The Guardian*, *The Independent*, *Granta*, and the *London Review of Books*, and has worked on TV and radio documentaries. She is also a part-time lecturer in the journalism department at City University, London. p. 292

ANDREW MEAD is a freelance journalist, writing on architecture, art, and landscape for a number of magazines. p. 283

JONATHAN MEADES has written and performed in some fifty polemical essays for BBC TV including the series *Off Kilter*. He is the author of seven books, among them *Pompey* and *The Fowler Family Business*. He is currently working on a memoir entitled *An Encyclopaedia of Myself*. p. 301

ROGER MICHELL is a film and theatre director of, among others, *Persuasion* and *Notting Hill*. p. 276

DAVID MILES is the chief archaeologist of English Heritage. p. 36

MATTHEW MILTON, a folk singer, free-improvisation violinist, music journalist, and editor, has lived in south London all his life. He has recorded albums for record labels such as Another Timbre, Matchless, and Creative Sources. pp. 184, 251

DAVID MLINARIC, now retired, was a partner at Mlinaric, Henry, and Zervudachi, an interior design and decoration company. He has worked on various museums and heritage sights in London and abroad, including the National Gallery, the Royal Opera House, and several British embassies, as well as on many private houses and flats around the world. pp. 55, 124

DEBORAH MOGGACH is a writer of screenplays and novels, including *These Foolish Things* and *Tulip Fever*. p. 146

WENDY MOONAN covers architecture, fine arts, and the decorative arts for *Veranda* and *Elle Decor*, as well as for several websites, including 1stdibs.com and VandM.com. She wrote a weekly antiques column for *The New York Times* for fourteen years. p. 92

ROWAN MOORE is architecture critic of *The London Observer*. He was editor of the architecture magazine *Blueprint* and founding partner of Zombory- Moldovan Moore Architects. Publications include *Vertigo*, *The Strange New World of the Contemporary City*, and *Building Tate Modern*. p. 187

FIDELIS MORGAN, writer and actor, is the author of a mystery series set in London in 1699 and featuring the Countess Ashby de la Zouche and her erstwhile maid, Alpiew. She has written books on seventeenth- and eighteenth-century English theatre history, and is also a playwright. pp. 67, 226

CAROLE MORIN has been writer-in-residence at Wormwood Scrubs prison and Literary Fellow at the University of East Anglia. Her books include *Lampshades*, *Dead Glamorous,* and *Penniless in Park Lane*. pp. 55, 60

NICHOLAS MOSLEY, novelist and biographer, won the Whitbread Book of the Year Award in 1990 for Hopeful Monsters. p. 282

PETER MURRAY, Hon FRIBA Chairman of Wordsearch, is also Chairman of the New London Architecture centre (NLA), and Director of the London Festival of Architecture. He is the author of

Architecture and Commerce: New Office Design in London and *The Saga of Sydney Opera House*. He is honorary secretary of the Bedford Park Society and founder-chairman of the Cycle to Cannes charity. p. 312

JEREMY MUSSON is an architectural historian, former architectural editor of *Country Life*, and presenter of BBC2's *The Curious House Guest*. He was born in London in 1965 and as a child lived on Abbey Road, made famous by the Beatles. pp. 33, 142, 170

RICHARD NOBLE lives in London. He writes about political philosophy from the eighteenth century to the present and the contemporary visual arts. p. 119

JOHN NOI is the editor of *Spektacle*, a magazine of fashion, music, and design. He also writes regularly for *Whitaker's Almanac*. p. 163

PHILIP OLTERMANN was born in Schleswig-Holstein, Germany. Since 1997 he has lived in London, where he works as an editor at *The Guardian*. He is writing a book on Anglo-German meetings. p. 161

AL ORENSANZ is a sociologist and semiologist, and the director of the Angel Orensanz Foundation, New York. pp. 49, 238

NADINE ORENSTEIN is curator in charge of Dutch, Flemish, and German Old Master prints in the Metropolitan Museum of Art, New York. pp. 41, 83

MAUREEN PALEY has had a gallery in East London for twenty-six years, dealing in contemporary British, American, and European art, and representing artists including the Turner Prize winners Wolfgang Tillmans and Gillian Wearing. p. 178

CORNELIA PARKER, artist, is known for a number of large installations including *Cold Dark Matter: An Exploded View*, where she suspended the fragments of a garden shed, blown up for her by the British Army, which was exhibited at the Tate Modern. Shortlisted for the 1997 Turner Prize, she has had major solo exhibitions in London, Paris, New York, Boston, Chicago, and Philadelphia. pp. 165, 168

RUTH PAVEY has lived and worked in London for twenty-five years, teaching art and English to inner-city children. She writes for national publications on contemporary fiction, crafts, and horticulture. She is the gardening correspondent for *Ham & High*. pp. 95, 116, 117, 281

CLAYRE PERCY is editor, together with her daughter, Jane Ridley, of *The Letters of Edwin Lutyens to His*

Wife, Lady Emily, and *The Letters of Arthur Balfour and Lady Elcho*. p. 16

ELIZABETH PISANI started life as a journalist with the Reuters news agency, when they were still based on London's iconic Fleet Street. She worked as a foreign correspondent in Asia for several years before happening upon epidemiology and becoming an authority on HIV prevention. Her book *The Wisdom of Whores: Bureaucrats, Brothels, and the Business of AIDS* was published by Granta. p. 140

PIERS PLOWRIGHT, who retired from BBC Radio in 1997 after thirty years as a producer, is a winner of several Prix Italia for radio documentary and of several Sony awards. He is a Fellow of the Royal Society of Literature. pp. 153, 212, 289

PETER PORTER, an Australian-born poet, won the Whitbread Prize in 1987. p. 82

ANNE PURCHAS is an architectural historian and a freelance lecturer and writer on architectural and garden history. pp. 222, 235

THEODORE K. RABB is Emeritus Professor of History at Princeton, and contributes to *The Art Newspaper*. pp. 34, 82

MICHAEL RATCLIFFE was literary editor and chief book reviewer of *The Times*, and theatre critic of *The Observer*. He has written on travel for *The New York Times* and contributes to *The Oxford Dictionary of National Biography*. pp. 14, 132

MARGARET RICHARDSON was the curator of Sir John Soane's Museum from 1995 to 2005. She is now a Council member of the National Trust, the Society of Antiquaries, and the Hon. Curator of Architecture at the Royal Academy. p. 72

SOPHIE ROCHESTER is the founder of the Literary Platform, a website dedicated to showcasing projects experimenting with literature and technology. p. 181

JUDE ROGERS writes for *The Guardian*, *The Times*, and the *New Statesman*, and is the co-founder of the quarterly magazine *Smoke: A London Peculiar*. p. 196

The late ALAN ROSS was editor of the *London Magazine* and author of memoirs, poems, travel books, and biographies. p. 254

GLEN ROVEN, four-time Emmy winner, has performed with orchestras around the world. He lives in New York City. pp. 23, 173

FRANK SALMON is head of the department of History of Art at the University of Cambridge and a Fellow of St. John's College, Cambridge. p. 191

ANN SAUNDERS worked on the restoration of Lambeth Palace

Library after the war. Her books include *Regent's Park*, *Art and Architecture of London*, and *St. Paul's Cathedral*. She is honorary editor to the London Topographical Society and, having retired from her position of editor after forty-one years, is now Editor Emeritus to the Costume Society. p. 288

JON SAVAGE is a historian of popular culture. His books include England's *Dreaming: Sex Pistols and Punk Rock*; *Time Travel: from the Sex Pistols to Nirvana*; *Teenage: The Creation of Youth 1875–1945*; and *The England's Dreaming Tape*. p. 315

MIRANDA SAWYER is a journalist and broadcaster. She is the author of *Park and Ride*, a personal history of suburbia. p. 79

MARJORIE M. SCARDINO is chief executive of Pearson PLC, owners of Pearson Education, the Financial Times Group, and the Penguin Group. pp. 56, 211

ERIC SCHLOSSER is an investigative reporter, the author of *Fast Food Nation*, an executive producer of the films *Fast Food Nation* and *There Will Be Blood*, co-producer of the documentary *Food, Inc.*, and a playwright whose work has been performed at the Arcola Theatre and Shakespeare's Globe. p. 288

MIRANDA SEYMOUR is a biographer, novelist, and critic. pp. 210, 312

SUSAN SILBERBERG-PIERCE is a classical art historian and photographer of ancient sites. p. 122

CLIVE SINCLAIR, born in London, is the author of novels including *Blood Libels* and *Cosmetic Effects*. He is a winner of the Somerset Maugham Award and the PEN MacMillan Silver Pen. pp. 136, 232

MARK SLADEN is a curator and writer based in London. p. 70

JOHN SLYCE writes on contemporary art and culture. pp. 130, 183

CHARLES SAUMAREZ SMITH is secretary/chief executive of the Royal Academy of Arts and lives in Stepney. pp. 60, 195

NEIL SPENCER is a journalist and scriptwriter, writing mainly for *The Observer*. He is the co-writer of *Bollywood Queen*, "London's first musical masala." p. 106

HANNAH STARKEY is a photographer whose work has been exhibited at London's Victoria & Albert Museum, the Tate Modern, the Seattle Art Museum, and the Centraal Museum, Utrecht. A book of her work, *Hannah Starkey Monograph 1997–2007*, was published by Steidl. p. 176

RALPH STEADMAN is a cartoonist, illustrator, printmaker, and writer. He has illustrated such classics as *Alice in Wonderland* and created prints on writers from William Shakespeare to William Burroughs. In addition, he has written books on Sigmund Freud and Leonardo da Vinci, and collaborated with Hunter S. Thompson on *Fear and Loathing in Las Vegas*. p. 235

LUCRETIA STEWART is the author of *Tiger Bam: Travels in Laos, Vietnam and Cambodia*; *The Weather Prophet: A Caribbean Journey*; and *Making Love: A Romance*. She is the editor of *Erogenous Zones: An Anthology of Sex Abroad*. pp. 125, 264

LADY STIRLING is a furniture and interior designer. She is the widow of architect Sir James Stirling. pp. 17, 89, 96, 122, 130, 144

SUSAN SWAN, a novelist, has had her fiction published in ten countries. Her books include *What Casanova Told Me* and *The Wives of Bath*. The film *Lost and Delirious*, based on this novel, premiered at Sundance. p. 88

A. A. TAIT, a professor of art history at the University of Glasgow, is the author of two books on Robert Adam, the architect, and on landscape architecture. A trustee of several museums and institutions, he lives in Scotland and London. p. 97

EMMA TENNANT was born in London and grew up in the borders of Scotland. Her novels include *Sylvia and Ted* and *The Beautiful Child*. She is a Fellow of the Royal Society of Literature. p. 233

SIMON THURLEY is chief executive of English Heritage and was formerly director of the Museum of London. He is an authority on sixteenth- and seventeenth-century English architecture. pp. 43, 160

EVA TUCKER'S novels include *Berlin Mosaic* and *Becoming English*. She writes for radio and various magazines and newspapers, and is a Fellow of the Royal Society of Literature. p. 249

ERICA WAGNER was born in New York and lives in London where she is Literary Editor of *The Times*. Her books are *Gravity*; *Ariel's Gift: Ted Hughes, Sylvia Plath and the Story of the Birthday Letters*, and *Seizure*. p. 146

MARINA WARNER is a writer of fiction and cultural history, a curator, and an art critic. Her books include *From the Beast to the Blonde* and *Phantasmagoria: Spirit Visions, Metaphors, and Media*. She teaches Literature and Creative Writing at the University of Essex. pp. 116, 273

JOHN WILTON-ELY, an art historian, is a Fellow of the Society of Antiquaries and the Royal Society of Arts. He is the author of *Piranesi as Architect and Designer*. pp. 300, 317

CECILIA WONG, formerly of Cecilia Wong Designs, Los Angeles, is an interior designer and art historian. p. 223

GABY WOOD is a journalist and critic. Her books include *Living Dolls: A History of the Quest for Mechanical Life*. pp. 22, 53

ROGER WOODLEY is the author of the *London Blue Guide*. p. 152

KAREN WRIGHT is the editor of *Modern Painters* and co-editor of the *Penguin Book of Art Writing*. pp. 19, 173

NICK WYKE is a journalist at *The Times* and has recently devised a foodies' walking tour of Belgravia in London. pp. 22, 48, 213

EVIE WYLD's first novel, *After the Fire, a Still Small Voice*, won the John Llewellyn Rhys Prize in 2009. She lives and works in south London. p. 298

Robert Kahn, creator and editor of the City Secrets series, is principal and founder of Robert Kahn Architect in New York City. A recipient of the Rome Prize in Architecture from the American Academy in Rome, Kahn has received numerous awards from the New York chapter of the American Institute of Architects (AIA). His work has been featured in *Architectural Digest*, *House & Garden*, *Metropolitan Home*, *The New York Times Magazine*, and *The New York Times*, among other publications. He has taught design at Columbia University, Ohio State University, and Yale University, where he held a Davenport Chair Professorship.

Tim Adams, editor of *City Secrets London*, is a staff writer at *The Observer*, where he was formerly Literary Editor. He lives in Highgate, North London, with his wife and two daughters.

A portion of the proceeds will be donated to Sir John Soane's Museum, the Whitechapel Art Gallery, and the Museum of London.

Sir John Soane's Museum was created as a residence by the architect Sir John Soane at No. 13 Lincoln's Inn Fields and has been a public museum since 1837. It survives as an integral whole, its interiors restored and its works of art displayed in the same authentic arrangements as they were in Soane's day. Many of its works of art, like the Hogarths, the Canalettos, and the Turners, are of great preeminence—as are its architectural collections of books and drawings by the leading architects of the seventeenth and eighteenth centuries. The Museum also holds changing exhibitions in its Soane Gallery. However, it still has the reputation of being a well-kept secret, with the majority of its visitors hearing about it by personal recommendation. It is still, as Henry James described it in 1889, "one of the most curious things in London . . . illustrating the prudent virtue of keeping." For more information, please visit www.soane.org.

The WHITECHAPEL ART GALLERY was founded in 1910 with the aim of bringing art to the people of East London. Now an internationally renowned independent gallery, the Whitechapel shows contemporary and modern art, by both well-known and local artists. For more information, please visit www.whitechapelgallery.org.

The MUSEUM OF LONDON is the world's largest urban history museum and tells the story of London's archaeology, history, and contemporary culture from earliest times to the present day. It maintains an active special exhibition programme as well as permanent galleries recording and documenting London's past. For more information, please visit www.museumoflondon.org.

A

Abbey Road Studios 253
Abbott, Ernest H. 76
Abernethy House 273
Abney Park Cemetery 289
Absolute Vintage 163
Ackroyd, Peter 129
Adam, James 97, 98
    Osterly Park 317
Adam, Robert 98
    The Adelphi 97
    Osterly Park 317
    Royal Society of the Arts 97
Adams, John 317
Adams, Maurice 313
Adelphi, The 97
A. Gold 160
Air Street 71
Aitchison, George 233, 234
Albert, Prince 314
    Memorial 225, 226
Albert Bridge 211, 218
Albion 179
Aldgate East Underground Design 55
Alexandra Palace (Ally Pally) 294, 295
Ali Bongo 132
Alma-Tadema, Lawrence 234
Amies, Hardy 213
Anderson, Lindsay 303
Andrew Edmunds 70
Andrewes, Lancelot, grave of 27
Andy's Guitars 66
Angel, The 261
Angel Pub 190
Apollinaire, Guillaume 112
Apsley House 227
Archway Tavern 265
Arcola Theatre 288
Ardizzone, Edward 15
Arnold, Benedict, home of 60
Arnold Circus bandstand 165
Arnos Grove Station 192
    Underground Design 55
Artisan Foods 26
Ashbee, C.R. 171

Ashcroft, Peggy 21, 172
Athenaeum Club 40
Atomica 179
Auerbach, Frank 249
Austin Reed Barber Shop 58
Avenue Restaurant and Bar 40
Ayrton, Michael 148

B

Bach, Johann Christian 108
Back to Basics 76
Baird, John Logie 71, 304
Baker Street Underground Design 55
Balfron Tower 196
Balla, Giacomo 264
Bank of England Museum 146
Bankside 22–25
    Open Spaces Trust 25
Banqueting House 43
Barbican Centre 153
Bar Italia 71
Barker, Robert 68
Barlow, William
    The Barlow Shed 106
Barnum, P.T. 88
Barry, Sir Charles 36
Bates, Martin Van Buren 88
Battersea Park 217
    Peace Pagoda 211, 217
Bat Walks
    Hampstead Heath 281
    Waterlow Park, Highgate 282
Baylis, Lilian 21
BBC Television
    Broadcasting House 73
    White City 240
Beatles 109
    Abbey Road Studios 253
    "Mad Day Out" 108
    Magical Mystery Tour 173
Beatles Coffee Shop 255
Beauvoir, Simone de 112
Beazley, Samuel 91
Beckford, William, birthplace of 68
Beckton gasworks 197

Bedford Park 312
Belgravia 212–219
Belsize Park Walk 250
Bennett, Arnold 137
Bentley, Sir John Francis
    St. Francis of Assisi 238
    Westminster Cathedral 49
Bermondsey 26–28, 190
    Early Morning in 27
    Market (New Caledonian) 27
Berry Bros. & Rudd 38
Betjeman, John 172, 312
Beyond Retro 163
Big Ben equestrian statues 36
Bird-watching
    Hampstead Heath 281
    Lee Valley Regional Park 292
    St. James's Park Lake 42
Black Friar Pub 141
Blackheath 307
Blackheath Park 308
Blake, William 33
    tomb of 128, 129
Blondie 163
Bloomsbury 106–124
Bloomsbury Cinema 118
Blue Bridge 42
Boadiccea, Queen, Statue 36
Boating, Ferries
    Cruise from Little Venice to
        Camden Market 255
    Crystal Palace Park 303
    Gunnersbury Park Museum 315
    Hollow Ponds 290
    Regent's Park 246
    River Running 26
    Tate Boat 22
    Thames Clippers 26
    A Trip Downriver 197
Boehm, Sir Joseph 234
Bond Street Couture Walk 53
Booth, William, tomb of 289, 290
Borough Market 26
Boucher, François 61, 62
Boundary Estate 165

Bowie, David 66
Bradley, Simon 146
Bradley's 79
Brailsford, H.N. 250
Brawne, Fanny, home of 275
Brentford Dock 318
Brew House Café 278, 279
Brick Lane
    Fashion Walk 163
    Market 163, 166, 185
Brick Lane Beigel Bake 165
Bridgemen, Charles 223
Bridgewater House 35
Brilliant, Fredda
    Gandhi Memorial 115
British Library 106, 109–115
    Reading Room 110, 122
    Shakespeare Statue (Roubiliac) 321
British Museum 84, 121
    Asian Art Collection 122
    Great Court 122
    Lindow Man 84
    Mexican and Pre-Columbian Art
        Gallery 122
    Mildenhall Treasure 84
    Reading Room (restored) 110, 122
    Temple of Artemis at Ephesus 121
British Treasury Building
    Cabinet War Rooms 45
Brixton's Covered Market 185
Broadway Bookshop 178
Broadway Market 177
Brockwell Park Lido 300
Brontë sisters, portraits of 86
Broughton, James 303
Brown, Charles 274, 275
Browns 53
Brummell, Beau 53
Brunel, Isambard Kingdom, grave of
    238
Brunel, Sir Marc 192
Brunel Museum Thames Tunnel 191
Brunswick Centre 118
Buchan, John 74
Bunhill Fields 128, 289

Bunyan, John, tomb of 128, 129
Burlington, Lord 57, 224, 313
Burlington Arcade 54
Burton, Decimus
  Constitution Arch 227
Burton, Robert 96
Bus No. 11, 168
Butler's Wharf 28, 190
Byron, George Gordon, Lord
  birthplace of 52
  portrait of 86

C

Cabinet War Rooms 44, 45
  Cabinet Room 46
  Chiefs of Staff Conference Rooms
    46
Cachao 248
Cadogan Hotel 205
Cadogan Square 206
Café Grove 239
Café Kick 132
Café Oto 184
Callcott, Frederick 142
Callow, Simon 172
Camden Lock 194
Camden Market
  Cruise from Little Venice to 256
Camden Passage Antiques Market 260
Camden Town 74
Camisards 129
Campbell, Colen 223
Canada Water Station Underground
    Outing 191
Canaletto 300
Canary Wharf
  Romantic Evening 162
  Station 48, 55
Canonbury Square 263
Caravaggio
  The Supper at Emmaus, 82, 85
Caravan 179
Carlyle, Thomas, home of 210
Carnevale 128
Cash X Change 265

Cat and Mutton, The 177
Cecil Sharp House 251
  Vaughan Williams Memorial
    Library 251
Cemeteries and Tombs
  Abney Park 289
  Bunhill Fields 128
  Giro's Grave (dog) 41
  Highgate 282, 283
  Hyde Park (dog) 41
  Kensal Green 238
  Nunhead 298
  St. John-at-Hampstead 270, 272
  St. Pancras Old Church 106, 107
  Southward Cathedral 27
Champagne Charlie 172
Changing of the Guard 224
Chapel Market 260
Charbonnel et Walker 53
Charles, Prince of Wales 56
Charles I 14, 16
  Statue (Le Sueur) 37, 90
Charlotte Street Hotel 77
Chatterton, Thomas 108
Chelsea 205–212
Chelsea Embankment 218
Chelsea Old Church 210
Chelsea Old Town Hall 235
Chelsea Physic Garden 209, 210
Chelsea Royal Hospital 207, 209
Chester, Eliza 276
Child, Francis and Robert 317
Children
  Blackheath (donkey rides, kites)
    307
  church bells song 93
  Coram's Fields (animals,
    playground) 119
  Crystal Palace Park (dinosaurs,
    playground, zoo) 302
  Finsbury (playground) 134
  Golders Hill Park (entertainment,
    playground) 281
  Hackney City Farm 178
  International Magic 131

Museum Trails 84
V & A Museum of Childhood 170
Chirico, Giorgio de 264
Chiswick House 313, 321
C. Hoare and Co. 100
Christ Church, Spitalfields 159
Christie's 204
Christmas, Oxford Street 52
Churches
    bells of 93
    Christ Church, Spitalfields 159
    Churches of London Walk 146
    Church Our Most Holy Redeemer
        133
    Church Row Walk (Hampstead) 271
    Farm Street 60
    French Protestant 67
    Kensington Church Walk 235
    London Russian Orthodox 211
    Notre Dame de France 67
    Royal Hospital Chelsea 207
    St. Aldgate 94
    St. Anne's Limehouse 159, 195
    St. Bartholomew-the-Great 147, 149
    St. Botolphs 153
    St. Clement Danes 94
    St. Clement Eastcheap 94
    St. Francis of Assisi 238
    St. George's Bloomsbury 123
    St. George's in the East 159
    St. James's 33
    St. Magnus the Martyr 153
    St. Martin-in-the-Fields 87
    St. Martin's Lane 94
    St. Mary Abbots 235
    St. Mary Abchurch 152
    St. Mary le Bow 94
    St. Mary's Lambeth 16
    St. Mary's Rotherhithe 191
    St. Mary Woolnoth 145
    St. Pancras Old Church 106
    St. Paul's Cathedral 16, 142
    St. Sepulchre-without-Newgate 94
    St. Stephen Walbrook 144
    Southwark Cathedral 26

Westminster Cathedral 49
Churchill, Clementine 46
Churchill, Winston 44, 46, 47
Churchill Bunker (Cabinet War
    Rooms) 44, 45
Churchill Museum 44
Church Our Most Holy Redeemer 133
Church Row Walk (Hampstead) 271
City, The 140–154
    Saturday Afternoon Walk 128
Claridge's 53
    Bar 55
Clark, H. Fuller 142
Clark, Samuel 135
Clarke, Samantha 135
Claude 300
Clerkenwell 128–137
Clerkenwell Green 130
Climpson & Sons 177
Clive of India Statue 45
Clive Steps 45
Cocteau, Jean 69
Cole, Sir Henry 202
    portrait of 203
Colebrooke Cottage 261
Collins, Joan 272
Columbia Road Flower Market 166,
    167, 178
Communist Party 186
Conan Doyle, Arthur 74
Concerts, Dance, Music see also
        Theatres, Cinemas
    Academy of St. Martin-in-the-
        Fields 87
    Cecil Sharp House (ceilidhs, folk
        dances) 251
    Costa Dorada (flamenco) 79
    Crystal Palace Concert Bowl 303
    Denmark Street 66
    Fabric (dance club) 151
    Kenwood House (summer
        concerts) 278
    National Opera 135
    Nick Leonidas (busker) 53
    Phoenix Theatre Bar 69

Royal Ballet 135
Sadler's Wells (dance) 132, 134
St. Botolphs (organ) 153
St. Magnus the Martyr (organ) 153
St. Mary Abbots Church
    (lunchtime concerts) 235
St. Paul's Cathedral 142
Sutton House 288
Wilton's Music Hall 172
Conrad, Joseph 198
Constable, John 274
    burial site 271
Constitution Arch (Burton) 227
Contemporary Applied Arts 77
Coq d'Argent 144
Coram, Thomas 116, 119
Coram Foundation 117
Coram's Fields 119
Cork Street 54
Costa Dorada 79
County Hall Restaurant 17
Covent Garden 91–99
    Underground Design 55
Coward, Noël, home of 216
Crane, Walter 234
Creswick, Benjamin
    Hat Factory carvings 78
Criterion Theatre 91
Cromwell, Oliver 90
Crystal Palace Park 302–304
    dinosaurs 302, 304
    Farm 303
    Museum 302
    National Sports Centre 303, 304
Cupola Room 224

D

Dahl, Roald 84
Daniel, Price, Sr. 38
Daquise Restaurant 203
Darwin, Charles, portrait of 86
Davies, Ray 266
Debenham House 232
Defoe, Daniel, tomb of 129
De Gaulle, Charles, home of 272

De Gustibus 26
Delius, Frederick 250
Denmark Street 66
Dennis Severs' House 161
De Quincey, Thomas 52
Derry and Toms department store 236
Design Museum 27
Devey, George 206
Devonshire, Georgiana, Duchess of
    313
Diana, Princess of Wales 34, 173
Dickens, Charles 28, 68, 107, 173, 198
    home of 74
    portrait of 86
Dilke, Charles Wentworth 274, 275
Dinosaurs (Crystal Palace Park) 302
Diploma Galleries (Royal Academy of
    the Arts) 57
Diplomat Hotel 214
Dixon, Jeremy 89, 96
Docklands 190–199
Docklands Light Railway 193, 196, 198
    Romantic Evening 162
Doherty, Maureen 212
Douglas, Lord Alfred, home of 271
Dove, The 177
Drayton Park stadium 265
Drury Lane, Theatre Royal 91
Duke's Head Yard 284
Dulwich Picture Gallery 208, 300
Dylan, Bob 66

E

East End and Hackney 158–186
East End Canal Walk 193
East London Stroll 178
Edgware Road 228
Edmunds, Andrew 70
Edward VI, portrait of 86
Edward VII 314
    equestrian statue of 37
    Manor House of 190
Eel Pie Island 322
Egg 76
Elephant Man (Joseph Merrick) 28, 171

Elgar, Sir Edward 254
El Greco
    Christ Driving the Traders from
        the Temple, 85
Eliot, T.S. 172
Emberton, Joseph 58
Emms, Dr., tomb of 129
Engels, Friedrich 131
English Folk Dance and Song Society
    251
Epping Forest 291
    Day Trip 293
Estorick Collection of Modern Italian
    Art 264
Estrela 12
Eurostar Terminus (Barlow Shed) 106
Evans, Edith 21
Eversleigh Road 212
Excursions see also Boating;
        Recreation, Sports; Walks,
        Strolls, Tours
    Bedford Park 312
    Blackheath 307
    Chiswick House 313
    Crystal Palace 302
    Day at the Spa 242
    Drive Through Norwood 301
    Driving Along the Westway 240
    Epping Forest Day Trip 293
    Fulham Palace Garden 312
    Garrick's Temple 320
    Greenwich Park 305
    Gunnersbury Park Museum 315
    Ice House 308
    Kew Gardens 318
    Lee Valley Regional Park 292
    Richmond Lock and Footbridge
        320
    Osterley Park 317
    Richmond Park 319
    Romantic Evening (Canary Wharf)
        162
    Saturday Afternoon (Clerkenwell)
        128
    Strawberry Hill House 322

Eyck, Jan van
    The Arnolfini Portrait, 83

F
Fabric 151
Fabrications 177
Fan Museum 305
Faraday Museum 57
Far Global 179
Farm Street Church 60
Farrell, Terry 13
Fatboy's Diner 196
Felt 206
Fenton House 273
Fenwick 53
Film Buff's Stroll 74
Finsbury
    Old Finsbury Town Hall 132
    Walking in 132
    Wilmington Square 136
Finsbury Health Centre 132
Fitzgerald, Penelope 28
Fitzrovia 72–79
Flask Tavern 277
Fleet River 108
Forbes, Leslie
    Fish, Blood and Bone, 169
Ford, John 100
Forest Gate Inn 293
Forest Hill 302
Forman's Fish Island 174
Fortnum & Mason 195
    St. James's Restaurant 32
43 Group 186
Foster, Sir Norman 121, 122
    Canary Wharf Station 48, 55
    Sackler Galleries 56
Foundling Museum 116
Fountains and Waterfalls
    Japanese Garden 233
    Leighton House Arab Hall 233
    Somerset House 96
    Triton Fountain 247
Four Aces 185
Fragonard, Jean-Honoré 62

Fred Bare 179
French Bookshop 204
French House 272
French neighborhoods 67, 107
    Francophile Walk 204
    French Connection stroll 67
    General de Gaulle home 272
French Protestant Church 67
Fresco 242
Freud Museum 270
Frink, Elizabeth
    mythical horse and rider statue 37
Frizzante 182
Fry, Maxwell 284
Fulham News 217
Fulham Palace Garden 312
Future Systems Bridge 162

G

Gainsborough, Thomas 117, 300
Gaitskell, Hugh, grave of 272
Gallions Hotel 198
Gallions Reach 197
Gambon, Michael 272
Gandhi Memorial 115
Garrick, David, home of 98, 321
Garrick's Temple 320
Geffrye Museum 169
    Café 169
George, Ernest
    Watts Memorial 148
George I Statue 123, 124
George VI, portrait of 46
Georgian houses 47
German Embassy (Foreign Office) 41
Gershwin, Ira 121
G. Heywood Hill Ltd. 58
Giant's Wedding 88
Gibbons, Grinling 153
    St. James's Church Font 33
Gibbs, James 89, 152
Gielgud, John 21
Gill, Eric
    Westminster Cathedral Stations of
        the Cross 49

Gina Shoes 55
Giordano, Luca
    Perseus Turning Phineas and His
        Followers to Stone, 85
Giro's Grave 41
Globe Theatre 23
Gloucester Place, No. 62, 60
Godwin, E.W. 313
Goldbeater's Building 75
Golders Hill Park 281
    Flower Garden 281
    Pergola 281
Goldfinger, Ernö 196
    Willow Road house 283
Gordon's Wine Bar 98
Gourmet Pizza Company 19
Grace, W.R. 304
Graham & Greene 239
Grand Union Canal 193
    Cruise from Little Venice to
        Camden Market 255
    Stroll from Windmill Lane to
        Brentford 318
Gray's Inn 99
Great Fire of 1666, 145, 150
Green Bridge 173
Greene, Graham 60, 75
Greenwich Park 305
    Fan Museum 305
    General Wolfe Statue 305
    National Maritime Museum 305
    Queen's House 305
    Ranger's House 306
    Royal Hospital (Old Royal Naval
        College) 305
    Royal Observatory 305
    sausage café 306
    Vanbrugh Castle 306
Grenadier, The 213
Gresham, Sir Thomas 317
Guinness, Alec 21
Gunnersbury Park Museum 315
    Gunnersbury House 315
Guy Fawkes Day Fireworks 295
Gwynne, Patrick 308

H

Hackney and The East End 158–186
Hackney City Farm 178
Hackney Empire Theatre 187
Hackney Old Town Hall 187
Haigh, Field Marshal, statue of 37
Hall, Peter 22
Halley, Edmond 306
Hals, Franz 279
    The Laughing Cavalier, 62
Hammersmith Underground Design
    55
Hampstead 270–285
Hampstead Heath 273–279, 284
    Bird Chorus and Bat-Watching 281
Hancock, Ralph 236
Handel, George Frideric 13
    bust (Roubiliac) 117
Hand Made Food 307
Hannay, Richard, Walk 74
Hanway Street 79
Happold, Buro 192
Hardiman, Alfred
    Haigh rocking horse statue 37
Hardy, Thomas 108
Harrison, George 254
Harrison, John 306
    grave of 272
Hastings, Jack
    Marx Memorial Library fresco 131
Hat Factory 78
Hawkins, Waterhouse 303
Hawksmoor, Nicholas
    Christ Church, Spitalfields 159
    Orangery 223
    Royal Hospital (Old Royal Naval
        College) 305
    St. Anne's Limehouse 195
    St. George's Bloomsbury 123
    St. Mary Woolnoth 145
Henry, Prince of Wales 101
Henry VIII 288
    King Henry's Mound 319
Hepworth, Barbara
    air and water sculpture 52

Heritage Lottery Fund 123
Hertford, Lord 61
    Wallace Collection 61
Hervey, Lord 313
Herzog and de Meuron 22
Highgate 283–285
    Architectural Stroll 283
    Queen's Wood 293
Highgate Cemetery 282, 283
Highgate Ponds 277
Highpoint I and II 283, 285
Hill, Heywood 59
Hill, Octavia 25
Hill Garden 280
Hitchcock, Alfred 74, 291
    Leystone Station Murals 290
Hitchcock, H.R. 58
Hitler, Adolf 44, 46
HMV (Oxford Street) 52, 58
Hoare family 100
Hodgkinson, Patrick 118
Hoesch, Leopold von 41
Hogarth, William 43, 161, 117
    Gin Lane, 124
    The Good Samaritan, 152
    Pool of Bethesda, 151
Holborn 99–102
Holden, Charles 192
Holland Park 232–237
Hollar, Wenceslas
    Long View of London from
        Bankside, 27
Holloway Express Shop 265
Holloway Road 264
Hollow Ponds 290
Holmes, Sherlock, Walk 74
Holmes, William 116
Holocaust Exhibition (Imperial War
    Museum) 15
Homer 232
Honthorst, Gerrit van
    Christ Before the High Priest, 85
Hopkins, Michael 48, 255
Horniman Museum 301
Horse Guards 43, 47, 224

Horses 36
Hotels
    The Cadogan 205
    Charlotte Street 77
    Claridge's 53
    Diplomat 214
    Marriott 17
    Midland Grand 106
    The Ritz 36
House of Charity for Homeless
    Women (St. Barnabas) 67, 68
Houston, Sam 37
H.R. Stokes 217
Hughes, Patrick 109
Huguenots 68
Hume, David, statue of 56
Hunter, John 95
Hunterian Museum 95
Hyde Park
    dog cemetery 41
    Sunday Softball 226
Hyde Park Corner 226
    Constitution Arch 227
    Machine Gun Corps Memorial 227
    Royal Artillery Memorial 227

I
Ice House 308
Immigration and Diversity, Museum
    of 158
Imperial War Museum 14
    Cabinet War Rooms 44
    Churchill Museum 44
    Holocaust Exhibition 15
Indian Ocean Tandoori 264
Inner Temple 99
    Prince Henry's Room 101
Inns of Court 99
Institut Français 204
International Magic 131
Islington 193, 260–266
    Stroll 261

J
Jack the Ripper Walking Tour 173

Jacques, Hattie 303
Jagger, Charles Sargeant
    Royal Artillery Memorial 227
James, Henry, house of 237
James I 101
Japanese Garden 233
Jarman, Derek 190
Jefferson, Thomas 317
Jeffreys, Judge 193
Jermyn Street Shops 34
Jeroboams 216
Jerusalem, Walk to 147
Jerusalem Tavern 147
Jewish neighborhoods 158
    Old Jewish Quarter Tour 173
Jiricna, Eva 192
Johanssons 298
John, Augustus 75
John, Elton 66
    portrait of 86
John Lewis Department Store 52
Johnson, P. 58
Johnson, Samuel 140
Johnston, Edward
    Underground Design 55
Jones, Adrian
    Peace in Her Quadriga, 227
Jones, Ed 89, 96
Jones, Inigo 43, 306
Jones Brothers department store 266
Jones Dairy 179
Joyce, James 115
Jubilee Gardens 17
Jubilee Line Extension 48, 191
Jubilee Walkway 16

K
Kate MacGarry 182
Kean, Edmund 21
Keats, John, House 274
Kendall, Kay, grave of 272
Kensal Green Cemetery 238
Kensington Church Walk 235
    No. 10, 237

Kensington High Street, Roof
    Gardens 236
Kensington Palace 222
    Cupola Room 224
    Green 222
Kensington Palace Gardens 35,
    222–225
    Orangery 222, 223
    Round Pond 223
    Serpentine Gallery 222, 225
    Sunken Garden 223
Kent, William 35, 36, 223, 313
    Cupola Room 224
    Horse Guards 224
Kenwood House 277, 278
    The Brew House 279
    Rembrandt Self-Portrait, 279
Kettners 67
Kew Gardens 318
    Palm House 318
    Waterlily House 318
Keybridge House 12
King Henry's Mound 319
King's Cross 107, 194
Kingsley, Charles 28
King's Road 169
Kinks 66, 266
Kipling, Rudyard 198
Knightsbridge 202–206, 215
    Underground Design 55
Knights Templar 187
Knot Garden 16
Kubrick, Stanley 198

L
La Bouchée 204
La Grande Bouchée 204
Lamb, Charles and Mary, home of 261
Lamb, The 120
Lambeth Bridge 16
Landseer, Sir Edwin
    The Old Shepherd's Chief
        Mourner, 203
Lasdun, Sir Denys 20
Lassally, Walter 303

Lauren, Ralph 213
Lawrence, D.H. 75, 115
Lawrence, Frieda 75
Leadenhall Market 147
    Walk from, to Jerusalem 147
Le Corbusier 241, 284
Lee Boo, Palau Prince, tomb of 192
Lee Valley Regional Park 292
Leighton House 233
    Arab Hall 233, 234
Le Mesurier, John 303
Lemonia 247, 248
Lenin, V.I. 131
Lennon, John 254
Lennox Gardens 206
Leonidas, Nick 53
Le Sueur, Hubert
    Statue of King Charles I 37, 90
Lewis, Wyndham 75
Leytonstone 290–292
Leytonstone Station
    Alfred Hitchcock Murals 290
Libraries
    British 106, 109–115, 122, 321
    Marx Memorial 130
    St. Bride Foundation 140
    Vaughan Williams Memorial (Cecil
        Sharp House) 251
Limehouse Basin 193
Lincoln's Inn 99
Literary Neighbours 237
Little Venice, Cruise to Camden
    Market from 256
Livingstone Studio 77
Lodge café 294
Lodging House 252
London County Cricket Club 304
London Development Agency 304
London Eye (Millennium Wheel) 17,
    19, 27
London Fields Lido 176
London Metropolitan Archives 133
London Review Bookshop 120
London Russian Orthodox Church 211
London Zoo 247, 256

Snowdon Aviary 250
Lonsdale, Gordon 74
Lord's Cricket Ground 255
Louis Pastisserie 284
Lubetkin, Berthold 133, 284, 285
Lunardi, Vencenzo 129
Lyceum Theatre 91
Lynch, David 28

M

Machine Gun Corps Memorial 227
Mackennal, Bertram
    Edward VII statue 37
MacMillan, Ron 131
Magna Carta 109
Maison Bertaux 67
Majestic Wine 12
Malaysia Hall Canteen 224
Manette House 67
Mantegna, Andrea
    The Agony in the Garden, 85
Marble Arch 52
Marcus Aurelius 37
Margaret, Princess 227
Markets see Shopping
Marks & Spencer (Oxford Street) 53
Marochetti, Carlo
    Richard the Lionheart statue 37
Marriott Hotel
    County Hall Restaurant 17
Marston, John 100
Marx, Eleanor 130
Marx, Karl 111, 131, 171
    grave of 282, 283
Marx House 130
Marx Memorial Library 130
Mary, Queen of Scots 288
Marylebone 60–62
Mason, Red 159
Massys, Quinten
    A Grotesque Old Woman, 86
Mather, Rick 40
May, E.J. 313
Mayfair 52–60
Mayflower Inn 190, 191, 192

McCartney, Paul 254
    portrait of 86
Meek, Joe 266
Mellon, Paul, Estate 123
Meo, Gaetano 232
Merrick, Joseph 171
MI6, 13
Michelangelo
    Taddei Tondo, 57
Middle Temple 99
Middle Temple Hall 100
Midland Grand Hotel 106
Mill, John Stuart 130
Millennium Wheel (London Eye) 17, 19, 27
Miller, Glenn 254
Milne, A.A. 86
Mitford, Nancy 59
Modigliani, Amedeo 264
Monmouth Coffee Company 24
Moore, Henry
    St. Stephen Walbrook Altar 145
Morgan, William de 232, 233, 234
Moro, Peter 308
Moro restaurant 135
Morris, William 130
Morton, H.V. 143
Mosley, Oswald 186
Mother's Square 289
Mozart, Wolfgang A. 68
Mr. Christian's Delicatessen 239
Mulready, William, tomb of 238
Museums, Galleries, Exhibitions
    Bank of England 146
    British Library 109
    Brunel, Thames Tunnel 191, 192
    Cabinet War Rooms 44
    Churchill 44
    Cork Street 54
    Crystal Palace 302
    Dennis Severs' House 161
    Design 27
    Dulwich Picture Gallery 208, 300
    Estorick Collection 264
    Fan 305

Faraday 57
Foundling 116
Freud 270
Garden History 16
Geffrye 169
Gunnersbury Park 315
Horniman 301
Hunterian 95
Imperial War 14, 44
Kate MacGarry 182
Kenwood House 277, 278
Leighton House 233
of Mankind (Royal Academy of Arts) 56
National Gallery 37, 56, 82
National Maritime 305
National Portrait Gallery 86
Netti Horn 182
Ranger's House 306
Sackler Galleries (Royal Academy of Arts) 56
Serpentine Gallery 222, 225
Sir John Soane's 92, 208
Somerset House 96
Sutton House 288
Tate Modern 22
Topolski Century 19
Trails 84
V & A, of Childhood 170
Vegas Gallery 182
Victoria & Albert 202
Vyner Street 182
Wallace Collection 61
White Cube 2, 168
Wilkinson Gallery 182
Muthesius, Herman 312

N

19 Princelet Street Synagogue 158
Nairn, Ian 197, 198
Napoleon Bonaparte 39
Napoleon III 68
Narrow Way 186
Nash, Paul 15
National Club 112

National Gallery 37, 56, 82, 85
    The Agony in the Garden (Mantegna) 85
    The Arnolfini Portrait (van Eyck) 83
    Belshazzar's Feast (Rembrandt) 85
    Christ Before the High Priest (van Honthorst) 85
    Christ Driving the Traders from the Temple (El Greco) 85
    Christ Washing the Feet of his Disciples (Tintoretto) 85
    The Finding of Moses (Poussin) 85
    A Grotesque Old Woman (Massys) 86
    Joseph with Jacob in Egypt (Pontormo) 85
    Perseus Turning Phineas and His Followers to Stone (Giordano) 85
    The Raising of Lazarus (del Piombo) 85
    Saint Jerome in a Rocky Landscape (Patinir) 85
    Samson and Delilah (Rubens) 85
    The Stigmatisation of Saint Francis (Sassetta) 85
    The Supper at Emmaus (Caravaggio) 82, 85
    Whistlejacket (Stubbs) 37
National Maritime Museum 305
National Opera 135
National Portrait Gallery 86, 89
    Portrait Café 90
National Sports Centre 303, 304
National Trust 284, 288, 317
Neal's Yard 26
Nelson, Richard 61
Netti Horn Gallery 182
New Caledonian (Bermondsey Market) 27
Newsstands 218
No-One 179
Norden, John 107
Norman Shaw, Richard 312
Northampton Lodge 264

Northern Outfall Sewer 197
North London 288–295
North Woolwich 198
Norwood 301
Notre Dame de France 67
Notting Hill 238–243
Notting Hill Books 223
Nunhead Cemetery 298
    Monument to the Scottish Political
        Martyrs 299

O

Oasis 79
Odette's 247
Old Bailey prison 94
Old Queen's Head, The 261
Old Royal Naval College (Royal
        Hospital) 305
Old Vic 21
Olivier, Laurence 21, 22
Olowu Golding 239
Olympic Games of 2012, 184, 292
Open Air Theatre 246, 247
Orange Amplifiers 66
Orangery 222, 223
Original London Walks 173
Orwell, George 47, 75, 264
    home of 263
Osterley Park 317
    Etruscan Dressing Room 317
Owen, Sir Richard 303
Oxford Street Walk 52
Oxo Tower Brasserie 20

P

Palladio, Andrea 313
Palumbo, Peter 144
Pantheon (Oxford Street) 53
Paolozzi, Eduardo
    Tottenham Court Road
        Underground murals 55
Parks and Gardens
    Battersea 211, 217
    Bedford 312
    Blackheath 307
    Chelsea Physic 209
    Chiswick House 313
    Coram's Fields 119
    Crystal Palace 302
    Fenton House 273
    Finsbury 134
    Fulham Palace 312
    Garrick's Temple 320
    Golders Hill 281
    Green Bridge 194
    Greenwich 305
    Gunnersbury Park Museum 315
    Hill 280
    Hyde 226
    Italian 247
    Japanese 233
    Kensington 35, 222–225
    Kenwood House 278
    Kew 318
    King Henry's Mound 319
    Knot 16
    Lee Valley Regional 292
    Mount Street 60
    Museum of Garden History 16
    Osterley 317
    Peace Pagoda 211, 217
    Pembroke Lodge 319
    Pirelli 202
    Postman's 147
    Queen Mary's 246
    Queen's Wood 293
    Red Cross 25
    Regent's 246, 247
    Richmond 319
    Roof Gardens 236
    St. George's 116
    St. James's Park Lake 41
    St. John's Church 187
    St. John's Lodge 246
    St. Pancras Old Church 106, 108
    Spring 12
    Trinity Green 170
    Victoria 183
    Victoria & Albert Museum 202
    Waterlow (Highgate) 282

Wilmington Square 136
Parliament
    County Hall Restaurant 17
    South Bank Stroll 16
    Westminster Walk by 48
Parliament Hill Café 276
Patinir, Joachim
    Saint Jerome in a Rocky Landscape, 85
Peace Pagoda 211
Pembroke Lodge 319
Penny Post 202
Pepys, Samuel 13
Peter Jones department store 169
Pevsner, Nikolaus 146
Phoenix Theatre Bar 69
Piccadilly Circus Underground Design 55
Pickering Place 39
Pilgrims 191
Piombo, Sebastiano del
    The Raising of Lazarus, 85
Piper, John 15
Pissarro, Camille, house of 240
Pitshanger Manor Museum 208
Plath, Sylvia 250
Pliny 124
"Plum Pudding Steps" 137
Polish neighborhood 203
Pontormo, Jacopo
    Joseph with Jacob in Egypt, 85
Poole, Henry 142
Porchester Spa 242
Portobello Morning 239
Postman's Park 147, 148
Post Office 87
Potter, Beatrix 86
Poultry, No. 1
    Le Coq d'Argent 144
    roof garden 146
Pound, Ezra, home of 237
Poussin, Nicolas 300
    The Finding of Moses, 85
Powell, Russell 143
Poynter, Edward 234

Primrose Hill
    Walk 248
    Walk from Belsize Park to 250
Primrose Hill Books 248
Prince Henry's Room 101
Prince's Arms, The 101
Princess's Theatre 52
Princi 69
Prinsep, Val 234
Public Record Office 202

Q

Quality Chop House 133
Queen's House 305
Queen's Wood 293

R

Ramsay, Allan 117
Ranger's House 306
Ravi Shankar Restaurant 253
Recreation and Sports see also
        Boating; Excursions; Walks,
        Strolls, Tours
    Alexandra Palace (ice rink) 294, 295
    Brockwell Park Lido (swimming) 300
    Crystal Palace Park (cricket, fireworks) 303, 304
    Drayton Park stadium 265
    Epping Forest (biking, cricket) 293
    Highgate Ponds (swimming) 277
    London Fields Lido (swimming) 175
    Lord's Cricket Ground 254
    National Sports Centre 303, 304
    Oasis (swimming) 79
    Porchester Spa 242
    Spa London 242
    Spitalfields bicycling 160
    Sunday Softball 226
Red Cross Garden 25
Redgrave, Corin 61
Redgrave family 21
Regent Hall 52

Regent's Canal 250, 261
Regent's Park 246–256
    Cruise from Little Venice to
      Camden Market 255
    Gardens of St. John's Lodge 246
    High Summer 246
    Italian Gardens 247
    Open Air Theatre 246
    Penguin Pool 247
    Queen Mary's Gardens 246
    Stroll 247
    Triton Fountain 247
Reith, Lord 73
Rembrandt 61, 300
    Self-Portrait, 279
Rendell, Ruth 75
Renoir Cinema 118
Restaurants, Cafés, Bars, Pubs
    Afternoon Tea 32
    Albion 179
    Andrew Edmunds 70
    Archway Tavern 265
    Avenue Restaurant and Bar 40
    Back to Basics 76
    Barbican Centre 153
    Italia, Bar 71
    Battersea Park (picnic) 217
    Beatles Coffee Shop 255
    Black Friar Pub 141
    Bradley's 79
    Brew House Café 278, 279
    Brick Lane Beigel Bake 165
    Broadway Market 177
    Browns 53
    Cachao 248
    Café in the Crypt (St. Martin-in-
      the-Fields) 87
    Carnevale 128
    The Cat and Mutton 177
    Cecil Sharp House 251
    Charlotte Street Hotel 77
    Claridge's Bar 55
    Climpson & Sons 177
    Columbia Road Flower Market 167
    Costa Dorada 79
    County Hall 17
    Daquise Restaurant 203
    The Dove 177
    Estrela 12
    Fatboy's Diner 196
    Flask Tavern 277
    Floral Hall (Royal Opera House) 96
    Forest Gate Inn 293
    Forman's Fish Island 194
    French House 272
    Fresco 242
    Frizzante 182
    Geffrye Museum 169
    Golders Hill Park Italian ice cream
      281
    Gordon's Wine Bar 98
    Gourmet Pizza Company 19
    The Grenadier 213
    Grove, Café 239
    Hackney City Farm 178, 182
    Hand Made Food 307
    Hoxton 170
    Imperial War Museum 15
    Indian Ocean Tandoori 264
    Institut Français 204
    Jerusalem Tavern 147
    Johanssons 298
    Kettners 67
    La Bouchée 204
    The Lamb 120
    Leadenhall Market 147
    Le Coq d'Argent 144
    Lemonia 247, 248
    Lodge Café 294
    London Review Bookshop 120
    Louis Pastisserie 284
    Maison Bertaux 67
    Malaysia Hall Canteen 224
    Mayflower Inn 190, 191, 192
    Monmouth Coffee Company 24
    Moro 135
    No-One 179
    Odette's 247
    The Old Queen's Head 261
    Old Vic 21

Orangery 222, 223
Oto 184
Oxo Tower Brasserie 20
Parliament Hill Café 276
Phoenix Theatre Bar 69
Portrait Café (National Portrait
    Gallery) 90
Prince Henry's Room (The Prince's
    Arms) 101
Princi 69
Quality Chop House 133
Ravi Shankar 125
Ridley Road Market 185
The Ritz 32
Rochelle School Canteen 166
Rosie's 27
St. James's (Fortnum & Mason) 32
St. John 130
Shepherd Market 59
Shoreditch House roof café 182
Smith's of Smithfield 151
Somerset House 96
South Kingsland Road Vietnamese
    170
Southwark Cathedral picnic 27
Sutton House 288
Tate Modern 23
Tayyabs 171
Ten Bells Pub 173
Tom's Deli 239
Victoria Park tea house 183
Victory Pub 183
Wallace Collection 61
Wapping Project 192
Westbourne Grove Restaurant Row
    241
Ziani's 207
Review Bookshop 298
Reynolds, Joshua 117
Ricardo, Halsey 232
Richardson, Ralph 21
Richard the Lionheart Statue 37
Richmond Lock and Footbridge 320
Richmond Park 319
Ridley Road Market 185

Rimbaud, Arthur 252
Ringmore Rise 301
Ritz, The
    Afternoon Tea 32
    Wimborne House 36
Riverside Stroll 190
Riverside Walk 210
R.J. Welsh 248
Rochelle School Canteen 166
Rolling Stones 66, 322
Roof Gardens 236
Rosie's 27
Rothchild family 315
Rotherhithe 190
    Canada Water Station to the
        Mayflower Inn 192
Rothschild, Lord 34, 35
Roubiliac, François
    Handel bust 117
    Shakespeare statue 321
Royal Academy of Arts
    Museum of Mankind 56
    Sackler Galleries 56
    Taddei Tondo (Michelangelo) 57
Royal Arcade 54
Royal Artillery Memorial 227
Royal Ballet 135
Royal College of Music 235
Royal College of Surgeons 95
Royal Corinthian Yacht Club 58
Royal Docks 197
Royal Hospital (Chelsea) 207, 209
    Chapel 207
    Stable Block 207, 208
Royal Hospital (Old Royal Naval
    College) 305
Royal Institute of British Architects
    (RIBA) 72
Royal Institution of Great Britain 57
Royal London Hospital 171
Royal National Theatre 20
Royal Observatory 305
Royal Opera House 89, 96
    Floral Hall 96
Royal Society of Arts (RSA) 97

Royal Terrace 97
Rubens, Peter Paul 300
    Banqueting House ceiling 44
    Samson and Delilah, 85
Rumbelow, Donald 173
Russian Baths 243
Russian Orthodox Church 211

S

Sackler Galleries 56
Sadleir, Sir Ralph 288
Sadler's Wells 21, 132, 134
St. Aldgate Church 94
St. Anne's Limehouse 159, 195
St. Augustine's Tower 187
St. Barnabas, House of 67
St. Bartholomew's Hospital Museum
    150
    The Good Samaritan (Hogarth) 152
    The Pool of Bethesda (Hogarth) 151
St. Bartholomew-the-Great 147, 149
St. Botolph's 148, 153
St. Bride Foundation 140
St. Clement Danes 94
St. Clement Eastcheap 94
St. Francis of Assisi 238
St. George's Bloomsbury 123
St. George's Gardens 116
St. George's in the East 159
St. James's Church 33
St. James's neighborhood 32–42
St. James's Park 47
    Blue Bridge 42
    Lake 42
St. John-at-Hampstead 272
    Graveyard 270, 272
St. John (restaurant) 130
St. John's (Hackney) 187
St. John's Lodge Gardens 246
St. John's Smith Square 47
St. Magnus the Martyr 153
St. Martin-in-the-Fields 87
    A Giant's Wedding 88
    Café in the Crypt 87
    recitals 87

St. Martin's Lane 94
St. Mary Abbots 235
St. Mary Abchurch 152
St. Mary le Bow 94
St. Mary's Lambeth 16
St. Mary's Rotherhithe 191
    Palau Prince Lee Boo tomb 192
St. Mary Woolnoth 145
St. Pancras Old Church and Gardens
    106, 107
St. Pancras station 106
St. Paul's Cathedral 16, 94, 142, 151
    Turner Monument (MacDowell)
        142
    Whispering Gallery 143
St. Sepulchre-without-Newgate 94
St. Stephen Walbrook 144
    stone altar (Moore) 145
Salvation Army 52
Samaritans charity 145
Sargent, John Singer 15
Sassetta
    The Stigmatisation of Saint Francis,
        85
Savile Row 54
Scott, Robert F. 198
Scott, Sir Giles Gilbert 22, 106
Scottish Political Martyrs Monument
    299
Seddon, J.D. 134
Serpentine Gallery 222, 225
Severini, Gino 264
Severs, Dennis 161
Sex Pistols 67
Shad Thames 28
Shakespeare, Edmund, grave of 27
Shakespeare, William 21, 23, 27, 100
    Garrick's Temple 320
Sharp, Cecil 251
Shaw, Fiona 172
Shaw-Lefevre, G.J. 294
Sheets, Kermit 303
Shelley, Percy Bysshe 108
Shepherd Market 59
Shopping

Absolute Vintage (clothes) 163
A. Gold (grocery, wines) 160
Andrew Edmunds (prints) 70
Artisan Foods 26
Atomica (furniture, lamps) 179
Bermondsey Market, New
    Caledonian (antiques, flea
    market) 27
Berry Brox. & Rudd (wines, spirits)
    38
Beyond Retro (clothes) 163
Blondie (clothes) 163
Bond Street Coutures 53
Borough Market (emporium) 26
Brick Lane Fashion Walk 163
Brick Lane Market (clothes) 163,
    166
Broadway Bookshop 178
Broadway Market (clothes, crafts,
    food) 177
Browns (clothing) 53
Burlington Arcade 54
Camden Market 256
Camden Passage Antiques Market
    260
Caravan (antiques, gifts) 179
Chapel Market (flea market,
    flowers, produce) 260
Charbonnel et Walker (chocolate)
    53
Christie's (art, furniture auctions)
    204
Claridge's 53
Columbia Road Flower Market 166,
    167, 178
Contemporary Applied Arts (gifts,
    postcards) 77
Cork Street (art galleries) 54
De Gustibus (bread) 26
Egg (gifts) 76
Fabrications (knit goods) 177
Far Global (Indian goods) 179
Felt (jewelry) 206
Fenwick (department store) 53
Forman's Fish Island 194

Fortnum & Mason (tea, jam) 33
Fred Bare (hats) 179
French Bookshop 204
Fulham News 217
G. Heywood Hill Ltd. (books) 58
Gina Shoes 55
Graham & Greene (furniture) 239
H.R. Stokes (books) 217
Imperial War Museum (books) 15
International Magic 131
Jermyn Street Shops 34
Jeroboams (cheese, wine) 216
Jones Dairy (bread, staples) 179
King's Road (clothes) 169
La Grande Bouchée (cheese) 204
Leadenhall Market 147
London Review Bookshop 120
Majestic Wine 12
Mr. Christian's Delicatessen 239
Narrow Way (Asian goods, phones,
    thrift shops) 186
Neal's Yard (dairy) 26
Newsstands 218
No. 11 Bus 169
Notting Hill Books 223
Olowu Golding (clothes) 239
Peter Jones department store 169
Post Office (gift stamps) 87
Primrose Hill Books 248
Review Bookshop 298
Ridley Road Market 185
R.J. Welsh (hardware) 248
Rosie's 27
Royal Arcade 54
Savile Row 54
Shepherd Market 59
Sloane Square (clothes) 169
Smithfield Market 147, 151
Specialty Shops Walk 76
Spitalfields Market (fashion, foods,
    interiors) 160
Steve Hatt Fishmongers 263
Tate Modern (books) 22
This Shop Rocks (clothes) 163
Tomtom Cigars 217

Turkish Food Centre 186
Two Columbia Road (furniture, fittings) 179
Vyner Street (art) 182
White Cube 2 (art) 168
Wild at Heart (flowers) 239
Shoreditch House roof café 182
Sickert, Walter 75, 261
    The Hanging Gardens of Islington, 261
Simpsons Piccadilly 58
Skinner, Thomas 294
Sloane Square 169
Smirke, Sidney 110
Smirke, Sir Robert 121
Smith, F.E., Earl of Birkenhead 40
Smith, John Saumarez 59
Smithfield Market 147, 150, 151
Smith's of Smithfield 151
Soane, Sir John 207, 208, 300
    Museum 92, 152, 208
Soho 66–72
Somerset House 96
    Courtauld Institute Gallery 97
    Gilbert Collection 97
    Hermitage Treasures 97
South Bank 12–22
    Stroll 16
South Kensington 202–206
South & Southeast London 298–309
Southwark Cathedral 26
Southwest and West London 312–322
Spas 242
    Day at the Spa 242
    Green Estate 132
    Porchester Spa 242
Spencer, Stanley 15
Spencer House 34, 35
Spitalfields Market 160
Spring Gardens 12
Stable Block 207, 208
Stanley Halls 301
Starr, Ringo 254
Statues, Memorials, Plaques
    Albert, Prince, Memorial 225, 226

Arnold, Benedict, plaque 61
Boadiccae, Queen 36
Brailsford, H.N., plaque 250
Bunhill Fields 129
Constitution Arch 227
Delius, Frederick, plaque 250
Gandhi Memorial 115
Garrick's Temple 320
Hat Factory figures 78
James, Henry, plaque 237
London's Horses 36
Machine Gun Corps Memorial 227
Meek, Joe, plaque 266
Mitford, Nancy, plaque 59
Orwell, George, plaque 75, 263
Plath, Sylvia, plaque 250
Postman's Park 147, 148
Royal Artillery Memorial 227
Scottish Political Martyrs 299
Texas Legation 38
Verlaine and Rimbaud plaque 253
Victoria & Albert Museum 202
Waterlow, Sir Sydney, statue 282
Watts, G.F., Memorial to ordinary people 148
Watts, Isaac, Monument 289
Wolfe, General 305
York, Duke of, Monument 41
Steve Hatt Fishmongers 263
Stevenson, Robert L., home of 273
Stirling, Sir James 144, 146
Stokes, H.R. 217
Strawberry Hill House 322
Strothard, Thomas, tomb of 128
Stuart, James 35
Stubbs, George
    Whistlejacket, 37
Studio House 283
Sun House 284
Sutton House 288
Swan, Anna 88

T

Tate Boat 22, 27
Tate Britain 22, 27, 152

Tate Modern 22, 27
    Auerbach painting 249
    South Bank Stroll 16
Tayler & Green 284
Tayyabs 171
Tea (High Tea)
    Ritz 32
    St. James's neighborhood 32
    Somerset House café 96
Temple Church 100
Ten Bells Pub 173
Texas Legation 37
Thackeray, William, grave of 238
Thames Barrier 198
Thames Clippers 26, 27
Thames River
    Battersea Park 218
    Garrick's Temple 321
    Path 190
    Richmond Lock and Footbridge
        Walk 320
    Riverside Walk 210
    Strawberry Hill House 322
    A Trip Downriver 197
    Tunnel 191, 192
Theatres, Cinema see also Concerts,
    Dance, Music
    Arcola 288
    Barbican Centre 153
    Bloomsbury Cinema 118
    The Criterion 91
    The Globe 23
    Hackney Empire 187
    Institut Français (cinema, lectures)
        204
    Lyceum 91
    Maison Bertaux tableau vivante 68
    Old Vic 21
    Open Air (Regent's Park) 246
    Princess's Theatre 52
    Renoir Cinema 118
    Royal National 20
    Royal, Drury Lane 91
    Theatre Architecture Walk 91
    Wilton's Music Hall 172

This Shop Rocks 163
Thomas, Hugh 115
Thorndike, Sybil 21
Thornycroft, Thomas
    Queen Boadiccae statue 36
Tintoretto, Jacopo
    Christ Washing the Feet of his
        Disciples, 85
Titian 61
Tolkien, J.R.R. 86
Tom's Deli 239
Tomtom Cigars 217
Topolski Century 19
Tottenham Court Road Underground
    Design 55
Townsend, C. Harrison 302
Tradascant, John 14, 16
Tradascant Sarcophagus 16
Trafalgar Square 82–90
    Afternoon 87
    Charles I Statue (Le Sueur) 37, 90
Trinity Green 170
Triton Fountain 247
Trollope, Anthony 12
Turkish Food Centre 186
Turner, J.M.W. 288
    Monument (MacDowell) 143
Twain, Mark 86
12 Bar Club 66
Twentieth Century Press (TCP) 130
Two Columbia Road 179

U
Underground (Tube)
    Architecture Outing 48
    Arnos Grove Station 192
    Canada Water Station 191
    Canary Wharf Station 48
    Design Tour 55
    Jubilee Line Extension 48
    Leytonstone Station, Alfred
        Hitchcock Murals 290
    Walk from Monument to Liverpool
        Stations 153
    Westminster Station 48

Urdang Academy 133

V

V & A Museum of Childhood 170
Vanbrugh Castle 306
Varah, Dr. Chad 145
Vardy, John 34, 35
Vauxhall Bridge 13
Vauxhall Walk 12–14
Vegas Gallery 182
Velázquez, Diego 61
Verity, Thomas 91
Verlaine, Paul 252
Vermeer, Jan 279
Victoria, Queen 89, 314
Victoria & Albert Museum 202
    Henry Cole portrait 203
    The Old Shepherd's Chief Mourner
        (Landseer) 203
    Pirelli Garden 202
Victoria Park 183, 193
    tea house café 183
Victory Pub 183
Virgin Hotels Roof Gardens 236
Vyner Street 182

W

Walbrook, Anton, grave of 272
Walks, Strolls, Tours
    Adam Brothers 97
    Air Street 71
    Architectural (Highgate) 283
    Architecture by Underground 48
    Beatles Tour 255
    Belsize Park to Primrose Hill 250
    Bermondsey, Early Morning 27
    Bond Street Couture 53
    Brick Lane Fashion 163
    Canada Water Station to the
        Mayflower Inn 191
    Chelsea Sunday Morning 207
    Churches 146
    Church Row (Hampstead) 271
    Clerkenwell Saturday Afternoon
        128

Connoisseur's Afternoon 216
Denmark Street 66
East End Canal 193
East London 178
Edgware Road 228
Film Buff's 74
Finsbury 132
Francophile 204
French Connection 67
Grand Union Canal Windmill Lane
    to Brentford 318
Hampstead Heath, Bird Chorus
    and Bat-Watching 281
Hanway Street 79
High Society 35
Holloway Road 264
Holmes and Hannay 74
Horses 36
Islington 261
Jack the Ripper 173
Kensington Church 235
King Henry's Mound 319
Leadenhall to Jerusalem 147
Literary Neighbours 237
Monument to Liverpool 153
Narrow Way 186
No. 11 Bus 168
Old St. Pancras 106
Original London Walks 173
Oxford Street 52
Parliament Hill Café 276
Pickering Place 39
Portobello Morning 239
Primrose Hill 248
Regent's Park 247
Regents Park High Summer 246
Richmond Lock and Footbridge
    320
Richmond Park 319
Ridley Road Market 185
River Running 26
Riverside 190
Riverside Chelsea 210
Romantic Evening 162
South Bank 16

Summer Evening 19
Theatre Architecture 91
Trafalgar Square Afternoon 87
Vauxhall 12
Vyner Street 182
Westminster 47
William Kent Royal Parks 224
Walk Along Oxford Street 52
Wallace, Sir Richard 61
Wallace Collection 61
    courtyard restaurant 62
    The Laughing Cavalier (Hals) 62
Walpole, Horace 322
Wapping Project 192
Waterlow Park 282
    Sir Sidney Waterlow statue 282
Waterstone's 58, 72
Watteau, Antoine 61, 300
Watts, G.F., Memorial 148
Watts, Isaac, Monument 289
Webb, Aston 68
Webster, John 100
Wellington, Duke of, home of 227
Wentworth Place 274
Wesley, John, tomb of 129
Westbourne Grove Restaurant Row
    241
West India Quay 162
Westminster 43–49
    Walk 48
Westminster Cathedral 49, 239
    Stations of the Cross (Gill) 49
Westminster Hall 100
Westway 240
Whiley, George Manning 75
Whistler, James 210, 218
White Cube 2, 168
Whitehall 37, 43–47
Who, The 66
Wild at Heart 239
Wilde, Oscar 68, 115, 205, 218, 235, 272
    house of 207
Wilford, Michael 146
Wilkinson Gallery 182
Williams, Osmund "Ozzy", 254

Williams, Vaughan, Memorial Library
    251
Wilmington Square 136
Wilson, Edmund 110, 111
Wilson, Sir Colin St. John 109
Wilton's Music Hall 172
Wimbourne House 35
Wolfe, General, Statue 305
Wood, Francis Derwent
    Machine Gun Corps Memorial 227
Woodrow Sculpture 109
World Monuments Fund 172
World War I 75
World War II 15, 41, 44, 46, 47, 59, 68,
    90, 149, 171, 272
Wornum, Grey 73
Wren, Christopher 146, 170, 191
    The Orangery 223
    Royal Hospital Chelsea 207, 209,
    218
    Royal Hospital (Old Royal Naval
    College) 305, 306
    Royal Observatory 305
    St. James's Church 33
    St. Mary Abchurch 152
    St. Paul's Cathedral 142
    St. Stephen Walbrook 144
Wright, Dr. Jules 193
Wyatt, Benjamin Dean 91

Y
Yeats, W.B. 108
York, Duke of, Monument 41

Z
Ziani's 207
Zoffany, Johann
    Garrick's Temple 321
Zoos
    Crystal Palace Park Farm 302
    Hackney City Farm 181
    London Zoo 247
    Penguin Pool 247

ACKNOWLEDGEMENTS

I am deeply grateful to all the contributors who have so generously and eloquently shared their insights, expertise, and love of London. It has been a privilege and an honor to receive each one of your entries. I would like to give generous thanks to Tim Adams, Helen Gordon, Ingrid Bromberg Kennedy, Robert Grover, Sarah Larson, and most especially my wife, Fiona Duff Kahn.

OTHER BOOKS FROM CITY SECRETS

CITY SECRETS ROME
"After using *City Secrets Rome*, you'll never want to go back to the standard guidebook." —*GQ*

"The best thing to happen to the Italian traveler since the Baedeker and Henry James." —*Financial Times*

CITY SECRETS FLORENCE, VENICE & THE TOWNS OF ITALY
"Architect Robert Kahn's *City Secrets Florence, Venice & the Towns of Italy* is full of interesting finds, even for those who know Italy well." —*Town & Country*

"They are the hot guide . . . Wonderful keepsakes."
—*Savvy Traveler*, Public Radio International

CITY SECRETS NEW YORK CITY
"In-the-know Big Apple-ites such as John Guare, Oliver Sacks, and Kate Spade share their city secrets . . ." —*Vanity Fair*

"*City Secrets New York City*, is the latest installment in architect Robert Kahn's invaluable series of insider guides for travelers."
—*New York Magazine*

CITY SECRETS MOVIES
"Surprising and revealing, *City Secrets Movies* is the instant response to the lament 'There's nothing to watch'."
—*Town & Country*

CITY SECRETS BOOKS
"So much concise and persuasive passion by such smart and interesting people about so many intriguing and unfamiliar works! My next several years are hereby, um, booked."
—Kurt Andersen, NPR radio host

City Secrets books may be purchased at special quantity discounts for business or promotional use. For information, please contact us at info@fangduffkahn.com.